EVERYBODY
WANTS
SOME

EVERYBODY WANTS SOME

THE VAN HALEN SAGA

IAN CHRISTE

BICENTENNIAL
1807
WILEY
2007
BICENTENNIAL

John Wiley & Sons, Inc.

Published by John Wiley & Sons, Inc., Hoboken, New Jersey
Published simultaneously in Canada

Wiley Bicentennial Logo: Richard J. Pacifico

Design and composition by Navta Associates, Inc.

For general information about our other products and services, please contact our Customer Care Department within the United States at (800) 762-2974, outside the United States at (317) 572-3993 or fax (317) 572-4002.

Wiley also publishes its books in a variety of electronic formats. Some content that appears in print may not be available in electronic books. For more information about Wiley products, visit our web site at www.wiley.com.

Library of Congress Cataloging-in-Publication Data:

Christe, Ian.
   Everybody want some : the Van Halen saga / Ian Christe.
      p.   cm.
   Includes discography (p. 285).
   ISBN 978-0-470-03910-6 (cloth)
  1. Van Halen (Musical group) 2. Rock musicians—United States. I. Title.
   ML421.V36C47   2007
   782.42166092'2—dc22

                           2007006572

Printed in the United States of America

10 9 8 7 6 5 4 3 2 1

I still think that, whatever people say,
you've got to read the book.

—*Edward Van Halen on how to do things right*

For Eugenia Van Halen, Sibyl Roth, Gladys Hagar,
Carol Sobolewski, Josephine Cherone,
and Valerie Bertinelli

And especially Carole Ann Bailey Christe,
1946–2006

CONTENTS

INTRODUCTION

LEARNING TO PLAY "ERUPTION"

I didn't think it would be fair to write this book without learning how to play "Eruption," getting a good idea of the mental and manual speed of Eddie Van Halen plus appreciating how much work and practice goes into playing, if not developing, his style. Basically, I wanted to write this epic story about Van Halen with at least a tourist's understanding of life in the land of big rock.

Like a lot of people, the first time I heard the guitar solo as a kid it sounded blatantly unplayable. I thought it was some kind of special effect, like a Star Wars laser blast, or a hi-tech synthesizer, or some combination of tape editing and video-game noises. That misconception only grew stronger with each successive challenge over the years—if no guitar hero could do better than "Eruption," then it was virtually untouchable. Anyone who could play even a little piece of it—they were obviously gifted beyond belief.

If Eddie Van Halen was the best guitarist ever, the next logical position to take was not to care. Since the minions throwing themselves on the sword of "Eruption" were mostly empty sounding, as a heavy metal punk teenager it made sense to me not to bother. "Eruption" became the calling card of a certain kind of douche bag who hangs around guitar stores waiting to be discovered, bullying younger players in the meantime.

But ten years passed and there was "Eruption," still retaining its magic, a brief postcard from some endless freak-out by Van Halen back in 1978, sounding miraculously fast and furious. On a whim, I leafed through a book of Van Halen sheet music and looked over "Eruption." That's when I realized it was even possible to play. I knew I could play the notes fast enough, but I had no clue where to begin—it seemed like trying to shake hands with the Tasmanian Devil. Guitar tablature uses an arcane system of notation to indicate finger slides, trills, and bent strings—and "Eruption" pretty much uses every trick in the book.

I feel much better writing this book after learning that "Eruption" was a carefully composed collection of techniques, not an off-the-cuff improvisation. Sitting down at home with my Jackson on my knee, I worked through the song, amazed with each tiny portion that I could extract from the version on *Van Halen*. When I finally pieced it all together after a few days work, it took me about twelve minutes to Eddie's 90-second journey from razor blues to neoclassical tapping to outer space.

The glowing finger-tapping section turned out to be one of the simplest parts, as it's all played on one guitar string. Memorizing the rapid-fire chord progressions behind all those notes, I'm sorry to say, took much longer. My progress was only hindered when I discovered over a thousand videos on YouTube of young kids blazing through the supposedly insurmountable "Eruption"—it must be the second most popular genre of video, next to clips of people falling off skateboards and animals biting people's crotches.

I finally got "Eruption" under control, however, and feels great. I've applied the skills and shortcuts to my own playing—unlike the brilliant Eddie, I should add, who was summarizing all the little things he did to make regular songs sound special. I want to say the reason nobody has ever attempted to write this book before is there was never a writer who could play "Eruption." Or maybe they all died trying.

PART I

RUNNIN' WITH THE DEVIL

THE ROTHOZOIC ERA, 1950–1985

May 8, 1953: Alexander Arthur van Halen born in Holland.

October 10, 1953: David Lee Roth born in Bloomington, Indiana.

June 20, 1954: Michael Anthony Sobolewski born in Chicago, Illinios.

January 26, 1955: Edward Lodwijk van Halen born in Holland.

Winter 1962: Jan van Halen emigrates with his family to California.

1967: Edward gets $100 Teisco Del Ray guitar from Sears.

1971: Alex and Eddie Van Halen form the Trojan Rubber Company.

Autumn 1973: David Lee Roth joins the Van Halen brothers in Mammoth.

Spring 1974: Mike Sobolewski joins Van Halen, becomes Michael Anthony.

May 1976: Gene Simmons "discovers" Van Halen at the Starwood, finances unsuccessful demo tape.

May 1977: Ted Templeman rediscovers Van Halen, signs band to Warner Bros.

February 10, 1978: Release of *Van Halen*; leading to tours with Journey, then Black Sabbath.

October 10, 1978: *Van Halen* goes platinum.

March 23, 1979: Release of *Van Halen II*; first headlining tour runs through October.

March 26, 1980: Release of *Women and Children First*.

August 29, 1980: Eddie Van Halen meets Valerie Bertinelli.

April 11, 1981: Eddie marries Valerie.

April 29, 1981: Release of *Fair Warning*.

April 14, 1982: Release of *Diver Down*.

May 29, 1983: Van Halen paid $1.5 million to play for four hundred thousand people at US Festival '83.

January 4, 1984: Release of *1984*, featuring band's first number 1 single, "Jump."

September 2, 1984: Final show by classic lineup in Nuremberg, Germany.

December 31, 1984: David Lee Roth releases *Crazy from the Heat*.

April 1985: David Lee Roth exits Van Halen.

THE IMMIGRANT SONG

L ike the stories of other great Americans from Henry Ford to Walt
Disney to Fievel the Mouse, the saga of Van Halen begins in an
ancient land, far from the United States and its constant supply of hot
water and electricity. As a narrator would say in the old movies: Among
the windmills, tulips, and wooden shoes of lovely Amsterdam, Holland,
there once lived a kindly musician named Jan van Halen.

Born in 1920, van Halen played saxophone and clarinet everywhere, from political events to radio orchestras to circus tents. During
World War II, he was reportedly captured while fighting the Nazis, and
forced to tour Germany as a prisoner playing propaganda music for the
hated Third Reich. When he was released after the war, he traveled to
Indonesia, where he met and fell in love with an Indonesian beauty,
Eugenia van Beers. She was older, born in 1914, but they married and
returned to Amsterdam, to Michelangelostraat, where a baby boy,
Alexander Arthur van Halen, was born on May 8, 1953.

Mr. van Halen worked his horns in every venue imaginable, but a
musician's life was unsteady and nomadic. Shortly after the birth of second son Edward Lodwijk van Halen, on January 26, 1955, the young

family moved to Rozemarijnstraat in Nijmegen, Holland. The proud father wanted his sons to someday become famous musicians, and he set the bar high for his second son—naming Edward Lodwijk after master composer Ludwig van Beethoven.

The van Halen house was alive with music. Always working on his tone, Jan played along with classical records at home, and the family always listened to his radio broadcasts together. When Jan joined the Dutch air force band, his little boys paraded through the house banging on pans and pot lids while their daddy practiced military marches. "The earliest memories I have about music are from our father," Alex said. "You couldn't help but be touched by music—we were surrounded by it."

Since Jan didn't have the patience to teach the boys about music, he sent them to lessons to become concert pianists. At six years old, Edward was already studying piano with a strict seventy-two-year-old Russian teacher. He and Alex remained in lessons, practicing Beethoven and Tchaikovsky, for nearly ten years. On one rare occasion when Alex didn't feel like practicing, he recalled his mother placing his hands on the kitchen table and rapping them sharply with a wooden spoon.

When they were old enough, Alex and Edward joined their father at his gigs. Reaching his finest form, Jan joined the Ton Wijkamp Quintet, which took top prize at Holland's esteemed Loosdrecht Jazz Festival in 1960. As they traveled all around Holland and sometimes across the border to Germany, the boys saw the practical aspects of a musical career firsthand, and on some of the more rustic and ribald nights they discovered the perks—Alex reported losing his virginity at age nine after one of his dad's gigs.

Letters from Eugenia's relatives told of a better life in the United States, and slowly lured the van Halens to try their luck in the land of opportunity. At the end of winter 1962, Jan and Eugenia gathered their two boys and the family's Dutch-made Rippen piano and set sail on a nine-day Atlantic passage with little more than seventy-five Dutch guilders in their pockets. Jan played with the band aboard the ship to pay for the expedition. Eddie and Alex also showed off their piano training, passing the hat among passengers for tips. And so the musical urchins arrived in the New World, all seasoned and ready to work.

A familiar part of many immigrant stories, Jan's first fateful move on reaching New York was to Americanize his surname, upgrading the antique "van Halen" to the slick "Van Halen," symbolically starting over as a new man. After the stopover in New York, the newly minted Van Halen clan boarded a four-day train to California, in the corner of the country where the American dream was still available for no money down. They found a small bungalow in Pasadena where they would live together as a family for almost twenty years.

Bushy-headed Alex and little Dutch boy Edward arrived in California with the splinters from wooden clogs still in their feet. Speaking almost no English, they smiled and said yes to anything. The second English word they learned was "accident." Edward remained extremely shy, and his bolder brother, Alex, protected him. The pair bonded tightly—comparing notes every day after school on what they'd learned on the playground. They began to blend in, riding bikes with neighbor kids, climbing into their tree house, and beating the hell out of each other.

Mr. Van Halen continued playing in wedding bands at night but kept several day jobs. He worked as a janitor, and when necessary walked five miles each way to wash dishes at Arcadia Methodist Hospital. He reinforced the boys' enthusiasm for music, smiling as they played along with the radio on cardboard guitars, using empty ice-cream tubs for drums. California was living up to its promise of paradise—if only there were more kids in the family: "I always asked my mom where our bass player was," Eddie said.

Around the holidays, the family played music together, with Eugenia seated at a huge electric organ. Yet Mrs. Van Halen was more traditional, and very concerned with taking care of the family. Though she pushed the boys to practice their music lessons, she hated the idea that they would eventually become musicians. Sometimes she was as much a mother to playful Jan as she was to her sons. "The whole time I was growing up," Eddie told *Guitar World*, "my mom used to call me a 'nothing nut—just like your father.' When you grow up that way, it's not conducive for self-esteem."

When they reached the fourth and fifth grades, the Van Halen brothers began imitating acts from *The Ed Sullivan Show* like the Beatles and the Dave Clark Five, whose "Glad All Over" awoke Edward to a new kind of popular music. These were the first bands to break into the pop charts because schoolkids liked them—and Eddie and Alex were schoolkids who could already play music. So at Hamilton Elementary School they formed their first band, the Broken Combs, with Alex on saxophone like his father, Edward on piano, and various schoolmates including Brian Hill on drums, Kevin Hill on an Emenee-brand plastic guitar, and Don Ferris on second sax.

Playing original songs like "Rumpus" and "Boogie Booger" at hot venues like the school lunchroom, Alex and Eddie overcame their awkwardness adapting to American ways. Forget about fitting in—now they were somebody special. "Music was my way of getting around shyness," Eddie later told *Guitar World*.

There were other ways to steel a timid heart. When Eddie was twelve years old, he was attacked and bitten by a German shepherd while on a family trip a few miles from home. To quell his younger son's distress and numb the pain, his father prescribed a shot of vodka and a Pall Mall cigarette on the spot—inducting the kid into two lifetime habits.

By junior high school, the Van Halen brothers had both picked up the violin, and Alex was good enough to make the all-city orchestra. But the television tempted them with a wilder kind of music. Eddie remembered sitting on the couch, plucking out the cool detective theme to *Peter Gunn* on his violin strings. Classical music didn't stand a chance—the boys wanted to play music standing up. Hoping to keep Alex's musical progress on the level, his parents bought him a nylon-string guitar and sent him to flamenco lessons.

Meanwhile, Eddie started a paper route. "The only honest job I ever had," he later joked. He bought a $125 St. George drum set and began studying songs by the Dave Clark Five.

Alex learned slowly on the guitar. He upgraded to a cheap electric and a Silvertone amp but remained frustrated by his progress. So while Eddie was out making collections for his newspapers, Alex slid behind the drums and started banging away, copying licks by Buddy Rich. Soon he mastered the primitive caveman rolls of "Wipe Out" by the Surfaris, a high mark of distinction in any school yard. Feeling somewhat frustrated at the unfair turn of events, Eddie picked up Alex's guitar to show that turnabout was fair play. When he impressed his older brother by learning "Blues Theme" by the Arrows, the true natural order of things quickly became obvious.

By age twelve, Edward owned a $100 four-pickup Teisco Del Ray electric guitar from Sears and was tackling instrumentals like "Walk Don't Run" by the Ventures. His first guitar amp was a chicken-wire model handmade by a friend of his dad's. Eddie's early guitar instructor in absentia was Eric Clapton, the heaviest player of the day, as Eddie figured out every riff and solo that Clapton recorded with the Yardbirds and Cream. He tried painfully to mimic the records but later admitted his versions never sounded quite right—his biggest fault was being unable to avoid his own style.

As they surrendered to the growing rock and roll scene, the Van Halens became infatuated with Jimmy Page in the Yardbirds, Jeff Beck from the Jeff Beck Group, and the unpredictable Jimi Hendrix. Surprisingly, considering the comparisons that came later, Eddie was not so into the wilder, free-form playing of Hendrix. "He used a lot of effects, and I couldn't afford the wah wah pedals and fuzzbox," he said.

Whenever Eddie broke the rules or neglected his piano, Eugenia Van Halen would lock his guitar in the closet for a week, the ultimate punishment. Friends at school also recalled Eddie getting in trouble for touching the sacred Steinway concert piano, the pride of the music department—but the penalties were light thanks to his aptitude and his impish grin. Remaining in lessons until age sixteen with a new, typically strict Lithuanian teacher named Staf Kalvitis, Eddie took top prize at Long Beach City College's youth piano competitions for three years running. The first year, he missed accepting the prize onstage.

Sitting in the stands when they called his name, he froze, pretending not to hear the announcement. He didn't know how to accept an accolade.

Though his fingers were dazzling, Eddie could never read sheet music as well as he should have. Alex was an excellent sight reader, but Eddie's performances were painstakingly crammed into his brain note by note, phrase by phrase, in advance. The judges at piano contests praised his unusual interpretations, but as far as he could tell he was playing it straight. "The only reason they ever wrote music down is because they didn't have tape machines," Eddie later complained. "Do you think Beethoven or Bach would ever have written things down if they had twenty-four-track tape machines?"

Since the Van Halen home was too small to host band practice, the brothers keyed into jamming with local kids whose houses had garages. They formed a band called Revolver, and progressed from the Ventures to heavier covers by Cream and Mountain—power trios centered around guitar and drums. "I approached the drums not as an instrument, per se," Alex remembered, "but more as an attitude—viciously attacking something" with the biggest, heaviest drumsticks available.

At thirteen, Alex began subbing for the drummer in his dad's wedding band, keeping time to jazz and salsa tunes driven by clarinet and accordion. Eddie frequently joined on bass, playing the oompah music lines. "One of Al and my first gigs together was with my dad at the La Merada Country Club," Eddie recalled. "We'd be the little freak sideshow while the band took a break. I would play piano or guitar and Al would play drums."

The first night on the floor, the boys passed a hat around to the dancing couples and collected twenty-two dollars. Their father gave each of them five dollars, and said: "Welcome to the music business, boys."

David Lee Roth was born on October 10, 1953, in Bloomington, Indiana, where his achievement-oriented father, Nathan, went to medical school. After the senior Roth graduated, he moved his family several times, first to a small ranch in Newcastle, Indiana, where Dr. Roth became the caretaker of a menagerie of horses and swans. Next the parents took David and his two sisters, Allison and Lisa, to the East Coast, settling on East Alton Court in Brookline, Massachusetts, outside Boston.

David was an energetic kid, but he was plagued by allergies and fought with health problems that forced him to wear leg braces from almost the time he could walk until age four. Then he was shipped off to therapy for the better part of a decade. At nine years old, he began three intensive years of clinical treatment for hyperactivity. He had a few healthy outlets—Roth's parents called his dinner-hour routines "Monkey Hour," when he acted out cartoons and sang revved-up vaudeville songs for dinner guests.

Though his mother, Sibyl, taught high school music and language classes, Roth claimed his parents were nowhere near as tuneful as the Van Halen family. "I had no musical influences to speak of," he told MTV. "My idols were always Genghis Khan, or Muhammad Ali, or Alexander the Great, or the guy who invented McDonald's hamburgers."

By his telling, he wasn't suffering from lack of concentration. Everyone else was simply having trouble playing their part in his continuous mental picture show, a fast, animated flipbook of *Mad* magazine and *Playboy*. Dave was obsessed with Bugs Bunny, Tarzan, and blackface song-and-dance man Al Jolson, whose songs he played on old brittle clay 78s. Later, he loved Elvis Presley—but not the music, just the movies.

While Roth's head was swimming in pop culture, his roots were knotted tightly around the Old World—his grandparents were Ukrainian Jews who traded the mountains and steppes of Eastern Europe for the sweltering cornfields of the Midwest. In fact, all four of his grandparents spoke Russian. "My great-granddaddy died dancing," he later joked with a TV interviewer, "at the end of a rope."

When Roth was seven, his movie-buff dad took him to see *Some Like It Hot*, the classic Billy Wilder film where Tony Curtis and Jack Lemmon dress in drag to get close to Marilyn Monroe. "Life turned into an ongoing quest to be in that movie, just somewhere in that movie," Roth told *Rolling Stone*. On the way home that night, while his eyes were still boggled, his dad detailed the plot to *Robin Hood*—the movie Mrs. Roth thought he was taking their son to see.

The rambunctious David found a kindred spirit in his uncle Manny Roth, a bohemian hepcat whose small Café Wha? on MacDougal Street was a nexus of New York's Greenwich Village beatnik scene in the early 1960s. Bob Dylan, Jimi Hendrix, Bruce Springsteen, Bill Cosby, and Richard Pryor all tempered their antiestablishment acts there before a highly engaged cosmopolitan audience. "New York certainly reflects the dinner table I grew up with," Roth later told an interviewer. "Obviously it encouraged me."

Summer trips to New York impressed on young David Roth that, guidance counselors and behavior therapists be damned, there was a big wide world that craved and coveted extravagant personalities. Uncle Manny bought him a radio for his eighth birthday, hoping to feed the kid some inspiration. "I put it on, and there was Ray Charles singing 'Crying Time,'" David said, "and I just knew I had to be on the radio."

The Roths left the East Coast for California in 1963, when Dave was ten, just in time to fall under the spell of the Beach Boys in their prime—America's only real defense against the Beatles. From his new home in Altadena, young Dave shuffled off with his tousled hair and tennis shoes to fourth grade at the Altadena School. Meanwhile, Dr. Roth's ophthalmology practice thrived—he became a successful eye doctor, and was also active in local theater productions. Throughout junior high, Roth remembered a poster hanging over his bed given to him by his father, picturing two chickens meeting a turkey above the caption "To thine own self be true."

After three years as a Tenderfoot Scout, Roth left behind his boyhood like the Van Halen brothers abandoning their tree house when he discovered his life's future work. He once reported losing his virginity on a beach in Tahiti at age thirteen, under a full moon and over a girl who didn't speak English. "She kept saying she liked me, she liked me.

I know she meant she *loved* me—but ever since I've had a complex."
Tahiti came to be Roth's catchall perfect setting for stories that may
have only taken place in paradise. In his memoir, *Crazy from the Heat*,
he reported another crucial moment in his early sex life—getting a blow
job behind the bushes in the suburbs while looking through someone's
living room window and seeing Johnny Carson on the TV.

As Dr. Roth's career bloomed, the family moved to the affluent section of Pasadena. When integrated busing arrived, Dave became a
societal guinea pig, sent to predominantly black schools from sixth
grade onward. He boasted of his ingrained blackness later, but at the
time being a fair-haired white hippie meant lots of fights. He put gobs
of Brylcreem in his hair, he liked to do headstands, and school became
an all-day talent show. Teachers didn't know what was wrong with him.

Despite his effusive personality, Dave was something of a loner, an
overly intelligent rich kid with delusions of grandeur. He felt perse-
cuted, and yet above it all. He had vulgar candy-sprinkled ideas of
sexuality, a by-product of learning about the world through the twisted
twin lenses of *Mad* and *Playboy*. Despite his father's money, he was
always a worker: at the end of his junior year at John Muir High School,
Roth bought himself a stereo with the dollars he earned shoveling dung
alongside Mexican gang members at a stable.

A bench-clearing brawl during a gym-class football game led to a
brief stint at boarding school. More rules only brought more resistance, so after one semester in uniform David rejoined the teen scene at
public school, his wild streak intact. "I never went to class, but I went
to school," he said. "I used to sit under a tree in the parking lot playing guitar." He attracted girls and cultivated a rep for his unusual
old-time repertoire and generally gleeful demeanor. While fighting a
constant cultural war at home with his attentive parents, he carefully
pushed his public image to the brink—his short-lived trademark was
a bleached skunklike strip down the center of his hair.

A native midwesterner like Roth, Michael Anthony Sobolewski was born on June 20, 1954, at St. Joseph's Hospital in Chicago. His family lived in a working-class section of what was then the breadbasket of blue-collar America. Michael was the second of five children, and the oldest boy. His dad, Walter, played in polka combos, gigging often at the Aragon Ballroom with musical prankster Kay Kyser, the popular band-leader who wrote "Praise the Lord and Pass the Ammunition." Walter encouraged Michael to play the trumpet too.

The Sobolewski family heeded the same clarion call that lured the Van Halens and the Roths westward, first testing the waters during a short move in 1963. In 1966, they left Chicago for good, settling in Arcadia, California, a town five miles east of Pasadena, where Jan Van Halen worked as a hospital dishwasher. Walt Sobolewski continued playing at dances, performing standards for other midwestern trans-plants and old-timers.

Michael became a long jumper at Dana Junior High. He played trumpet in the marching band, and stayed active in sports, going out for baseball. After his older sister, Nancy, brought home psychedelic acid-rock bands like Electric Flag, Cream, and Blue Cheer, Michael's attention wandered to the loud, animal side of music. He learned the walking bass line to Electric Flag's "Groovin' Is Easy" and admired the band's bassist, Harvey Brooks. Straying from the conformity of the high school band, he idolized bassist Dickie Peterson of Blue Cheer—an iconoclastic hippie whose tough attitude was basically one giant mid-dle finger to the world.

At fifteen, with younger brother Steve on drums and friend Mike Hershey on guitar, Mike formed Poverty's Children, later known as Balls. His bass was a cheap Japanese Teisco guitar belonging to Her-shey—they removed the two highest strings to create a "bass" guitar. Though he played catcher on local baseball teams as a left-hander, he considered himself ambidextrous—in fact, he started playing bass as a lefty, and switched sides because a right-handed instrument was eas-ier to find.

Since Michael wasn't sure how to tune a bass, he tuned the four strings to an open E chord for the first year. He soon acquired a Fender P-bass copy at a local flea market. Like Alex Van Halen, Michael also played with his father's band, a polka combo, tooting a trumpet for pocket money up until college.

〰〰〰〰〰

By their midteens, Alex and Eddie were regularly performing live sets of covers by Black Sabbath and ZZ Top, while joining their dad for his regular gig at the North Continental Club in North Hollywood, acting as designated drivers when needed. They were several inches, many dollars, and quite a few decibels short of where they wanted to be, but they were resourceful and shameless enough to beg or borrow any equipment they needed for their gigs.

In 1971, the Van Halen boys formed the Trojan Rubber Company, a power trio with neighbor Dennis Travis on bass. Already the boys were little-league outlaws. They smoked cigarettes like European street kids—their mom, Eugenia, even bought them packs to smoke. They had to call themselves the Space Brothers to get permission to play a Catholic high school—the priests and sisters found cosmic drug references more acceptable than a band named after condoms.

By any billing, the Van Halen brothers became known for their spot-on impersonations of cool hard rock bands like Cream and Cactus. Eddie had been playing through a 100-watt Marshall guitar amp from the time he was fourteen. Competing in a local battle of the bands against kids eight to ten years older, Alex was already stealing shows with a bombastic set piece—Ginger Baker's entire fifteen-minute-plus drum solo from "Toad."

While other kids were dating, experiencing heartbreak, getting into fights, and enduring the endless social humiliation of high school, Eddie sat most of those years out. Sequestered in his bedroom, he entered into a long-term relationship with his guitar. "Everybody goes through their teens getting fucked around by a chick or not fitting in with the jocks at school. I just basically locked my room for four years," he said.

His mind may have been with his guitar, but his skill as a guitarist made him popular. He experienced sex at an early age, and girls were always interested in this sweet, shy boy. In the eleventh grade, his steady girlfriend became pregnant. "It was very confusing," he told writer David Rensin in *TeenAge*. "We didn't even have enough money to go to a doctor to see if she was pregnant. And getting out of school to take care of it was a feat in itself. Luckily I had a friend in the school office who gave me blank admit slips."

The potentially life-changing event was over quickly, before gravity really kicked in for the young couple. "She wanted an abortion," Eddie said. "We went to Planned Parenthood and talked it over. We were worried about her parents and my parents finding out, about getting busted for cutting school. Eventually her parents did find out, and their reaction surprised me. It was 'why didn't you come to us and let us help?' I thought they'd call us scum."

Stashing the experience in the back of his mind, Eddie stayed focused on his guitar and his band with his brother. Though their schoolmates were already wild about them, at one show they completely changed the life of a kid from a nearby school, Dave Roth. He was a sponge for all forms of culture, high and low, mass and micro, and followed every dance craze from the Twist to the Freddie—yet he was somewhat sheltered. His parents forbade him to go to big rock concerts—until he was nineteen and snuck off to see Humble Pie. So when teenage Roth first saw Eddie Van Halen playing guitar, he saw the light.

"Eddie was kind of a mentor," Roth later told a TV interviewer. "I saw what he did with his fingers, and I knew that's what I wanted to do with my feet, and with my voice." Praise be and hallelujah.

RATS IN THE CELLAR

By the time Alex Van Halen graduated from Pasadena High School in 1971, he and his brother were well-regarded fledgling musical professionals. Continuing to direct and manage his band with Eddie, Alex started music classes at Pasadena City College. He signed up for a composition class, where he arranged *West Side Story* for a fourteen-piece jazz orchestra, and was still subbing with his father's wedding band when needed. "I was surprised by how well Alex played our kind of music—polkas and waltzes," said Richard Kreis, a regular bassist in Jan Van Halen's group. "He carried the rhythm of the band! And while we set up before the bar opened, he'd watch the door while I got the beer from the tap."

The brothers had outgrown their neighborhood bands—the Trojan Rubber Company closed shop after bassist Dennis Travis moved away. In 1972, Alex and Eddie formed a new group with bassist Mark Stone. They wanted to call themselves Rat Salad, the title of a Black Sabbath instrumental from the ultra-heavy, groundbreaking new *Paranoid* album. Instead, the Van Halen brothers chose the name Genesis—the optimistic beginning of a musical career of biblical scale.

As Genesis began playing backyard parties in Pasadena, a friend jokingly drew up a poster announcing "Genesis at the Forum"—summoning a hilarious fantasy that the band would ever be big enough to play L.A. Forum. Then one sad afternoon Eddie came home from the record store and glumly informed Alex that their band already had an album out—he had discovered the latest record by the British progressive rock band Genesis on the new-release shelf.

Afterward they became known as Mammoth, a wild and woolly beast that promised a heavy step. For a while, the Mammoth lineup included a keyboard player, which Eddie hated because the electric piano filled up the sound and tied down his guitar playing. Besides playing guitar, Eddie also sang lead vocals in Mammoth, though singing was not his strongest point.

"Rock Steady" Eddie, as he became known at school, soon followed Alex to Pasadena City College, where he studied composition with Dr. Truman Fischer, also a former teacher of Frank Zappa's. Fischer was a follower of the visionary composer Arnold Schoenberg's stern belief in learning the rules so you could completely ignore them. From this professor, Eddie received his lifelong creative license: If it sounds good, it is.

While setting up on stages in high school gyms and auditoriums, Mammoth met fellow heavy travelers like Snake, boogie rockers who played ZZ Top and Foghat covers. Snake also lent the Van Halen brothers equipment—which was to be expected. Alex remained perpetually a few pieces of gear short of the bigger, better show, and he was shameless about borrowing what Mammoth needed to slog onward.

Snake's leader, vocalist and bassist Michael Sobolewski, had graduated from nearby Arcadia High in 1972. He crossed paths with Alex Van Halen at Pasadena City College, studying psychology until his father gave him permission to switch to music. Even on rudimentary originals, Mike's powerful lungs, expanded by blowing trumpet and running track, were an obvious strong point.

Another of Alex's classmates at Pasadena City College, Dave Roth, frequently supplied Mammoth with a PA system, but at least he had the good sense to charge ten bucks a night for rental. At one point, Roth auditioned for Mammoth, but the band was unimpressed with his free-wheeling renditions of Cream and Grand Funk Railroad standards. At that ill-fated meeting, a nervous Eddie left the room so older brother Alex could break the bad news.

Undiscouraged, Roth formed the Red Ball Jets, an R&B-influenced act that played old rock and roll covers like "Johnny B. Goode," a band where a huge horn section wouldn't have been out of place. They rehearsed in the basement of Dr. Roth's office building in San Marino, and frequently faced off against Mammoth in local battles of the bands in public parks. "It was never about the music for him, it was about the show," Eddie recalled. "He was like an emcee, a clown. He was great at what he did."

Biding his time with theater courses in junior college, Roth was a big personality for a small suburban city. His constant manic energy grated on the down-to-earth teenage rock scene. He wore ridiculous costumes, talked constantly, and strutted and preened like the sex god he obviously believed he was. Mike Sobolewski's first reaction when meeting Roth was, "Jesus Christ, get this guy away from me!"

Borrowing liberally from his inspirations, Roth built his singing voice from an articulate palette of screams, including the primal roar of Ian Gillan from Deep Purple, the orgiastic squeals of the Ohio Players and Cold Blood, and a whole bag of tricks from obscure midwestern soul singers like Major Lance. Jim Dandy Mangrum of Black Oak Arkansas, a godfather of cock rock, claims that Roth asked permission to film his shows at a Hollywood club. If true, Roth was learning stagecraft from a lurid master. "It's better to steal," Roth later told MTV. "Inspiration doesn't come from nowhere. You don't lie in a dark black room and a burst of light appears with the hand of the Lord offering you a song. It doesn't happen like that. You have to steal it from somebody. You change this and you change that—if it was good enough for Beethoven, it's good enough for me."

Reconsidering his early rejection, Alex Van Halen sensed a fellow warrior in Roth. Besides, his brother was struggling as lead vocalist of

Mammoth. Though his voice would have been adequate in any other local act, compared to the wunderkind's magical guitar his singing sounded dodgy. Not only did Eddie's playing shame other guitarists, it shamed his efforts as a frontman. Alex started to envision a whole package. Besides his boundless drive, Roth came with a rehearsal space, an Opal Kadett station wagon for transportation, plus the PA system that was currently costing Mammoth plenty of dough. So in late 1973, David Lee Roth joined Mammoth, and the band ditched the Blue Cheer/Cream power-trio configuration that had gone out of style in the late 1960s, becoming a quartet like Led Zeppelin—the template for the 1970s.

As Eddie's reputation spread, his picture-perfect renditions of the guitar gods gave way to a fluid yet unpredictable style he described as "falling down the stairs and hoping I land on my feet." "I sometimes wonder myself when it was that I turned the corner and went my own way in playing," he told *Musician*, "because the last thing I remember was playing 'Crossroads' and being Eric Clapton. All of a sudden, I just changed."

Shortly after David Lee Roth joined Mammoth, their hapless keyboard player was given the boot. The next business was a name change—"Mammoth" sounded too ponderous. Roth suggested "Van Halen," a cool, memorable moniker like Santana that would stand out on a poster next to other local bands like Snatch or Kuperszyth. Next, Van Halen devised their first band logo—loopy, with descending lines that looked like musical notes.

Graduating from high school auditoriums, the next step for a fledgling hard rock band was playing the informal backyard party scene. Rock ruled for California teens in 1974, and massive crews of kids in tank tops and cutoff jean shorts passed the hot summer nights with kegs of beer and ample opportunity to score cheap grass. By the time Van Halen played their first backyard party, they were already able to muster nine hundred paying heads.

In demand from the start, Van Halen played everywhere they could draw electricity—outdoor parks, the backyards of mansions, and roller rinks. Where extension cords couldn't reach, they took electric generators. The locations became familiar—Huntington Drive, Arden Road, Colorado Avenue, Hamilton Park, and Madison Avenue—all announced on mimeographed party flyers with hand-drawn maps. Friends remember an early flair for showmanship, like Eddie sticking his cigarette in the headstock of his guitar in emulation of Keith Richards. Eddie's lead guitar playing was unrivaled. He usually closed shows with an extended firestorm based perfectly on the electric blues boogie "Goin' Home" by Ten Years After—no easy task, as their guitarist Alvin Lee had been billed the "fastest guitar in Britain."

Inevitably the police arrived to bust the backyard parties, sometimes in helicopters, to keep the revelry from going too far over the edge. For the kids, it was all part of the light show, and "crime scene" videotapes made by the police remain the ultimate unseen early documents of Van Halen. When the cops broke up the show, the kids would scatter, spreading out into suburban neighborhoods, scrambling in their sneakers through culverts and vacant lots, evading the long arm of the law, hoping to regroup before night's end. If they were lucky, Van Halen would arrive at the next party, and Eddie would seize whatever guitar was available and reel off a few choice tunes in the living room.

There were minimal distractions at that time—no video games, no VCRs, no Internet chat rooms, and no cable TV. There were barely even any skateboards. When they outgrew GI Joe dolls and Evel Knievel action figures, live rock bands gave kids a setting to entertain one another. While the adults of California partied with cocaine in hot tubs, the children got wild in the streets with cheap beer and little plastic sandwich baggies stuffed with green grass. Not only was AIDS not an issue, there was no War on Drugs, and the drinking age was for all practical purposes nonexistent. "Back in 1972 I OD'd on PCP, thinking it was cocaine," Eddie later told radio interviewer Mark Razz. "That's when I first got exposed to that stuff, and I didn't know what it was."

Along with neighborhood divisions came territorial rivalries. Van Halen represented the San Gabriel Valley and fought for turf against the

San Fernando Valley's Quiet Riot, who dressed in polka dots and showcased their own guitar prodigy, Randy Rhoads. Innocent but extremely headstrong, Van Halen weren't above a bit of sabotage, unplugging amps to steal the thunder of opening bands and hurry themselves onto the stage. "What's a party without any guests?" Dave taunted from the stage. "A Quiet Riot concert!"

As wild Pasadena parties and Eddie's guitar wizardry put the band in demand, Van Halen's repertoire of cover songs grew to a hefty two hundred tunes—three hundred if you count blatant hack jobs. Their set list ranged from pounding proto-metal by Deep Purple, Queen, Black Sabbath, and the little-known Captain Beyond, to boogie rock by ZZ Top and Grand Funk Railroad. To broaden their appeal beyond Pasadena, Roth insisted they learn soul jams that could move the dance floor, like James Brown's "Cold Sweat" and KC & the Sunshine Band's "Get Down Tonight." As late as 1976, Van Halen would still pull off a left-hand turn like Stevie Wonder's "Superstitious."

Eddie still felt frustrated when the covers sounded too much like Van Halen, not enough like the originals. Part of the problem was that Roth never bothered to learn the words—he faked the rhythms phonetically and improvised the rest. As he recalled one of his colorful uncles telling him, "Dave, the key to success is sincerity. Once you can fake that, you've got it made!" The band would fight over the set list outside the venue until the last minute, but when they hit the stage it was all smiles and high fives.

Sensing opportunity in upscale San Marino near Pasadena, they struck up a band business spray-painting house numbers onto curbs for five bucks a pop. Appearing on doorsteps in blue overalls holding stencils, they informed housewives of an obscure and imaginary city requirement for visible street addresses. The proceeds from this quasi-scam went straight back into the band to buy gas, drumsticks, and guitar strings.

Van Halen never heard of a basketball court or a basement too small to jam. They played in a parking lot to publicize the opening of a new supermarket. This around-the-clock commitment became a pain in the ass for bassist Mark Stone. Unlike the Van Halen brothers, for whom school was a promotional opportunity, Stone was a straight-A student with career aspirations beyond this backyard rock band. Obviously, he had to go. The fall from local celebrity to face in the crowd was difficult for him. "For a long time, it really hurt," Stone said.

During the spring of 1974, Mike Sobolewski was invited to become part of the Van Halen gang. He apologized to his bandmates from Snake, and then bounded away to join the offputting Roth and the friendly Van Halen brothers. Sometime between leaving the high school marching band and meeting David Lee Roth, good-natured Mike Sobolewski became known as Michael Anthony, a crazy bass wildman, one step closer to the musical all-star team. "When my father found out I'd joined, he got really angry and kicked me out of the house for dropping out of school," Michael said.

Besides bringing a rumbling bottom-end sound that complemented Alex's thunder perfectly, Mike was also an unrivaled backup singer. His uncanny high-end harmonies expanded the available range of cover songs, and eventually crafted the Van Halen sound significantly. More coveted for the time being, however, was a system of light pedals he rigged to play using his feet. He met the requirement to help the band's career by advancing their stage show.

With the addition of Dave Roth from Red Ball Jets and Michael Anthony from Snake, Eddie and Alex had swallowed the local competition. Van Halen now featured the main guys from the three most happening bands in the region. Possessing more than just musical ability, they were outgoing people who knew how to use a telephone, how to draw a crowd, and how to put on a great show. Plus they all had great smiles.

Billing themselves as "the pride and joy of Southern California," Van Halen were a homegrown grassroots phenomenon whose popularity grew by word of mouth. As it was for the local hardcore punk bands Black Flag and the Germs, and later Sunset Strip glamsters Guns N' Roses and Poison, the grapevine was all-important in the spread of the band. They ruthlessly promoted their appearances with cheap ads in local news circulars, and especially through flyers and handbills. Before a show, the hustling Van Halen would put thousands of hand-drawn flyers printed for a penny apiece into every locker in local high schools—and not just their high schools but also the dozens of others within an hour's drive.

The backyards were better than the bars for building a fan base— you didn't have to be twenty-one to get loaded underneath a palm tree and pass out on the lawn. But eventually Van Halen landed gigs playing as many as four sets a night at beer bars like Walter Mitty's Rock N Roll Emporium. "To me that was the epitome of a rock and roll club," Alex said. "And every night we played there I had this vision that we were playing some sort of large arena."

Los Angeles is a big city with a lot of neighborhoods. Several nights a week Van Halen played at Perkins Palace, Walter Mitty's, the Proud Bird, the Civic Auditorium, Barnacle Bill's, the Swiss Park, or the occasional pizza parlor. And as the band grew up and started playing more clubs, its audience came of age or got fake IDs and followed. For some reason, Van Halen still couldn't get booked in Pasadena bars. "We couldn't even get work at the local club, the Handlebar Saloon!" Eddie later told *Creem*.

After failing the audition at least once, Van Halen won a regular spot beginning in April 1974 at Gazzari's Teen Dance Club in Hollywood, playing cover songs for over three hours a night. Eddie bought platform shoes for the occasion and nearly broke his ankles. As documented in *The Decline and Fall of Western Civilization 2*, Gazzari's was a bawdy, go-go scene relic that survived into the 1970s with rock excess and a touch of vaudeville. The best dancer in the crowd won thirty dollars—incentive to copy the moves on *Soul Train* and *American Bandstand* and hopefully bump into the girls standing nearby.

Roth honed his stagecraft by emceeing the dance contest between singing songs. His joining the band had opened the door to Hollywood—club owner Bill Gazzari famously called him "Van," assuming the band was named after the singer. Though considered by many to be obnoxious, the band's only impediment to sure success, Roth was already choreographing stage and lighting moves that made every little lick memorable. The Van Halens handled the music, and he took care of the rest.

"We're playing dance music for people who like to party tonight," Roth chatted up a Pasadena crowd. From his earliest moments onstage, he was riffing on song titles, talking a mile a minute, looking to burn through his awkwardness as fast as possible and become a seasoned stage master. "No sense trying to be high-class and play nonsense shit. We'll play something maybe you can relate to. At least you can get up and dance, man, find out if that honey you've been looking at wants to look at you."

With his windblown hair and hairy exposed chest thrust outward, Roth was a fusion of pop icons Farrah Fawcett-Majors and Burt Reynolds—but he wasn't hanging next to Robert Plant on bedroom walls just yet. In 1975 he was still a loose, chatty kid, rattling off stage raps just to hold back the hecklers. He taunted rocker boys to "get mellow and imitate *Soul Train*," then laughed when they shouted their disdain for soul music. Nevertheless, while the strong bass lines and Alex's drums punctuated the California air, the young ones danced boldly.

Even as the band scored entry-level Hollywood showcase gigs at Gazzari's—a glamorous position compared to the bowling alleys of Pasadena—they were taking home less than a hundred bucks a night, hardly enough for four guys in their twenties to keep their enterprise rolling. Eddie's mother badgered her baby to take his future more seriously. With her musician husband cheering the boys' progress with every step, it was up to Mrs. Van Halen to think sensibly. She insisted that Edward allow her to sign him up for computer classes at the DeVry Institute of Technology in Phoenix, Arizona.

If Eugenia Van Halen had won that family fight and Eddie had applied his talents elsewhere, Phoenix might have become the center of some kind of unorthodox revolution in personal computing. Instead, under Eddie Van Halen's influence, Southern California would soon become the holy land of hotshot guitarists and big hair, and he would be the messiah.

～～～～

Combining New World ambition with Old World discipline, Eddie spent hours every day practicing guitar. He sat with a six-pack of Schlitz while his older brother went out to party, and he'd still be hitting the strings when Alex came home in the wee hours of the morning. Eddie's style was ultramodern but deeply musical. He fired off familiar lead guitar licks so fast that they sounded new, without pause, a torrent of sounds and musical ideas that kept listeners pinned to the wall. He appeared to be mentally three steps ahead of his instrument, wailing and flailing his way to mastery.

After seeing Led Zeppelin play in 1971, Eddie began experimenting with a finger-tapping technique, inspired by the fluttery noises of Jimmy Page flopping his violin bow against his Les Paul. Eddie held his pick between his thumb and middle finger, where most guitar players use their thumb and first finger, like holding a pencil. When he played a fast solo, he would tuck his middle finger underneath and extend his index finger to tap out high notes on the guitar neck. He could play high- and low-note combinations or triads, using the fingertips of both hands. As he built up speed, the effect was dazzling—completely ballistic and brand-new sounding, yet undeniably musical.

Though years of piano prepared him for the technique, Eddie Van Halen did not invent the finger-tapping approach to guitar. Back in 1971, Steve Hackett of the English band Genesis tapped on several songs on the album *Nursery Cryme*. Electric blues player Harvey "the Snake" Mandel tried two-handed tapping in 1973 on his *Shangrenade* album. Brian May of Queen made finger-tapping motions in a 1975 video for "Bohemian Rhapsody." Even more concretely, Emmett Chapman invented a two-handed tapping instrument called the Chapman Stick in 1969—an electric ten-stringed curiosity played without strumming, just using fingertip pressure like Eddie did in his solos.

But none of the forerunners pushed tapping to Eddie Van Halen's precision and velocity. Eddie was self-critical and extremely hard on himself and his playing. His mind was wrapped so tightly around the electric guitar that he was thinking holes straight through his instrument—how the strings were twisted, where to apply oil, what kinds of frets gave the right sound. He kept his low-grade arsenal in a constant state of reinvention, accidentally destroying many guitars by ripping out their frets or trying to alter their body shape with a saw. For a while he played a Fender Strat in honor of Jimi Hendrix, rewired with a Gibson PAF humbucker pickup to fatten the sound. He also cut the vibrato bar on his Gibson ES-335 in half, so only the top three strings whammied. After the solo break, he could finish the song with the bottom three strings still in tune—a clever modification.

Like Hendrix before him, Eddie was a technical innovator who reconfigured the instrument to suit his needs. Unsatisfied with stock instruments, he essentially invented the modern shredder guitar by taping together various parts to create a lightweight, high-output weapon suitable for his soon-to-be trademark attack. In 1975 he bought a budget Boogie guitar body for fifty dollars and a maple neck for eighty dollars, stamped in some Gibson frets stripped from a less fortunate donor axe, and Krazy-Glued a single humbucker pickup at the bridge position for maximum sustain and resonance. He also rewound pickups with extra copper wire, to balance the sounds from the sharp rear pickup and the mellow front pickup until they suited his ear.

Eddie's cobbled-together guitars could be as temperamental as they were innovative. Roth called these creations "Dennis the Menace bits of trouble." To minimize problems while performing, in 1975 Eddie took on guitar tech Robin "Rudy" Leiren, a junior high school friend who remained his six-string valet for more than a decade. Eddie delighted in throwing his guitars around, however, horrifying onlookers who expected the guitar whiz to treat his instruments gingerly.

One ongoing problem was volume—Eddie only liked the sound of his amp when it was pushed to full output, which created countless problems. He tried aiming the amp at the wall, stuffing it with padding, and covering it with a plastic hood before discovering that he could overdrive it at a lower volume if he starved it for voltage using a Variac variable power supply. Eddie dialed the Variac well below the standard 110 volts to artificially overload the vacuum tubes, allowing him to reach his favorite resonant feedback tones without deafening clubgoers or his parents. "Those amps used to blow like every other gig, and you have to retube them every other day, but they crank!" he told *Guitar Player*. An earlier experiment with variable voltage using a light-switch dimmer blew out the power in his parents' house.

Through a friend of Michael Anthony's, Eddie met a guitar maker named Wayne Charvel in San Dimas, California. Operating a small custom shop, Charvel was one of many kindred spirits Eddie would find among instrument makers. His shapes were especially light and sounded rich. Eddie ordered a body, specifying where he needed holes to be routed for one single humbucker pickup and a tremolo bar. From Charvel, Eddie also learned how to reduce feedback by dipping his pickups in hot paraffin—the same substance used to wax surfboards. In fact, Charvel and tinkerers like him were a unique product of Southern California garage culture, joined by surfboard shapers, hot-rod mechanics, electronic keyboard makers, and the nascent home computing kit scene. Like Eddie, they all believed there were crazy reasons at the end of the rainbow to do things perfectly—they were all trailblazing personalized directions to paradise.

HOTEL CALIFORNIA

Van Halen played Gazzari's basically three times a week for the next two years, cutting their teeth on cover tunes the same way the Beatles and Black Sabbath did during their record-setting residencies at the Star-Club in Hamburg, Germany. With a tight rhythm section delivering heavy artillery, a flamboyant lead singer, and a hotshot prodigy guitarist, Van Halen were biding their time until they became stars. Until then, Schlitz Malt Liquor and Camel Filters fueled champagne dreams.

The boys were organized in their dogged way. They drove beat-up jalopies and secondhand vans with crooked wheels and barely enough room to haul gear. They began recording demos, though on their shoestring budget it was difficult. They bartered and scraped together enough cash for sessions at Cherokee Studios and Hound Dog Recording Studios on Colorado Boulevard. Among the earliest tracks recorded were during 1974—the tenderly corny "Angel Eyes" with insufferable vocals by Roth, and the hot, rocking "Believe Me," with Claptonesque leads by Eddie. The thundering "Simple Rhyme" and bass-heavy boogie "Take Your Whiskey Home" from the band's third album also originated on these early tapes.

After two years of hustling at Gazzari's, Van Halen took a slot on May 9, 1976, opening for the lethal British rock squadron UFO at the Golden West Ballroom in Norwalk. Usually Van Halen were happy to slip one or two originals into the playlist, but that night they made a major decision to perform mostly their own songs. Besides a midset block of songs by Aerosmith, ZZ Top, and Led Zeppelin, they played "On Fire," "Last Night," and "Somebody Get Me a Doctor"—plus a flashy guitar solo Eddie had developed called "Eruption," which show-cased his two-handed tapping style.

These early tracks would resurface over their first five albums, and bits and pieces would appear in reworked form for another decade. Most of Van Halen's material was unique, heavy, and ready to go. Roth remained something of an ugly duckling, and the band was slightly off-kilter yet ridiculously good. Gigging disco covers, they had honed their background vocals, with Eddie and especially Michael shooting high-pitched harmonies to counter the missing horn section. When they started writing their own songs, those harmonies became a hallmark of the Van Halen package—Michael Anthony earned the nickname "Cannonmouth."

Local impresario Rodney Bingenheimer liked the band's originals at the Golden West Ballroom and recommended them for a booking at the Star-wood—a den of ill repute in West Hollywood with several spaces, including a rock room that held a thousand. Slash from Guns N' Roses hung out there as a teenager, selling Quaaludes, he told *Musician*. Unlike the Top 40 bars Van Halen had been playing, the Starwood didn't want covers—or bands tainted by the stigma of playing Gazzari's. From then until the end of 1976, Van Halen straddled the line, appearing at more prestigious gigs at the Star-wood while still playing covers on alternating nights for old man Gazzari.

At that point, older brother Alex handled the band's booking and management, and for years he would remain a band authority figure. The outgoing Roth played a different kind of leadership role, constantly repackaging the band's image for the outside world with stage cos-tumes, flyers, and publicity stunts. The music, the image, and the work ethic all flowed naturally from the same quarreling four heads—young dudes jumping down one another's throats but united for a just cause.

"We were always disagreeing about what was the appropriate thing to do, but it was that belligerent, confrontational chemistry that created the music you grew up to," Roth said. "Rather like all those folks who spent time at law or med school, it wasn't something we got right away. It had to be whittled away and worked at."

When it came time to register their first original songs with ASCAP, the band sat around a table at Dr. Roth's house and discussed how to split the songwriting credits. They voted as a band to share the proceeds among all four members. "That was before we found out I'm the only one who writes," Eddie later told *Musician* with a laugh. It goes without saying, though, that at the time the net proceeds were zilch.

Through their patron Bingenheimer, Van Halen were introduced to the way-out Hollywood in-crowd—tastemakers like Kim Fowley, who brought them to the Rainbow Bar & Grill in Hollywood. They began playing his song "Young and Wild," which eventually popped up on a record by his protégés the Runaways. "Van Halen is a six-pack of beer, a big-breasted woman, cruising down the highway running over animals," Fowley said admiringly. In fact, they were cruising across Highway 101 nearly every night, heading home from West Hollywood to Pasadena.

Van Halen saw behind the mask of the big leagues later in 1976, when Gene Simmons of Kiss took the band under his batlike wing. Looking to sink some of his new wealth into producing young bands with his company Man of a Thousand Faces, Simmons unexpectedly scouted Van Halen at the Starwood while out one night with rock courtesan Bebe Buell. When Simmons introduced himself, the band was overjoyed. Their other allies were way less glamorous. "They had a potential backer who was a yogurt manufacturer," Simmons recalled in his autobiography.

Eddie called Simmons that very night after packing up his gear, and a few hours later Van Halen were ensconced at Village Recorder Studios in West L.A. Simmons talked a mile a minute at them, preening their rough edges with the wisdom of his rock-star polish. Interestingly, Simmons's offer preempted his original intention—to produce a band who played earlier that night called the Boyz, featuring future Dokken hero George Lynch on guitar.

"Hey, it was our gig," Lynch later said with a laugh to *Guitar World*. "All I cared about was that they didn't suck and drive people away before our set. Then to see everything you thought you knew about guitar playing change right before your eyes at your very own show? Talk about depressed!"

To complete some guitar overdubs, Simmons sent Van Halen to Electric Lady Studios in Greenwich Village in New York City—Dave's adolescent stomping grounds. Though the purpose of New York trip was for Eddie to record more disciplined solos, Simmons also claimed he took the band shopping for hipper clothes and bought them leather pants. The pants were fine, but Eddie hated overdubbing (recording his guitar parts twice). The process created a thicker sound, like on a Kiss record, but playing exactly the same parts twice in a row drove Eddie nuts.

When the ten songs for the Van Halen demo were finished, Edward and Alex helped Simmons with three new Kiss songs, including a take of the unreleased "Christine Sixteen." Simmons later claimed in the book *Kisstory* that Kiss guitarist Ace Frehley replicated Eddie's solo faithfully on the *Love Gun* album. Roth thought that Simmons wanted Eddie to leave Van Halen and join Kiss, which Simmons denies. "In 1977, there was certainly no talk of anyone leaving Van Halen. They seemed to be getting along well in those days." Yet whenever Simmons invited Eddie to the studio or to a party, Roth made sure he was also there—and suspiciously his name was usually not on the guest list.

From the sessions came a polished studio demo featuring a thicker, more muscular production—a little like Kiss—that essentially captured what the band would sound like on its first album. Back in L.A., Roth took the tapes to Rodney Bingenheimer. His *Rodney on the ROQ* show became the first radio program to air Van Halen's "Runnin' with the Devil," complete with Roth's original tremulous, quivering vocals and Edward's snappy, fully developed version of the famous lead.

Ultimately, nothing happened. Unconvinced by Roth's commercial prospects as a frontman—he wasn't especially cute and his voice was far from smooth—Gene's manager, Bill Aucoin, passed on the project, opting in favor of Piper, a more manageable and marketable Stones-

influenced act led by guitarist Billy Squier. Aucoin also thought Van
Halen sounded too similar to Black Oak Arkansas. Eddie and Roth
remembered Aucoin having his shoes shined during the meeting. Afterward, Simmons handed Van Halen back the demo tapes and wished them
the best. Before ending the fling, the Kiss bassist offered some career
advice—he urged Van Halen to change their name to Daddy Longlegs, and
presented them with a new band logo picturing a spider wearing a top hat.

The band remained a hot L.A. attraction despite the career misstep. The
front end of 1977 found Van Halen gigging every six weeks at the
Whisky a Go Go, a bank building turned temple of hedonism on
the Sunset Strip in West Hollywood where the Doors had been the
house band until being fired for lewdness. The cover charge was a
respectable four dollars, and Van Halen would usually be sandwiched
between acts like Berlin Brats and Orange. They shined in a locale that
billed itself as the birthplace of caged go-go dancing.

    After the brush with the big time, their ambitions expanded, along
with their original repertoire. They were constantly dangling new inven-
tions during the act, ranging from the sturdy metal of "We Die Bold" to
an acoustic Humble Pie cover between Eddie and Dave called "79th &
Sunset," a kind of protégé for later album cuts like "Could This Be
Magic." They played every cover song as their own, and they treated
every Van Halen song as if it were already a huge hit.

    Showing their versatility, on March 13, 1977, the band went back to
the Golden West Ballroom in Norwalk for a "Punk Rock Ballroom Blitz"
where they played first on a bill of three bands headlined by the
Ramones. Though Van Halen were a different breed than the punks, they
played with punk bands at the Whisky often and they branched from
some shared influences: the Sweet, Black Sabbath, and the Shangri-Las.

    Van Halen's image in 1977 was still very glam, swathed in satin and
mirrors. As Roth said many times, "We try and look like the music
sounds." In moments of extreme glitter excess, Eddie bought a pink satin

bell-bottom suit that made him look like a disco pimp, and Mike donned a glitter gold jumpsuit. Sometimes Eddie wore a cape. "Eddie never needed that stuff," local musician John Driscoll explained to *The Inside*, Van Halen's fan quarterly. "He sounded great playing in backyard jam sessions, pinching off lightning quick riffs and smiling sheepishly while David Lee Roth pranced and strutted and generally tried to hog the scene."

Unlike other club bands, Van Halen weren't too cool to put on a show. Besides the spandex and spangles, they experimented with smoke bombs and lighter fluid. Former high school jock Michael Anthony did somersaults while playing bass. Alex bought a board rigged with horns taken from different cars, which he abused to create sound effects during "House of Pain" and "Runnin' with the Devil."

During 1977, the band started playing almost monthly at the Pasadena Civic Auditorium before an audience of three thousand per show. They didn't need to paper the town with flyers anymore—the promoters did it for them. An advance team of fanatics became the self-enlisted Van Halen Army. Led by a giant kid named Danny who drove an old Ford Econoline van with the words "Van Halen" painted on the side, the Army encamped outside gigs, tailgating from late afternoon until the band hit the stage, wherever the next battle might be. Van Halen were hometown heroes—and that pride only increased as those wild teenage partiers grew up to be the social pillars of Pasadena.

Already the backstage was becoming a social focal point. The goal was for everyone to outdo the others, whether it was with girls, gusto, guitars, or graffiti. When all else failed, Alex could be counted on to act weird, popping open beer bottles with his teeth and draining them without using his hands, pushing a party over the edge. He was especially fearless, like a six-foot-tall version of Animal the drummer from *The Muppet Show*.

While the young men of Van Halen started to feel like rock stars, they were still rehearsing in Dave's parents' basement. Except for the filth and noise of their practice room, the nine-bedroom Roth mansion was a glamorous Mediterranean spread. Though Dave's dad may have hoped for something more stable for his son than singing, Dr. Nathan Roth himself began to venture beyond ophthalmology around this time.

Bitten by the show business bug, he began renting the family grounds for film and television shoots, then got into acting himself, winning bit roles in *The Bionic Woman* and a couple of beachside bikini movies.

The realities of a band fighting its way up from the gutter were too harrowing for prime-time TV dramas. There were countless close calls, potentially the stuff of Hollywood tragedies. After witnessing a disembowelment on the dance floor following a knife fight at an early show, Van Halen learned that setting their amps two feet away from the wall gave them room to hide if necessary—in effect, they built their own secret safe tunnels for when a gig got rough.

To distinguish himself from the crowded field of flashy rivals and imitators, Eddie decorated his guitar with a roll of tape and some spray paint, creating a trademark stripe motif that would eventually be used by the band to market everything from keychains to foam beer-can cozies. Eddie later applied the pattern to his golf cart. For the time being, it was just Eddie being different.

One of his peculiar stage tricks came from simple paranoia. Hoping to keep his innovative method of finger tapping to himself, Eddie began playing with his back to the crowd. The move didn't work—word had already spread among the other guitarists on the scene—and it wasn't necessary, as none of the others could touch his mastery of the technique. In any case, it was great showmanship, drawing the lay audience into his guitar cult.

As his arsenal of secret weapons grew, Eddie modified an Echoplex tape echo box to create a slower, lower delay, and then transplanted the guts into an Army-surplus torpedo dubbed "the Bomb." Standing nearly as tall as Eddie, the big metal ordnance-cum-reverb-chamber took center stage during Eddie's guitar solo, "Eruption." He later claimed that playing with his back to the audience was only partially an attempt to shield his two-handed tapping technique from prying eyes—he also needed to face the Bomb to twiddle the knobs.

Alex added a second bass drum to his kit, creating a double bass tower behind which he was a monster. Double bass drums were not common at the time, but Alex's idols Ginger Baker of Cream and Keith Moon of the Who had pioneered the practice. During Deep Purple's early-seventies tours, Ian Paice played two bass drums on the song "Fireball," but the Purple roadies would bring out the extra kick drum for that number only and remove it after the song was done.

All the California kids knew about Van Halen by now—the word was out among high schools, guitar stores, and hangouts all over Los Angeles. Finally, on a rainy weekday night in 1977, again at the Starwood in West Hollywood, Van Halen were discovered for the second and last time. A nephew of Milton Berle, talent manager Marshall Berle, showed off Van Halen to two big shots: Doobie Brothers superproducer Ted Templeman and Warner Bros. president Mo Ostin—the label exec who signed Jimi Hendrix at the Monterey Pop Festival in 1967.

Templeman had apparently watched Van Halen from the shadows the previous night, taking a good look at the band before bringing Ostin down to view the merchandise. He had apparently been searching unsuccessfully for his own guitar hero for some time. "That's why he signed [the band] Montrose," said former Van Morrison guitarist Doug Messenger. "Ronnie Montrose could write good songs and play, but he didn't have Eddie's superstar quality."

Van Halen played it cool, allegedly signing a letter of intent on a bar napkin and then letting Warner Bros. simmer for a full twenty-four hours before delivering their reply. Roth estimated the initial advance at $26,000, and said that Warner Bros. recommended the lawyer who looked over the deal for the band. Eddie later called the initial terms of the contract "a Motown deal"—a kind of indentured servitude unique to the entertainment industry. But at the time, they were thrilled, and they hired Berle as their manager.

Unknown to Van Halen, Warner Bros. had reservations about the band's singer too. The label brass conferred with house producer Templeman about substitutes, someone more polished who could take their new rock act over the top. Alex Van Halen claimed the band didn't learn about these boardroom discussions until the early 1980s, but one of the possible replacements for Roth in 1977 was recently liberated Montrose singer Sammy Hagar.

Hard rock was so far out of vogue in Hollywood that it hurt, as clubs mostly booked singer-songwriters and punk acts. Van Halen were not a formula hard rock band, however, and Warner Bros. hoped that the rest of the United States would embrace them. Contemporaries like Quiet Riot were stunned to see Van Halen signed. "We were more popular than they were," singer Kevin Dubrow later told *Creem*. "They had a better rhythm section than we did. We had a great guitar player—they had a great guitar player. I thought for sure, after they got signed, we'd be next. But we weren't. I was furious." While hard rock waited to take off from the Sunset Strip, Van Halen enjoyed a five-year head start.

In late 1977, Van Halen played their last self-promoted party, for thirty-three hundred people who paid a cover charge of five dollars each. Van Halen were now sharply honed by hundreds of gigs and were in amazing form. Cover songs fit seamlessly between battle-tested originals and Eddie's spectacular solo breaks. Roth's randy crowd raps were far improved. In particular, the call-and-response part of the show by late 1977 between Eddie's flickering fingers and Roth's mile-a-minute mouth was spellbinding. "We did work really hard," Eddie says. "It's not like we were born with guitars and drumsticks in our hands."

The local kids were proud—after all, they had won the turf wars, producing the baddest band in the region. Though the Pasadena party scene continued into the 1980s, it was the end of an era. Police and parents' groups frightened by one too many ABC *After School Special* cautionary tales kept kids on the run, and the quality of bands slipped back down to more ordinary high school levels.

Funny that nobody in Van Halen had been born in California, because the band played the part perfectly, selling a bigger, better, and more liberated version of sun and fun. They were outsiders who had bridged the gap, and the great unwashed hordes would soon respond by the millions. After years in the trenches, now Van Halen could die happy. "My fondest memory of working with Van Halen is it was a group that was aimed in a single direction," David Lee Roth later recalled. "We played a lot of different kinds of music in the bars for a number of years, and that was a great education. We didn't do it for money. We did it because we really loved the music."

BAT OUT OF HELL

For all their regional success, in 1977, Van Halen were still just a promising club act. They were gaudy, sweaty hard rockers in an era of sleek disco and fashionable punk rock. Refining the edges on these square pegs was now the job of producer Ted Templeman, who had wrangled rockers Montrose, cooked mellow hits for the Doobie Brothers, and harnessed the frenetic Captain Beefheart.

Templeman sought the live excitement, beginning by bringing Van Halen to the studio to record demos of two to three dozen winners from their stage repertoire. Plenty of tough jams like "Young and Wild" and "We Die Young" from those sessions never made the grade, but "Runnin' with the Devil," "Atomic Punk," and "On Fire" were perfect. Other early live favorites needed major tweaks and were set aside for the time being. "House of Pain" and "Voodoo Queen" would surface again in coming years. The giddy energy and humor on the demo recordings were evident—at the end of "Little Dreamer," Roth mocked Alex's trippy cymbal splashes, cooing, "Are you experienced?" in his best Hendrix baritone.

Templeman soon installed Van Halen at Sunset Sound Recorders, where he had steered the Doobie Brothers to a slew of gold albums. There the band labored to record a white-hot debut loaded with unabashed charisma and a powerhouse of electricity. Usually Roth sang his lead vocals live in an isolation booth at the same time the band played the music in the main studio—an uncommon practice during an era when perfectionists like ELO and Boston were creating lush studio soundscapes one meticulous tape splice at a time.

The band jumped around and put on a show for themselves in the studio. The brothers bickered often over whether Alex was keeping steady time, and he countered by accusing Eddie of playing out of tune. In fact, Eddie was tuned down a quarter step to somewhere between D-sharp and E, a sweet spot low enough for Roth's vocal range but high enough so Michael Anthony's bass sounded tight.

Mike's bass guitar was somewhat downplayed by Templeman, except for the "doomp doomp doomp doomp" at the start of "Runnin with the Devil," a big-bottomed prelude that became iconic for Michael and the band. "When we recorded our first album, Ted Templeman was so into Eddie playing. Everything had to be oriented around the guitar," Mike told *Bass Frontier*. "I had to be really basic. But from the first time I ever picked up a bass, everyone always said it's not a glamorous instrument. You're going to stand there like Bill Wyman in the back and just play. I don't care. I love the way the bass felt, the way it makes your pants and everything else shake."

There was almost no studio magic behind the band's flashy technique. Eddie pleaded with Templeman not to force him to relive the headaches of the Gene Simmons demo sessions. Of ten songs, Eddie claimed he recorded overdubs on only two or three, including the solos to the cover of John Brim's "Ice Cream Man" and "Jamie's Cryin'"—a song that was written in the studio. "When 'Jamie's Cryin'' was picked," Alex told the *Album Network*, "everybody's memory of it now is 'Oh, what a great song.' And yes, it was a good song, or else it wouldn't have made it on the record. But we were more into 'I'm The One,' the hyperkinetic stuff. We were heavy."

Lacking time to hone the song on the Hollywood grindstone—the usual weekly club dates—Roth was unsure how to approach "Jamie's Cryin.'" Not wanting to screw things up, he put down the Camel Filters and laid off drinking for a day beforehand, hoping to sweeten his raspy voice. After a couple takes, Templeman came down on him for sounding weak. When he heard Roth's explanation, Templeman prescribed an immediate return to form—so the singer quickly applied the necessary medications, and soon his voice was suitably thrashed and ready to roar.

Slowed way down, a tape of three of Alex's car horns became the special-effect intro to the record. Eddie recorded a cheap electric sitar to faintly fill out the sound of the guitar solo on "Ain't Talkin' 'Bout Love," the band's manifesto to being young, dumb, and full of cum. The song's simplicity made a mockery of punk rock, using a complicated picking strategy to rip two chords wide open. At the same time, the feel-good vocal harmonies of "Feel Your Love Tonight" put a more racy sexual thrust into the good vibrations of the Beach Boys, the older generation's consummate California crew.

The dynamics of *Van Halen* were fantastic, power rising from a hushed whisper to a full-on blaring wall of guitars, often within one song. On the soft side was "Ice Cream Man," an old blues song of John Brim's by way of Elmore James. Though out of place, the tune was a throwback to Dave's days playing guitar in the high school parking lot. A dexterous picker in his own right, he played the acoustic first verse, and he played it live.

Eddie was awakening the higher brains of a generation with its feet stuck in the primeval mud of heavy rock. His archetypical guitar solo, "Eruption," was done in two or three takes. Basically a showcase of his live soloing, "Eruption" was a slight variation on a composed solo piece for electric guitar. He would flash his chops throughout the live set, wiggling them between songs. Once committed to vinyl, "Eruption" became associated indelibly with Van Halen's crunchy stop-start version of the Kinks' "You Really Got Me." Eddie thanked Templeman for even including "Eruption"—the producer heard him practicing it in the studio and demanded he cut a version for the album. A slight fade in the middle muted a squall of amp feedback—otherwise the unedited ninety-second stroke of genius appeared as performed.

The end of "Eruption" burst into a decimating boom that threw down the gauntlet to all other musicians calling themselves guitar players. The solo elevated electric guitar wankery from its slavish devotion to the blues. The middle finger-tapping section was almost like a flowing saxophone riff—maybe gigging with Jan Van Halen had rubbed off. Eddie's sound was aggressive but natural. His guitar tone became known as the "brown sound," a description Alex originally coined to describe his specifically tuned snare drum. Eddie wasn't shooting for silvery robotic aggression—he wanted earthy noise. "I want my guitar to sound like Al's snare," Eddie said with shrug. "Warm, big and majestic."

Not having heard "Eruption," you could argue that music is more than just an athletic competition. You could talk about feeling, and how good music isn't how many notes you play, but about which ones you really feel. You could look at Eddie Van Halen in his shag haircut and shiny pants and say that he was everything wrong with music. But Eddie wasn't a nascent guitar god because his pick moved faster. He put more ideas together quicker but still poured more feeling into his playing, expressing a higher level of excitement and euphoria than anyone before him.

After twenty-one days in Sunset Sound, Van Halen rested. The band left the sessions with dozens of songs remaining from the preproduction demo, including "Peace of Mind" and "Babe Don't Leave Me Alone." Not many of them stayed on the shelf for long, as the band would tap the creative well of their club days several times over the course of Van Halen's first six albums.

The photos for the album sleeve that introduced the band members to the big bad world beyond Southern California were shot at the Whisky a Go Go. The guitar on the album cover was one of Eddie's $200 specials cobbled together from a pile of cheap guitars—what he called a Frankenstrat. The front pickup was just for show, to fill the hole—only the rear, bridge pickup was actually wired for sound, because after all his hot-rodding, Eddie couldn't figure out how to solder the switch back in place. The guitar also had bike reflectors attached to the back to throw lights around onstage, like something from an episode of *The Little Rascals*.

For "Runnin' with the Devil" and a couple other songs, the band filmed flashy music videos at the Whisky, hoping to capture the dazzle of their live show so the videotape could travel places they couldn't. In the clip for "You Really Got Me," Eddie wielded an Ibanez Destroyer he had crudely sawed some chunks out of to make a star shape, in the process ruining the guitar for actual music. For the band's press bio, David convinced the others to shave two years off their age in order to seem younger. As if the old guard didn't have enough cause for jealousy, Van Halen wanted to kill them completely.

Warner Bros. chose "You Really Got Me" to herald the coming of the new colossus. Bummed that their first single would be a cover instead of an original, Eddie recalled playing a tape of the finished album for drummer Barry Brandt from the rival Sunset Strip club act Angel, only to learn a week later that Angel were in the studio bashing out their own hard rock version of the Kinks' song. Templeman and Warner Bros. scrambled to rush Van Halen's single into stores first.

Standing atop the Hollywood rock club scene, Van Halen crowned 1977 with a New Year's Eve date at the Whisky a Go Go, playing a best-of club days set, including "On Fire," "Bottoms Up!," "Summertime Blues," a three-and-a-half-minute version of "Eruption," and several unreleased songs like "No More Waiting" and "Bullethead." Dave polled the audience about how 1977 had been for them, then drawled: "I judge the year on how good the Thai sticks were, and they were pretty good this year! Let's hear it for Thailand! Let's hear it for Colombia! Let's hear it for Mexico! Let's hear it for Edward!"

Wasting no time, in January 1978, Warner Bros. sent radio stations five songs from *Van Halen* pressed on a special red vinyl record. The standard cardboard sleeve pictured a pointy Van Halen logo that looked like a mountain range, while the flip-side label on the record featured Elmer Fudd climbing out of the famous Looney Tunes/Merrie Melodies spirals used by Warner Bros. cartoons. "You Really Got Me" snuck up on a few rock radio stations and soon took hold nationally. Angel had been smart to try to snake the song—the precision-tooled cover took Van Halen into the Top 40 pop charts in United States and the United Kingdom, a sort of American invasion. Eddie was at home when he heard the song on the radio for the first time at 2 A.M. He ran into his parents' bedroom and woke them up shouting, "Mom! Dad! We're on the radio!"

The full album hit the new-release shelf in record stores nationwide on February 10, 1978, complete with a fetching new VH inverted triangle logo. Van Halen sold the California lifestyle and the world bought it. "We celebrate all the sex and violence of the television, all the rocking on the radio, the movies, the cars, and everything about being young or semi-young or young at heart. That's Van Halen," David Lee Roth told *Waxpaper* shortly afterward.

The album was not an instant hit but a slow and continuously rising success. At the end of May, it was certified gold. After a thousand nights in the beer halls, the cover band from Pasadena was finally about to be taken seriously.

〰〰〰

Warner Bros. found Van Halen a production manager, Noel Monk, fresh off the road wrangling the previous year's self-destructive great white hope, the Sex Pistols. He and acting manager Marshall Berle arranged an eight-man team to get the Van Halen convoy rolling. On March 3, Van Halen hit the road opening for Journey, a light rock band from San Francisco whose audience ranks were swollen with females. "People say this is Van Halen's first world tour," Roth cackled. "This is our first world vacation, man!"

At first they felt out of their element, no longer basking in the approval of thousands of hometown fans. They left home wearing three-inch platform shoes, pushing Eddie and Michael up toward six feet, where Roth stood in his socks. Alex decked himself out in a black-studded leather jumpsuit, his hair a nappy UFO that jived with his reputation as the wildest banana in the bunch. The whole band wanted so badly to look ace that observers remember even the crew wearing platforms. Before the first month was over, it was back to more practical sneakers for the band and Capezio dance slippers for the high-leaping Roth.

Everyone thought that Van Halen should consider themselves lucky to be earning a few hundred dollars a night, playing brief thirty-minute sets with dodgy sound, but they were used to raking in thousands selling out clubs back in Hollywood. The desire to succeed had brought them to the top of the barrel—now they flopped over into the very bottom of a much bigger pool. With sets as short as six songs some nights, no catering or sound check, the band soothed themselves by stealing food and girls from Journey's backstage area while the host band was onstage. Eddie, out from under his parents' watchful eyes for virtually the first time in his life, later admitted to "squeezing everything that walked" in 1978.

For half an hour each night, Van Halen bounced across the stage as if they were weightless on the surface of the moon. David Lee Roth worked his body into contortions and then sprang airborne with vertical splits. And those legs were straight—the corrective braces he had worn on his legs for two years as a toddler did their job. Roth allowed no resistance to his existence, except the tiny internal pilot light that told him it was all turbulence ahead. His was an ever-renewing energy that could be toxic when pointed in certain directions, but there is no underplaying how high his hyperactivity lifted the band upward.

At the time, few people thought rock would still exist in five years. Yet Van Halen played as if they didn't yet realize that in rock and roll, nobody expected them to be this consistently good. Eddie traveled with a suitcase of guitar parts, often found open and scattered across motel rooms as his compulsive search for the perfect weapon continued. He continued composing new song parts into the wee hours, though he admitted to Jas Obrecht that often he was jamming just for the sake of it. "Most of the time I'm so high I forget them!" he said, laughing.

The stage effects in the Army-surplus bomb guaranteed chaos as the round, heavy, unstable war artifact toppled over and rolled around during nearly every show. That torpedo, a strobe light on Roth's spinning scarf, and a logo banner fit for announcing a half-price pizza sale were the sum total of the production value for that tour.

The name Alex Van Halen soon dominated damage reports issued by band management, detailing lamps that had been drummed to pieces, smashed hotel room mirrors, bathroom doors off their hinges, toilet seats found in the parking lot, telephones hanging out the window, and room service carts wrecked from Mississippi to California. The rest of the band and their support staff and road crew made frequent guest appearances on the deduction sheets as well—Roth traveled with a wrench to open windows in hotels that tried to exercise climate control. He claimed he needed fresh air.

In Wisconsin, the touring menagerie trashed the seventh floor of the Madison Sheraton. There were no girls on the scene, nothing but a band of California wildmen set loose in the snow, tossing furniture out of a window several stories above ground. When Eddie found his room empty, he snuck into Roth's room and swiped the table and chairs to replace his own. The adventure led to an apology of sorts in the liner notes for the next album, a gesture that also extended to "all the hall managers who waded through the rubble of Van Halenized backstages across the world."

It paid to remain alert around the Van Halen encampment, especially after someone figured out how to build rockets by stuffing aluminum hotel towel rods with firecrackers. One uneventful evening, Alex was inspired to re-create one of his famous pyro displays in a motel parking lot. He found a pile of black rubber tires and, salivating at the idea of filling the sky with wretched black smoke, tried to light them on fire with a pack of matches, oblivious to the policeman waiting nearby with his gun drawn. "Finally, he says 'what are you doing?'" Alex recalled, and the stunt was thwarted.

After Alex finally lit his hair on fire by accident onstage, he no longer doused his sticks and entire drum set with burning lighter fluid. The band decided to leave pyrotechnics to the professionals. His drum hardware also needed to be welded together, to support the weight of the singer jumping off the kit. "Drummers are people who make their living beating things with sticks," Roth said admiringly. "Alex has got to be the main spirit of Van Halen—we named the band after him."

Hitting Holland that May—where record shops couldn't decide whether to file *Van Halen* under "V" or "H"—the California quartet with two Dutch-Indo brothers was welcomed with curiosity. They appeared on

DJ Alfred Lagarde's influential "Concrete Hour" show on national VARA radio, speaking Dutch with marked American accents. At the Amsterdam-area concert, the band added a cover of "Summetime Blues," and won over an audience heavily populated by aunts, uncles, and proud cousins.

Van Halen were so good opening for Black Sabbath in England in 1978 that Sabbath toppled and broke apart immediately afterward. Their singer, Ozzy Osbourne, became completely demoralized and left the group. Sabbath bassist Geezer Butler later quipped sardonically that it was the first time after eight albums that Warner Bros., their American label, had ever bothered to come see the band—and then only for the sake of catching Van Halen.

To Sabbath's credit, the metal forefathers recognized they were imploding on their own problems, and they bore the Californians no grudge. There was none of the sabotage that Van Halen had come to expect as an upstart opening act—in fact, Osbourne invited them to his home after a Birmingham show for a night of madman-style drinking. Roth recalled seeing Ozzy's wife bring out his children in the morning to kiss their father good night, the helpless Ozzy sprawled unconscious on the couch.

The torch had been passed. When David Lee Roth victoriously opened bottles of champagne over the British crowd, he left Black Sabbath little room but to mop up after Van Halen's party. The only cloud over the parade was that Sabbath's British audience was just too male. Van Halen made up for lost time with an old-fashioned romp through the red-light district as soon as they hit Paris.

In Aberdeen, Scotland, the group learned of their first gold sales award. Celebrating both the gold record and their introduction to Glenmorangie scotch, they trashed their hotel room during a six-hour fire extinguisher fight. Since they had little to no Top 40 singles chart activity, the success of the album caught them by surprise. When the foam cleared, baton-wielding bobbies escorted the band out of the country, and Van Halen were not invited back to Scotland for almost two decades.

Van Halen were ushering in a huge change—they were a heavy metal band with obvious crossover appeal. But for all their black leather posturing and heavy metal riffage, they were equally at home onstage alongside the radio dreamboats in Journey. The secret formula was made up of equal servings of rebellious fire and old-time schmaltz like "Ice Cream Man." The boys came for the guitar solos and flaming drums, the girls came for the bulging trousers and the winning smiles, and everyone went home happy. "Most of our songs you can sing along with," Eddie explained in his first interview, "even though it does have the peculiar guitar and end-of-the-world drums."

"I think a lot of Van Halen's music could be construed as heavy metal," Roth said. "A lot of it can't be construed as any specific thing, except what we call 'Big Rock.' In essence that's high-velocity music— we use volume to drive out the evil spirits. I see a lot of these categories as being based mostly on haircuts and shoes. My haircut's alright for heavy metal, but baby my shoes are all wrong."

Van Halen trekked to Japan for seven shows in late June, where they were hailed as conquering heroes. Jetting straight back to the States, the band arrived in Dallas, to play the first ever Texxas Jam on July 1. The other bands on the bill were strictly representative of the 1970s— including Cheech and Chong, Mahogany Rush, Eddie Money, and the Atlanta Rhythm Section. Arriving before their equipment, not for the first time Van Halen needed to borrow gear for the show. Funny, considering the later mass obsession over Eddie's exact setup, Van Halen ripped apart eighty thousand Texas rockers with an early-afternoon detonation using rented equipment. "It was the most awesome show ever," said Vinnie Paul of the Texas metal band Pantera, then a teenager.

Playing with Boston and Black Sabbath before fifty-six thousand people at Anaheim Stadium in California, Roth conceived a parachute stunt where a quartet of acrobatic skydivers would plummet from the sky onto the stage. During the mass confusion of the moment, the real wig-wearing daredevils ducked behind the amps, and Van Halen rushed onstage to fanatical enthusiasm wearing skydiver suits. Though he didn't dive from a plane, Alex still managed to twist his ankle during the episode, tripping over a massive cable.

At the Day on the Green festival in Oakland, California, in July 1978, Eddie encountered a rock upperclassman, former Montrose singer Sammy Hagar. Eddie asked him why he quit his band, and Sammy told him that Ronnie Montrose, the bandleader, wouldn't let him play guitar. "Ronnie Montrose was the type of guitarist who didn't want another guitarist in the same building," Sammy said.

After Van Halen's show that day, Eddie granted what famously became his "first major interview" with writer Jas Obrecht of *Guitar Player*. Eddie seemed almost unsure that he deserved the attention. "I'm always thinking music," he said. "I'm always trying to think of riffs, using my head. Like sometimes people think I'm spacing off, but I'm not really. I'm thinking about music."

Van Halen were assaulting the monsters of rock on their own terms and winning. The other young bands playing Hollywood in 1978 were mostly punks or new wavers like Devo, X, and the Germs, who attacked from below—the punks couldn't beat Peter Frampton at his own game, so they changed the rules successfully. Van Halen went gunning for the majors head-on. They knew all of Aerosmith and ZZ Top's tricks—they had been practicing them for years in backyard parties.

In October, *Van Halen* went platinum, a stunning mark for a debut album. It would remain on the *Billboard* charts for over three years—a total of 169 weeks. Edward bought a Porsche 911e Targa and practiced not smashing himself into pieces with it.

At the end of the year, Warner Bros. threw a party for their newest platinum playthings at the Body Shop strip club in Hollywood. Newly annointed manager Marshall Berle wheeled out his legendary uncle Milton to present Van Halen with their shiny wall plaques. Afterward, the Van Halen brothers went back to their parents' small house, where the whole family still lived. Thanks to the amazing math of the record business, where every limo and light bulb is eventually charged back to the band, for their labors Van Halen now owed Warner Bros. close to a million bucks for expenses paid on their behalf.

BACK IN THE SADDLE

The production plan for Van Halen's second album was simple: If at first you succeed wildly, retrace your steps and try, try again. The band returned to Studio 1 at Sunset Sound Recorders on December 10, 1978, within a week of completing its first world tour. Eddie was stressed out trying to bring the band down from full party mode. "I was trying to wake the guys up," he said, "saying 'Hey guys, we've got to chill out a little bit, because we've got another record to do'"

Within a week the album was nearly finished—despite the success of the first record, their label allegedly gave them a smaller recording budget the second time around. Many of the tracks used were first takes. Though Eddie publicly mentioned his desire to bring electronic synthesizers into the mix, no such drastic changes were made. If anything, the songs were more focused, pointed rockers—probably because the more dynamic songs had been cherry-picked into service for *Van Halen*.

Van Halen II kept the party rolling at close to full steam. At Sunset Sound they recorded with an old Putnam 610 console, a not at all state-of-the-art mixing desk that dated to the 1950s. Everyone from

Frank Sinatra to the Doors to Walt Disney's animated movies had recorded using that same equipment—a good representative survey of Van Halen's forefathers and influences.

There were fewer dizzying peaks than the debut, but the debauchery was more up front. The record was more fun, showing that the band wasn't just some lethal-precision hit squad from Southern California. They laughed at themselves during a bebop bit in "Bottoms Up!" and offered a timeless pop single in "Dance the Night Away." Written on the spot in the studio, the song was inspired by a drunk woman who had sex with her boyfriend in the back parking lot of Walter Mitty's in full view of the band, then danced for hours in the front row of the club with her jeans put on backward.

Though Roth's aerial spread-eagle jump on the back cover was supposed to look like just another day at the dude ranch, it was a staged stunt for the photo shoot. On the third try, the singer landed sideways and broke a bone in his foot. The last panel in that Bazooka Joe comic could be found inside the sleeve—a photo of Roth with his bare foot bandaged, holding a cane while entertaining a bevy of nurses.

Released thirteen months after the first album on March 23, 1979, *Van Halen II* went gold the following month, and platinum the month after that. It peaked at number 6 on the strength of "Beautiful Girls" and the Top 20 success of "Dance the Night Away."

The record kicked off with Clint Ballard Jr.'s "You're No Good," also the lead track on a number 1 1974 album by California soft rocker Linda Ronstadt. Now the boys of noise were repurposing her broken heart for their own needs. Stepping lightly with a volume-swell guitar intro, the track kicked in like a comeuppance to all the feel-good mellow fellows of the West Coast music establishment.

Alex identified "Light Up the Sky" as the band's true musical direction at the time, or at least his personal preference—a swerving metallic number with a tender underbelly, stop-start rhythms, and a flashy guitar solo. He dismissed "You're No Good" as "somebody else's idea of a hit single"—presumably Templeman, who remained a record company man at heart, always looking to deliver chart action from the bands he produced.

Eddie's guitar ran thick through the mix, deftly spinning pirouettes around the thrust of the songs. He still declined to double his rhythm tracks. To thicken his "brown" guitar sound, he preferred to turn up the volume, overdrive the circuits, and let the amplifiers crackle with natural warmth. The beautiful bell-like intro to "Women in Love" would stand as one of his proudest moments.

For "Spanish Fly," another of Eddie's high points, he played on an ordinary Ovation nylon-string guitar. An acoustic flamenco-style answer to the electricity of "Eruption," the one-minute solo still relied self-referentially on tapping. While guitarists were still reeling from his finger-tapping innovations on the first album, now Eddie was admonishing his acolytes with tapped harmonics, opening another vocabulary for lead guitar.

The band returned to the demo sessions for the first album, bringing back club-pleasers like "Somebody Get Me a Doctor," "D.O.A.," and the Deep Purple–influenced "Bottoms Up!" with its blasting backup vocals. Likewise, "Outta Love Again" was one of the oldest Van Halen songs, dating to before Mike had joined the band. "Beautiful Girls" had also appeared on the Templeman demos under the name "Bring On the Girls"—the album version made the band's horny teenage approach to courtship a little nicer.

More than on the first album, producer Templeman's mellow Doobie Brothers chops shone through. Yet according to Roth, "When *Van Halen II* was recorded and ready to go, everybody at Warners thought it was a failure." Van Halen were succeeding underneath the radar of their own corporate masters.

From March to October 1979, Van Halen embarked on their first headlining tour, suitably dubbed the "World Vacation." No longer only along for the ride, they were doing heavy lifting—thirty-six tons of gear were required to get the show on the road. Streamlining their operation, they did lose a little luggage by firing Marshall Berle and promoting Noel Monk to band manager as a reward for his success as road manager.

The band now dressed in striped overload—thin stripes, thick stripes, vertical stripes, and horizontal stripes. "We know that people come to see bands that look and act special," Roth said, "and that's why we dress in some outrageous costumes and put on a visual show, live right in front of your naked steaming eyeballs. We've got the tightest pants in the business."

He was right—to kids who switched off the tube ten seconds before heading to a Van Halen concert, the band looked like *Charlie's Angels*—two shag brunettes and a feathered blonde with a short, squat Bosley on bass guitar. The Van Halen generation was raised on *The Partridge Family*, where every family had a rock band in their garage. Now Van Halen were trying to put on a pop spectacle that could compete with *The Six Million Dollar Man* and *Love, American Style*. They blessed their crowds with the gracious bounty of everything rock and roll and a little technology could offer, then hoped the fans would provide the rest.

The tour started with a roar, and the second week the band played before 106,000 at the California World Music fest, joining heavyweights Aerosmith, Toto, UFO, Cheap Trick, and Ted Nugent—bands that Van Halen would have stood in line to see just a year earlier. That night, Van Halen and three hundred close friends arrived in a convoy of sixteen limousines. David Lee Roth presided over the backstage, joined by a chimpanzee dressed like him and two little persons hired as bodyguards.

The band concocted an elaborate stunt for the show, at the expense of Aerosmith. On a grassy incline behind the stage, visible to the crowd, a $100 yellow Volkswagen was parked throughout the day. Periodically, someone at the soundboard would make an announcement asking for "someone in the Aerosmith organization to please move their car." Van Halen had arranged for a Sherman tank to roll out onto the field before their set and crush the "Aerosmith" car, but apparently word leaked to Aerosmith and the caper was curtailed before any military hardware could be deployed. The party still stormed well into the next day, leaving many casualties, including Dave—he fainted onstage in Spokane, Washington, five days afterward. He later blamed a stomach virus.

Their quest for carnage was soon satisfied in July at the Illinois State Armory in Springfield. According to the *State Journal-Register*, the band destroyed a limousine there and started a fire that caused $2,000 worth of damage. They were stopped overnight for a police investigation, forcing a cancellation of the Cincinnati show the next night.

Tour mishaps became growing experiences as the band struggled to keep up with its success. Backstage sex movies, drug abuse, and clashing egos came with the territory—though the Van Halen brothers remained close, often sharing hotel rooms. "When we started out, the emphasis was on sex, drugs, and rock and roll," Alex told *Guitar Player*. "Forget the drug part, we'll drink ourselves to death. You do your tour— two hours onstage—and then get the hell out of there so you can get laid!"

The band took rock hedonism to new levels. When they found something that made them laugh—like a sex shop in Cleveland overloaded with inflatable love dolls—they shared it with the audience, hanging a full harem of lingerie-laden air hoochies from the lighting rafters. The fans got laid, the band got laid, and their crew and business associates got laid. Even the journalists sent out to cover the band got laid. "What happens after our show isn't that different than [what] happens on a lot of tours," Dave explained. "It's just that we're the ones who will let you take a picture."

A Van Halen concert was a constantly shimmying rock variety show packed with as many highlights as imaginable. When you went to see the Who, you had to wait a while to see Pete Townshend's windmills. At a Led Zeppelin show, Jimmy Page didn't break out the violin bow for his guitar until the second hour. But with Van Halen, the money shots started the moment Roth made his stage entrance with the bang of the lights and flying aerial splits off the drum riser.

The impact of Van Halen's early streaks across the United States was tremendous and far-reaching. Kirk Hammett of Metallica saw them play in Oakland in 1978. Henry Rollins—then still Henry Garfield— and his pal Ian MacKaye, the future leader of Minor Threat and Fugazi, watched Van Halen open for Ted Nugent and were amazed. And not only the young minds were impressed. Leslie West of Mountain, a band Van Halen had covered, was deep into drug problems, and claimed he had all but abandoned playing guitar until witnessing Eddie Van Halen opening for Journey in 1978.

Also apparently fallen under the spell of Eddie was guitarist Rick Derringer, who began copying Eddie's guitar solo while opening shows for Van Halen on the tour. He crossed the line when he began ending his sets with a certain Kinks cover. "After the show, we're sitting in the bar," Eddie told *Guitar Player*'s Jas Obrecht. "I said 'Hey Rick, I grew up on your ass. How can you do this? I don't care if you use the technique—don't play my melody.' And he's going, 'Yeah, yeah.' The next night he does my solo again, and he ends the set with 'You Really Got Me,' which is exactly what we do. So I kicked him off."

Not everyone appreciated the hot-dog approach to making music. Seasoned rock fans saw all the glitz and powder as a distraction, a sugary substitute for the integrity found in rock songwriters like Bruce Springsteen or Patti Smith. "There is a lot of wizardry and technique at work here," Roth defended himself during a TV interview. "We just don't bang on it and bang on it to show you how artistic we are. But hey, we're from California!"

A measure of respect arrived when Eddie was voted guitarist of the year in *Guitar Player* in 1979. By now, there were legitimate guitar manufacturers betting their entire business on single-pickup models based on Eddie's homemade Strat. The band celebrated with friends by going out for pizza and beer. Unlike Roth, Eddie was not the type of person to put himself on a pedestal. The world would be glad to do that for him. *Billboard*'s year-end chart for 1979 placed both Van Halen albums in the Top 40.

〜〜〜〜〜〜

For the third album, *Women and Children First*, the band ran on momentum, even spinning its wheels a little. If *Van Halen* was an approaching comet, and *II* was the heat of that approach, then *Women and Children First* was a kind of afterglow—a chance for everyone to gather their wits and take stock of everything that had happened.

The instrumental tracks were recorded in four days and the vocals added afterward in six days. Inside of a week later, they had a finished record. "I don't think we'll ever be confused with Fleetwood Mac or Steely Dan, who spend jillions of dollars and years in the studio just to make one record," Roth guffawed in *Hit Parader*. "How boring can you get, man? I like to think that all we're really trying to do is capture some of our youthful enthusiasm."

Missing some of the overall energy of the first two records, *Women and Children First* showed signs of road fatigue. However, the record benefited from three great tracks on side one: the slow-motion power anthem "And the Cradle Will Rock," the explosive "Everybody Wants Some," and the frisky "Romeo Delight," which became the band's new show opener. Notably, for the first time there were no cover songs.

The powerhouse opener, "And the Cradle Will Rock," featured the band's first use of keyboards, an old Wurlitzer disguised by bristling distortion that came from playing it through a Marshall guitar amp. No longer allowed the endless club dates that had honed their past material and defined the songwriting process, Eddie and Alex played the main riff to the song together in Dr. Roth's basement two hours a day for two weeks to fuse the feeling in all the right places.

"Everybody Wants Some" was a hymn to horniness, with Roth launching off-the-cuff into some trash talk directed toward a woman visiting the studio control room. The song's subtext was the band blowing off steam about a syndrome they were experiencing of former friends, rivals, and complete strangers hitting them up for handouts. Onlookers saw the silver outfits and limousines and started thinking about what they could get from Van Halen. While the band had recently played L.A. Forum, for example, some scheming stoners had broken into Jan and Eugenia Van Halen's house and stolen two dozen framed platinum albums, thinking the awards were cast from precious actual platinum.

Still dipping into the fertile songwriting well of their formative years, "Fools" was a thumping track that had been with Van Halen since before Michael Anthony. A basic blues bomp, the song had character, but it was easy to see why it had been passed over on the first two albums. A better early track resurfacing was "Take Your Whiskey Home," which the band had already recorded as early as 1974—one of the first songs Michael Anthony learned.

Moving beyond his former heroes Eric Clapton and Jeff Beck, Eddie now championed the playing of jazz-fusion virtuoso Allan Holdsworth, whose slapping technique was predicated on funk. Eddie had maxed out on speed and flashy technique, and was trying to push his playing in more subtle ways. "I ain't no extrovert," he said. "I'm a quiet person. That's probably why I do all these weird things on guitar."

"Tora! Tora!"—which Eddie had wanted to call "Act Like It Hurts"—began with backwards guitar before lurching into a Sabbathy dirge that introduced the spastic "Loss of Control." Though Eddie had written the music the same day as "Ain't Talkin' 'Bout Love," Roth's lyrics were still incomplete, so he improvised a helicopter pilot transmission at the start of the song. MTV was more than a year away from launching in the States, but the band produced a strange concept video for "Loss of Control" in Europe with Roth vamping onstage in a hospital gown and white gloves, groping and grinding with a pretty young nurse. The rest of the band wore green surgical scrubs, and Alex had X-ray films taped all across his drums.

Templeman suggested that Eddie use a guitar slide for "Could This Be Magic?" creating the old-timey bottleneck sound that made this original song sound like a traditional sea shanty. David Lee Roth, whose parking-lot fingerpicking skills remained unsung, joined on second guitar. This neo-skiffle treat also featured harmony vocals by former Linda Ronstadt session vocalist Nicolette Larson. She was repaying a favor, as at the end of 1978 Eddie had stealthily recorded a guitar solo for her hit *Nicolette* album against Roth's wishes.

The album ended with an untitled twenty-second muscular vamp that the band referred to sometimes as "Tank" or "Growth." If the band was not rushed to finish the album, the mystery riff would probably have been developed into a full song. Instead the idea was to let the riff fade out, then start the next album by fading it back into a full song—a plot that was never hatched.

The guitar pictured on the album cover was the Ibanez Destroyer lent to Eddie by local Pasadena guitarist Chris Holmes, later of W.A.S.P., made from highly desirable and resonant korina wood. Not by coincidence, the guitar was a great stunt double for the instrument Eddie used to record most of *Van Halen*—which he had inadvertently wrecked by sawing halfway apart. Holmes had bought the Destroyer in the first place to emulate Eddie. "When I got it back," Holmes told *The Inside*, "the bridge was turned around backwards and all that intonation. It was just backwards to the way I would have had it. I just don't see how he played it that way, but he did. I've been to a few Van Halen shows and I put on Ed's guitar and it's just the complete opposite of the way I set up mine. He'd have the strings about a mile off the fret board. He likes his whammy bar so loose that he Super Glues the nut on the back so it spins around."

Boosted by the two million albums sold before it and Van Halen's heavy touring, *Women and Children First* landed in the Top 10 the week after its release on March 26, 1980. Peaking at number 6 like its predecessor, the album went platinum within ten weeks, the band's third million-plus-selling effort. Eddie and Alex bought themselves jeeps, Eddie invested $10,000 in what he knew best—two vintage Les Paul guitars—and the boys retired their parents from ever working again.

The record was not a critical darling. Even *Creem*, the black sheep of the mainstream rock press, offered a letter from a reader: "I want to write for your magazine. I hate David Lee Roth. Do I qualify?" The smart-aleck magazine answered, "You and an astonishing number of our readers."

Roth mercilessly sized up his opponents, boasting that Van Halen platters were designed to spill over the turntable and melt all the other records in the house. As he told *Creem* and everyone else, "All I got to say is that the reason why so many critics dislike Van Halen and like Elvis Costello so much is because they all look like Elvis Costello."

Never shirking the responsibilities of a sex symbol, Dave wanted to prove he was more than a himbo with a scream. After cornering photographer Helmut Newton at a Beverly Hills hotel, he participated in an S&M-tinged photo shoot that was out of step with his California-boy image and the band's party appeal. Shirtless and bound in black straps, Roth crouched chained to a chain-link dog pen in his backyard. Except for the excess hair on his heaving bosom, he looked like a submissive princess from a Frank Frazetta fantasy poster, not a leonine conqueror.

Exactly for those reasons, and to stir up controversy, the photo became a yard-high poster folded into every copy of *Women and Children First*. "That poster made it to more ceilings than *paint*," Roth joked. Thrilled with the results, Newton charged Roth only $45, which he paid to the art students who worked as photo assistants on the shoot.

Traveling to Japan in late 1979, Van Halen appeared on TV lip-synching to "You Really Got Me" with canned overdubs of squealing teenage girls. Smiling for an audience of schoolgirls in uniform, the woozy-seeming band looked surprised that the hosts were mostly interested in the singer. Roth, doused in pancake makeup, was asked about the future of rock. "I think that Van Halen is the future of rock and roll for the United States, and for the world! This is the 1980s—everybody up for the kickoff and *fasten your seat belts*!"—the end of the message coming in four-part harmony. The 1970s had been a wonderful training ground, but Van Halen couldn't wait to get out of the decade and into an era they could truly call their own.

The 1980 tour was suitably called "Invasion"—fitting considering the massive resources now mobilizing behind hard rock music. In England and Europe, heavy bands were already invading all aspects of the music scene, and the United States would soon follow. Before hitting the road, the band took over a massive sound system belonging to the Bee Gees. After all, disco was dead or dying—the Brothers Gibb didn't need a few thousand watts as much as the Brothers Van Halen.

The show typically opened with the upbeat "Romeo Delight," a hectic pacesetter about taking whiskey to the party every night, looking for a body to squeeze. "Tonight I'm going to teach you how to drink for yourself," began one of Roth's new crowd lines. "Next year when we come back I'll teach you how to drink for other people!" Like the letters scrawled on Roth's shirt, the backstage passes and Mike's blood-spattered bass all boasted: "W.D.F.A."—We Don't Fuck Around.

To re-create the monstrous Wurlitzer sound of "And the Cradle Will Rock"—which most people assumed was Eddie's guitar—Michael Anthony snuck to the side and played keyboards. You would think the crowd would notice a band member slipping away to pound on a five-hundred-pound Wurlitzer and a Minimoog, but hardly anybody knew the difference.

Almost immediately, the tour made headlines. In Cincinnati, Roth was ticketed for urging the audience to "light 'em up" in the nonsmoking arena during "Light Up the Sky." The city was taking no chances after eleven people were trampled to death in the same stadium at a Who concert five months earlier. Roth was cited by police and given a court date a few days later. He pleaded innocent, and the misdemeanor charges were dismissed, but the band got its money's worth in free publicity. "Police said Roth was charged with complicity to violate Ohio's fire codes, after many in the audience lit matches and lighters at the urging of the performer," the national Associated Press wire reported and hundreds of regional papers reprinted the news.

A mishap at the University of Southern Colorado in Pueblo revealed a curious Van Halen quirk. A new shock-absorbent floor on the arena proved a poor foundation for the umpteen tons of stage, amplification, and lighting trusses built for the show. Though the booking contract stated the requirements clearly, Van Halen's gear crumpled to the floor, causing tens of thousands of dollars' worth of damage. At the same time, the band members had gone ballistic backstage, kicking holes in the walls and smashing mirrors in their dressing room.

Apparently, Van Halen had appended a rider to their standard performance contract asking for a bowl of M&M's, strictly forbidding any brown ones. When Roth arrived and found the offending candy, he felt compelled to wreak havoc. Given the situation on the main floor, the band was able to claim that their "no brown M&M's" clause was a type of quality control. The same slipshod operations that would overlook a detail in the candy department would also likely neglect to fulfill obligations in a more crucial department—such as rigging safety, transportation security, or making sure the stage didn't sink through the floor.

The *Los Angles Times* had reported in March 1978 on rock bands requesting no yellow M&M's backstage at the Cal Jam II festival five years earlier. "The thing about not having any brown M&M's is part of the old tradition," Roth mused. "I think Caruso didn't allow anyone to whistle backstage." Yet press reports sloppily confused the backstage damage with the floor damage, and the band were soon accused of causing $80,000 worth of damage in a tantrum over candy. Pueblo promptly banned rock concerts, and Van Halen's hatred of brown M&M's entered into American folklore.

Seeking new ways to attract attention, Roth was now inverting himself before concerts, picking a conspicuous spot backstage to hang upside down like Richard Gere with his gravity boots in *American Gigolo*. While still presenting himself as an athletic specimen, Roth broke his nose jumping during a photo shoot in Italy. The lights went down and he went up several times without a problem—until his luck ran out and his face smacked into a low-hanging disco ball. He was treated for concussion and slapped some bandaging tape across the bridge of his nose for the next few shows—a rock and roll nose job.

Roth felt that his parents had more respect for the black limo that picked them up before a concert than they did his music, but he was very proud of keeping the mood light. "When you're on the road for nine months a year and you always have all these cute little chiquitas running around in their halter tops, it's kind of hard to worry about things like nuclear proliferation." Forget the topical songs, Van Halen were going for some kind of timeless celebration of life—or at the very least celebrating Roth's life. "I'll never have all the women I want," he quipped, "but I'll get all the women who want me!"

The spectacle of Van Halen was already eclipsing the genuine furor over their music. As the band became not just rock stars but celebrities, Roth soon opened his boudoir to actresses, older socialites, punk rock chicks, and fledgling models. Now under the athletic supervision of an L.A. Lakers trainer, he attempted to protect his body with a paternity insurance policy from Lloyd's of London, claiming in his petition that fast and frequent fornication was "necessary to his work."

Inspired to document some of the carnage with a concert film to challenge Led Zeppelin's *The Song Remains the Same* and the Who's *The Kids Are Alright*, Van Halen dabbled in filmmaking. They reported hiring a "Dutch cinematographer" supposedly named Snade Krellmans—an in-joke based on rock-star slang for cocaine. Though the footage never surfaced, it may have inspired the new song "Dirty Movies"—an eerie midpaced narrative about a small-town girl appearing in porn films.

"Van Halen is definitely a ladies' band, and we've got the Polaroids to prove it," Roth said with a smirk. Still, when defending Van Halen's appeal, he could go more than skin deep. "When the crowd goes crazy, it's because they're actually physically enjoying themselves. It's as simple as that." Van Halen's songs were becoming anthems, as important a piece of the American teenage dream as a chrome tailpipe on a muscle car, latex miniskirts on flirty girls, and a bag of really good marijuana on a summer Saturday.

Offstage, Van Halen behaved like a team of superheroes with separate storylines. In February 1980, Roth explored his Tarzan fantasies during the first of several outback excursions with the Jungle Studs. This pack of self-identified alpha males—CPAs, MBAs, Vietnam vets, research scientists, and with Roth one rock star and his girlfriend— sought out high-impact survival experiences that would justify their massive egos and make them forget the pressure of their day jobs.

On one adventure, the Jungle Studs hired a guide for a thirty-eight- day trek up the steep jungle cliffs of the Hindenburg Wall in the Star Mountains of New Guinea. Roth claimed he started on one side of the island with brand-new combat boots and emerged a month later on the other side wearing rotten scraps of leather. "I get some really dramatic and colorful emotional response out of myself, and maybe I can put that onto plastic when we make a record," he said. "Your life depends on how many little things you can notice and remember. That to me sends chills up and down my spine. Now when somebody tells me the stage monitor has blown up—it's really no big deal."

As a kid, Roth had been fascinated by the Rolling Stones because "they were someplace I couldn't be." Now he and Van Halen seemed to have all-access passes everywhere they went.

GIRLS ON FILM

I n Shreveport, Louisiana, during the 1980 "Invasion" tour, TV actress Valerie Bertinelli came backstage with her gaggle of brothers, enthusiastic Van Halen fans who hoped to meet the band using their sister as a giant life-size party pass. She came bearing bags of M&M's for everyone in the band and before long found herself in the quiet backstage universe of the band's musical prodigy, Edward Van Halen. Valerie had just ended a miserable two-month publicity relationship with Steven Spielberg. She said she had always thought Eddie looked nice in pictures. She must have been reading *Creem* and *Circus*, since despite three platinum albums *Rolling Stone* had passed over Van Halen for its cover repeatedly in favor of figures like Jackson Browne.

Valerie turned up again the next night in Baton Rouge, Louisiana. Afterward the couple seemed inseparable, with Valerie joining the Van Halen tour at every chance. In Phoenix, Eddie came to bed with the news that *Guitar Player* readers had voted him best player yet again, and so had *Creem*, but Roth had rubbed Eddie's nose in the dirt about the kudos. Eddie had been holding back on having sex with his actress girlfriend, but this night he began crying and, according to Valerie, she jumped his bones once and for all. Afterward, the *One Day at a Time* theme came blaring over the TV.

Eddie proposed to Valerie on New Year's Eve 1980. The union of these lookalikes had probably been ordained since they met. While they held hands and looked into each other's eyes for hours that first night under the Louisiana moon, Michael Anthony and one of the Bertinelli boys had trashed a hotel during a drunken fire extinguisher battle.

Eddie Van Halen and America's sweetheart Valerie Bertinelli were married on April 11, 1981, at St. Paul the Apostle Church in Westwood, California. Roth bought Eddie a white-tailed tuxedo to wear. Now a member of Eddie's circle of friends, Van Halen collaborator Nicolette Larson sang a song in French she had written for the ceremony. Smiling shyly, the impish newlyweds looked almost like siblings, or Kewpie dolls that should have been standing on the cake.

There was a fantastic feeling to this union of rockers and TV actors. Michael Anthony later joked about being freaked out meeting actress Bonnie Franklin, Valerie's mom on *One Day at a Time*. "She was just like she is on the show!"

"I know people hear my name and they think I'm Barbara Cooper, that little girl on TV, and I'm not any more," Valerie told *Entertainment Tonight*. Soon after her real-life wedding, the producers of *One Day at a Time* married off her character on the show to a dentist.

Eddie panicked the day of the wedding, drinking heavily and nearly collapsing into his groomsmen's arms several times. At the crucial moment, however, he jumped into matrimony happily. Afterward, he moved out of his parents' house for the first time in his life, moving into a large house in the Hollywood Hills with his wife and his rapidly expanding collection of sports cars.

The public immediately wondered if Valerie would be Van Halen's Yoko Ono, steering Eddie down a secluded path and stealing their hero. "We see a lot less of Valerie Bertinelli than people are led to believe," Roth told *Rolling Stone*. "I'm sure some folks out there feel like she's moved into the studio with the band or that she takes an active participation in what the stage show is going to be like. I think I've seen Valerie once in the last five months."

Michael Anthony followed Eddie down the aisle, marrying his high school girlfriend, Sue, who proposed to him while they were waiting in line at a McDonald's drive-through window. As a self-professed fan of the most insanely squeaky clean TV show in history, *Leave It to Beaver*, Mike's interests were considerably domestic, revolving around pet dogs and a growing collection of Mickey Mouse memorabilia. If he was clinging for dear life to something resembling normalcy, he was in for a shock—Disney and Van Halen were just two rival cartoon attractions in the wonderland of Southern California.

When Roth privately became concerned that wholesome marriages would weaken the band's image as lust-starved marauders, Eddie sensed a celebrity effect. "I think it pissed him off because all of a sudden I got a whole other side of the limelight that he wanted. The tabloids and *People* magazine kind of shit—some people thrive on all that attention." Sure enough, the band bounded in popularity as Eddie-loves-Val stories in the *National Enquirer* pushed the band's names into shopping market checkout lines, hairdressers, and doctor's office waiting rooms.

"I'm so tired of saying I'm fine, my marriage is fun, that I don't care anymore," Valerie told *Entertainment Tonight* the following year. "I think what happened is both of us got each other's personalities. I got to be a little more crazy, and he felt more comfortable being sane."

Marriage delayed work on the band's fourth album. Torn between his new domestic bliss and a helter-skelter career in Van Halen, Eddie grew disillusioned with the band and wanted to quit. In his book *Kiss and Make-up*, Gene Simmons reported that a distraught Eddie at least halfheartedly made motions toward defecting Van Halen and joining Kiss as a second guitarist. "We thought Kiss with Eddie Van Halen on second guitar was an exciting idea," Simmons wrote, "but if it came to pass what would his makeup character be?"

Certainly Eddie's qualms were serious enough that Alex later claimed to have convinced Eddie to keep Van Halen together. "On the whole album I was angry, frustrated, and loose," Eddie admitted. It was a dark time for him personally.

Consequently, *Fair Warning* was a major departure from the playfulness of *Women and Children First*. Before work began in the winter of early 1981, Roth had spent a few royalty checks for a glamorous jungle adventure to Haiti and had been punched with an emaciated paw in his conscience. He saw poverty and corruption in doses unavailable in Pasadena or Indiana, and he came back to the fractious Van Halen camp ready for a revolution of his own.

The record brought back the dynamics of the debut album, the silences and rhythm-section showcases that formed the full heavy metal machine. At the same time, it was much denser. Musically, almost every song had thick overdubs on the rhythm and lead guitar tracks, and the band recorded using smaller studio amps to control the sound instead of capturing it directly from typical high-decibel stage rigs. The sunshine backing vocals were held to a minimum.

The album cover was also odd, a collection of drawings of violent street situations, each panel loosely corresponding to a song on the album. The images were chosen and arranged by Van Halen's lighting designer turned all-purpose creative director, Pete Angelus, based on paintings by troubled Canadian-Ukrainian prairie artist William Kurelek. Alex had discovered the paintings, and instead of a collage he initially was interested in only one image: a man ramming his head into a wall.

This tough fourth album declared the band's reign over the rising tide of heavy music. They were pictured uncharacteristically wearing black leather, nodding to the British metal sound just arriving in the United States. Yet Van Halen remained wary of the term "heavy metal." They had Americanized heavy metal, styling their hair and projecting exuberance and confidence instead of the dour attitudes of their European counterparts. As Roth said, "This is not like Judas Priest and Black Sabbath—that's for young boys. I maintain that Van Halen is for everybody."

Oozing with menace, *Fair Warning* was the closest Van Halen ever came to a thematic concept album, a suite of songs about life in the ruts. The opening cut, "Mean Street," became an anthem. Beginning with Eddie's fast-motion slapping pattern on high and low E strings, a technique he adapted from funk bass, the track stepped into skid-row territory instead of strolling down Main Street. The main riff was lifted from the band's midseventies staple "Voodoo Queen," while the funky transitional riff came from "She's the Woman." Now past the point of reusing old songs, Eddie was chopping and rearranging the hot moments of his back catalog.

Fair Warning was a masterpiece made in the studio, not honed like past albums in the clubs before recording. While demoing the song as a work in progress, Dave slurred the lyrics in a monotonous jive, hustling the band toward a bang-up heavy metal can-can finale, far flashier than anything used on the album.

Eddie again picked up a guitar slide for "Dirty Movies," though he had trouble reaching the high notes on his SG-shaped Gibson Les Paul Junior. Ever one to bend his tools to fit his needs, he sawed a chunk off the vintage guitar so he could play the song the way he thought it should sound.

Eddie claimed "Push Comes to Shove" was a nod to dub reggae, instigated by Roth. If so, the template for dread-rock fusion was years ahead of similar sultry tracks by Rastafarian punks Bad Brains or the Red Hot Chili Peppers.

Saved as a big punch for the start of side two, "Unchained" was the biggest riff since "Runnin' with the Devil"—a barrel-chested headbanger built on crunchy guitar, Roth's screams, and a plowing bass line that left Michael Anthony free for high-pitched backing vocals. At the end of the guitar solo, the band pulled back while Roth ribbed the control room like a street-corner wiseguy running a friend through the dozens. "Hey man, that suit is you! You'll get some leg tonight for sure!"

"C'mon Dave, gimme a break," Ted Templeman punched in from the control room, and a legendary ad-lib was born, a peek behind the curtain of the Wizard of Van Halen. As with most of the band's off-the-cuff turns, however, each peck of brilliance was meticulously rehearsed. On the preproduction versions of "Unchained," Roth delivered the "Gimme a break!" line himself.

Eddie and Templeman often came to screaming fights about overdubs, with Templeman refusing to allow multitracking that the band could never re-create onstage. He nixed a version of "Unchained" where Eddie had split his guitar with a harmonizer so that the sound in the right speaker was a muddy octave lower. Some days they were best friends, sometimes Templeman was the enemy. Eddie later admitted to sneaking into the studio with engineer Donn Landee behind Templeman's back. Significantly, Eddie's need for more control pushed him to begin plans to build his own home studio with Landee's help.

Though brief instrumentals like "Eruption" were now part and parcel of a Van Halen package, *Fair Warning*'s "Sunday Afternoon in the Park" was a complete departure. Composed quickly by Eddie on an Electro-Harmonix synthesizer, allegedly for his new wife, the funky two-minute track fit the album's mood perfectly. The synth rock pulsed as hard as any rudimentary electro music, resembling squelching European synth devils like the Italian horror soundtrack group Goblin or England's cold-blooded Gary Numan.

Closing the record was "One Foot Out the Door," a fast rocker built on another burbling synth line. The song was reputedly captured in one take as the band was literally heading out the door of Sunset Sound after finishing the record.

After a reviewer in *Rolling Stone* predictably tore up the album, Valerie Bertinelli threw the band a congratulatory celebration. Regardless of what a magazine that had yet to put them on the cover thought, *Fair Warning* established the band artistically and proved Van Halen mattered beyond a party environment. At one point or another, all four members later declared it their favorite early Van Halen record and defended its virtues.

Launched in April 1981, *Fair Warning* set a new chart high for the band by peaking at number 5 on the *Billboard* chart. The problem was there was no obvious radio hit. "Mean Street," "Push Comes to Shove," and "Unchained" all cracked the Top 30 rock list, but the mainstream pop hit that the record label wanted eluded them. In the eyes of the band's business partners, that was a flaw. As much as the music industry pretended to be results-driven, there was a pack mentality that craved marketable hits.

Roth liked to say that Van Halen had played Lima, Ohio, and Lima, Peru, Paris, Texas, and Paris, France, and every place in between. But except for rehearsal sessions in Halifax, Nova Scotia, and a few subsequent gigs north of the border, the *Fair Warning* tour in 1981 never left the country. The band's operation had become too massive, requiring a small city of support staff and hardware. The four weeks of tour rehearsal alone cost almost $100,000 in crew salaries plus stage and gear rental. The actual tour budget named expenses like $5,000 for an "ego ramp" reaching into the crowd, $1,000 for Alex's fire effect, a whopping $4,000 for backstage passes, and $2,500 for dance lessons.

Instead of burning audiences in the corneas with a straightforward light show, the *Fair Warning* stage setup brought the bad side of town to the suburbs. A bluesy urban street scene unfolded on a massive backdrop while Van Halen ripped through darker material like "Sinner's Swing." Meanwhile, Alex acquired a massive gong behind his kit, which he lit in a circle of flame and bashed repeatedly to bring the show to a climax.

During 1981, the band sold out three nights at the Philadelphia Spectrum and two nights at the Capital Centre in D.C. The *New York Times* gave the band's Madison Square Garden appearance a respectful nod, describing the three-ring circus administered by Roth with the help of "right hand man" Eddie Van Halen. The newspaper of record even credited "the heavy-metal brand of hard rock" with keeping the record business afloat.

Though the full tour was too expensive to haul to Europe, Van Halen appeared on Dutch television. On the streets of Amsterdam, Dave was comically brushed off by passersby, except for a well-meaning elderly man who thought he was a French tourist. Dave found his bandmates near a wurst wagon and mock-interviewed them about Van Halen. Eddie and Alex began rapidly discussing the band in Dutch. They pretended to be starstruck by the arrival of bassist Michael Anthony—a man so unpresumptuous that he still admitted to being thrilled when fans asked him to sign autographs.

Dave continued questioning the band as they cruised the Amsterdam canals. Eddie replied in his native Dutch: "The best city in the world, with the best beer and the best romance." He and Alex glowed with pride, enjoying the royal treatment twenty years after leaving the country as small boys.

Par for the course, *Fair Warning* was platinum by year's end, but sales of each of the band's first four albums pointed toward a slight downward trend. The band shot a music video in a foggy forest near a giant brontosaurus sculpture, but the footage was never edited because the record label saw no need to promote an album without a single. That insatiable appetite for airplay would hang over the band during their next record.

Van Halen now presided over a great reawakening of hard rock music and were already surpassing many of their idols. Among the monoliths of the 1970s, only Queen still thrived, and that was by making forays into dance and funk. Led Zeppelin had disbanded in December 1980 after the sad death of drummer John Bonham. Black Sabbath had split with their original singer, Ozzy Osbourne, and were in a commercial stalemate. Kiss had lost drummer Peter Criss and guitarist Ace Frehley, and their latest studio album, *Music from the Elder*, was a confusing hodgepodge of medieval horns and Gregorian chants. Even Aerosmith were suffering lineup changes and commercial doldrums, and were about to enter a period of inactivity.

On the ground in Hollywood, however, the situation was exploding. Though hard rock had been passé when Van Halen arrived at the Starwood, the club scene they left behind was now crowded with baby Halens with outrageous lead singers and flashy guitar heroes. "I used to sit on the stage at the Whisky, and Van Halen would be exploding all over the place," singer Stephen Pearcy of Ratt recalled.

Dokken, Mötley Crüe, Quiet Riot, and Ratt were all on the verge of minting platinum records, and they owed much of their stage acts to Van Halen. Singers like Vince Neil of Mötley Crüe bleached their hair to look more like David Lee Roth, and everyone practiced their guitars twenty-four hours a day to be more like Eddie. Those lacking in charm and talent made up for it in stagecraft, incorporating storefront Satanism, strippers, and fake blood into their acts. "I'm not that goofy, am I?" Eddie asked *Musician* about his more obvious imitators.

Some of the glamsters had old connections to Van Halen—Chris Holmes from W.A.S.P. hailed from the Pasadena party scene, and George Lynch from Dokken had inadvertently steered Gene Simmons to see Van Halen in 1976. The link between the band Hollywood Rose and Van Halen was truly special—in the early seventies, drummer Johnny Kreis's dad, Richard, had played with Jan Van Halen in a polka band, with Alex often playing drums. Though Hollywood Rose didn't leave behind any albums, their singer Axl Rose and guitarist Izzy Bell split in March 1985 and founded Guns N' Roses.

As Eddie's guitar cult became legion, every band in L.A. required an Eddie clone. The Guitar Institute of Technology (GIT) in Hollywood had launched in 1977 and began mass-producing guitar prodigies with master classes in finger-tapping. Eugenia Van Halen should have been proud—instead of going to DeVry, her son now had a technical institute dedicated to his study.

As the artistry of *Fair Warning* proved, Edward still blew smoke rings around the competition. "What bothers me is that often the kids don't even notice when I'm bad," Eddie told *Rolling Stone*. "I come off-stage and get compliments up the ass. That's so frustrating." He expressed his impatience by wearing a T-shirt onstage with a crossed-out picture of Bozo the Clown: No Bozos.

While prowling the night, David Lee Roth befriended Mötley Crüe, and he introduced them at the Troubadour in June 1981. Afterward, he cornered the band's singer—Roth-a-like bleached blond Vince Neil—

and lectured him on the music business. Neil recalls being shell-shocked—a year earlier he was selling bootleg Van Halen shirts at Long Beach Arena just to scrounge up enough money for a concert ticket.

The next afternoon, Roth met Neil for lunch. He arrived in a dark Mercedes-Benz with a skull and crossbones painted on the hood, then proceeded to brain-dump on the young singer the lessons of seven hard years. "Don't go with a small distribution company," Roth urged. "You have to have your records in Tahiti. If they aren't in Tahiti, they aren't anywhere else." Neil promptly ignored the advice, and says he soon learned Roth was right.

Not every fellow traveler in Hollywood was a superstar in waiting, however. Somehow Van Halen were charmed, gliding straight across the fly-infested molasses of exploitation. The sticky sidewalks of the Sunset Strip had a dangerous way of dissolving dreams like industrial solvent, and the also-rans became the stuff of Hollywood's darker legends.

While seducing Southern California one bikini at a time, Van Halen were tempered by the mood of the Me Generation: if it felt good, they did it. But in the hands of lesser mortals, sometimes "anything goes" went to a dark place. Depravity tainted the decadence of the Hollywood rock clubs. Using drugs as bait, real predators hunted underage foxes, young girls with fake IDs and a willingness to try new things. David Lee Roth recalled sixty-year-old Bill Gazzari using rudimentary videotape equipment in the mid-1970s to videotape himself getting blow jobs from the teenyboppers who worked at his club.

The Sunset Strip was filled with the flotsam and jetsam of the star machine, and the cautionary stories of runaways and junkies could be chilling. In 1982 the Starwood Club, where Van Halen had been discovered, burned down under mysterious circumstances. The previous year, Starwood owner Eddie Nash had made headlines—not for his support of the local music scene, but for his involvement with an infamous quadruple homicide in Laurel Canyon known as the Wonderland Murders. Drug-addicted porn star John Holmes went to jail for refusing to testify to his involvement in the crimes; Nash was also imprisoned.

Even outside the seedy gravity of Hollywood, criminals sought out Van Halen's families. Posing as a patient, a man named Danny Angel Vega entered Dr. Nathan Roth's office and kidnapped Dave's father at gunpoint. Seizing a chance, Dr. Roth clocked the interloper and ran, and the man was captured. Vega spent the time in jail grousing about his imaginary injuries at the hands of the Roth family. In early 1987, he escaped and was killed hours later after pointing a .357 Magnum pistol at police. "He died under a Toyota," Dave said.

The situation was not a joke. Several year later, for example, basketball star Michael Jordan's father was robbed and shot to death on a North Carolina interstate, his body dumped in a swamp and his NBA championship rings taken. After the incident with his own father, Dave bought himself a gun, security against the increasing dangers of mounting fame. "You buy the land, you get the Indians," he said resignedly.

Paranoia mounted as the band members became aware that their gilded lives could be easily threatened—hurdling the pitfalls became part of what made excessive partying so much fun. To protect his fort, Roth hung a sign outside his house in Pasadena, his deadly sense of humor intact: "Attention: There's nothing here worth dying for."

JUKEBOX HEROES

Van Halen had good musical genes, and they were photogenic. Now the tide of history seemed to be turning in their favor. MTV wanted fashion plates, and most of the heavy hitters of the 1970s were slobs. Like stage actors adapting to the dawn of motion pictures, Van Halen redeployed their formidable stage charisma for the small box.

As early as 1982, MTV singled out talkative, witty David Lee Roth as the focal point of Van Halen. While the others were understandably less than thrilled about being relegated to sideman status, Roth made himself readily available. "We really don't train for this kind of thing," he explained to Martha Quinn. "I like sports, but I'm no good at any of them. I don't have the discipline for it. I was raised on a steady diet of radio and television, so I need a commercial every ten minutes in my life. I've never really kept after any one thing. Most of the moves that I do onstage are taken from television or from comic books."

Touring at maximum velocity, traveling through the dense jungles of the South Pacific, and witnessing the rampant weddings of the men of his musical tribe only seemed to make Roth more fearless. He threw himself into designing merchandise, plotting videos, and masterminding the nonmusical aspects of the band. "If there's any kind of image here, it's a nonimage," he said. "We control all our press and media. We aren't controlled by a fat cat manager. We're actually doing what we want, and acting how we want. That's the integrity of Van Halen—if there's any to be found."

Though MTV was heavily pushing British new wave and new romantic bands like the Eurythmics, the Police, and Duran Duran, the channel also adored Van Halen's flashy, campy video clips. Prior to the *Diver Down* album in 1982, the band nodded to MTV by filming "the most lavish home movie ever made" at a Malibu movie set for their update of Roy Orbison's "(Oh) Pretty Woman." The video had the magic touch, with a storyline scooped out of little kids' minds in the middle of the night when they're dreaming in their bedrooms. Basically, when two midgets are spotted abusing a damsel in distress, Van Halen come to the rescue—Michael Anthony in samurai armor on horseback, Alex in a loincloth with a bone necklace, and Eddie done up as Billy the Kid. Roth poked fun at his own egomania, dressing as a campy Napoleon Bonaparte, the quintessential costume of a megalomaniac nut.

Incredibly, programmers in Japan were offended by the samurai likeness, and Australia thought the woman in distress was a blow against women's rights—even though the supposedly pretty woman is unwigged at the climax and revealed to be a transvestite. After a few dozen showings, deluged by irate cards and letters, MTV pulled the video from rotation, another notch on the band's outlaw record.

Van Halen's funny, charismatic screen presence terrified the 1970s rock generation, visually moribund with their beards and beer bellies. The band had nearly owned the live arena, and now it totally took over television. They weren't really competing with rock and roll bands any-more, but with video games and all thirty-two channels of cable television. "I'm sorry, I'm stoned—hey, why do you think I'm wearing sunglasses?" Roth said with a laugh during a televised interview, and the audience laughed along with him. He brought the party culture nationwide, just as Dean Martin had once made an older generation chuckle knowingly at his ever-present cocktail tumbler.

While the band sought a break from one another in early 1982, Warner Bros. released the toss-off cover of "(Oh) Pretty Woman" as a single. Unexpectedly, the song strutted up the Top 40 catwalk to number 12 on the singles chart. Van Halen rushed to Amigo Studios to make *Diver Down*, the first album recorded outside the hallowed rooms of Sunset Sound Recorders. Warner Bros. owned Amigo, so they could make it available on short notice, and it was cheaper for them, only costing about $46,000.

Diver Down was created one song at a time over twelve days, collecting little pop vignettes instead of presenting an overarching statement like *Fair Warning*. The cover was equally simple, a deep-sea semaphore flag marking where divers are swimming beneath the waves—an invitation to go more than skin deep with the band, signaling all kinds of activity under the pleasant surface.

Included in the song list were a slew of covers. Besides Orbison's "(Oh) Pretty Woman," another Kinks number appeared, "Where Have All the Good Times Gone?" The band had learned it during the cover band days along with "You Really Got Me" and a few others after Dave bought a K-Tel collection of Kinks songs for research purposes.

The band pointed toward Roth and Ted Templeman to explain why so many other people's songs were on *Diver Down*. Originally done by Martha and the Vandellas, "Dancing in the Street" was one of Roth's musical inspirations as a boy listening to the radio. The keyboard line, played on a Minimoog, was something Eddie had first written for "(Oh) Pretty Woman." Though Alex defended the choice—"It's not so much the song as the way you play it"—his gut feeling was that the song was not right for Van Halen.

"They're rather like send-ups, which is why there are words missing and choruses missing," Roth told *Creem*. True—somehow the most watched guitarist in the United States, Eddie Van Halen, allowed "(Oh) Pretty Woman" on the street without a guitar solo, an oversight that bothered him afterward.

Among the originals was a revamped version of "Last Night" from the 1977 demo session with Templeman. Musically, the song was virtually unchanged in five years. It had never made the cut before due to its lame dialogue, with Roth endlessly nagging a girlfriend, "Where were you last night?" Rewritten with epic western horse rustler lyrics, "Hang 'Em High" befittingly became a legend.

"Secrets" was a more recent leftover from the *Fair Warning* sessions, and it featured all the layered melodies and rhythmic motion of that hallmark album. Roth reportedly wrote the words using taglines from postcards and greeting cards he found at a truck stop in New Mexico. On this song, Eddie expanded the "brown sound" with a growing arsenal of guitars. Among them was a heavy double-necked Gibson, the polar opposite of the light wood models Eddie favored. "No wonder Jimmy Page has a slouch!" he joked to *Guitar World*.

Diver Down abandoned a long-standing Van Halen production quirk. On the first four albums, Eddie's guitar was hard-panned to one side, to create a realistic impression that he was playing live on one side of a stage. Eddie hated that. He reckoned that half the kids driving around in Ford Pintos only had one speaker connected, so there was a fifty-fifty chance they were missing almost all of his playing. On the other hand, plenty of junior Eddies were turning the balance control to the max and jamming in their bedrooms with the other three-fourths of the band—the same trick he had used to learn Cream songs.

"Intruder," the drum, synth, and guitar-noise intro to "(Oh) Pretty Woman," picked up where "Sunday Afternoon in the Park" left off: a paranoid electronic soundscape for a generation just getting hooked on Space Invaders, Gorf, and Defender. According to Roth, he wrote it on an Electro-Harmonix membrane synthesizer in about an hour as a filler preamble for "(Oh) Pretty Woman," because the video ran three minutes longer than the song.

Outside a hotel in Memphis on the *Fair Warning* tour, a fan named David Petschulat gave Eddie a one-third-scale miniature replica of a Les Paul. Spotting a good stage gag, Eddie wrote "Little Guitars," and its Spanish feel inspired Roth to write a love song to a señorita. "Little Guitars" was one of Eddie's self-professed finest moments. Along with "Cathedral," it was a rare example of his needing ten takes to get a perfect performance.

Usually, what came down on record was exactly what Eddie played live in the studio. The process was not meticulous, though—before Eddie ripped into "Little Guitars (Intro)," Templeman asked if he wanted to "do the electric thing first?" Eddie was prepared for a virtuoso performance of any kind, but was still incredibly hard on himself. "I'm fucking nervous," he squeaked before completing "Little Guitars" with a stellar take.

Only slightly beneath the surface, "Big Bad Bill (Is Sweet William Now)" allowed Roth to ride Edward's marriage, singing about Big Bad Bill's conversion from wild child to pussy-whipped husband, doing the dishes and mopping the kitchen floor. The song, a hit from 1924 by Milton Ager and Jack Yellen, also featured guest Jan Van Halen playing clarinet. Probably the only recording of Mr. Van Halen as a soloist, the playful woodwind lines are a brief glance into the whimsical hand that guided two of the modern era's best-known musicians. Mr. Van Halen hadn't even played clarinet in ten years, after losing one of his fingers in an accident. The band sat in a circle with sheet music during the session, and Eddie remembered his father being extremely nervous. "My dad would get tears in his eyes every time he saw us play. He loved it. He lived through us because he never really made it."

The TV sugar rush came with "Happy Trails," a sing-along from *The Roy Rogers and Dale Evans Show* in the early 1960s. "If you laugh, don't worry," Roth instructed the others when the tape started rolling. "If you hit a flat note don't worry—as long as there's exuberance." The lighthearted breather was one of dozens of songs—including the Mounds and Almond Joy candy bar commercials—the band could sing in four-part harmony, and "Happy Trails" became a heralded and beloved show-closer.

Diver Down's back cover showed a photograph of the band leaping to greet 150,000 fans while opening for the Rolling Stones in Orlando, Florida, one week before Halloween 1981. The triumphant performance was one that nearly didn't happen—Alex had broken his hand in four places, and affixed a drumstick to his arm with tape and shoelaces so the show could go on.

Diver Down was like soft colorful Lycra compared to the leather gloves of *Fair Warning*, but held together with the same robust stitching. The few overdubs were done mostly for quiet sounds like Dave's harmonica. The whole episode was barely over thirty minutes long, slightly longer than a TV sitcom—the band pleaded with the press to accept their argument that higher audio fidelity demanded wider grooves and a shorter playing time. Eddie claimed they had even dropped two old club days originals recorded for the album, "Big Trouble" and "House of Pain."

The way the producer and the singer ran roughshod over this rush job did not sit well with the musical members. "What Eddie and I do is we argue," Roth told *Creem*. "We come from different backgrounds, musically, philosophically, socially, our hobbies. I have trouble understanding, more times than not, why he does what he does. There are meeting grounds, of course. But on the musical end, there is no meeting ground. We're arguing. Somehow we reach a compromise. No one is ever happy except the public."

Though *Diver Down* lacked the impact of the first four albums, MTV and the fun song selection successfully goosed record sales. It inched slightly higher up the charts than its four older siblings, peaking at number 3 during a lengthy sixty-five-week run in *Billboard*. "Dancing in the Street" joined "(Oh) Pretty Woman" in the American Top 40. Though the record rang in platinum status after just ten weeks, for at least ten years it remained Eddie's least favorite Van Halen album.

When 1982's "Hide Your Sheep" tour began that July, Eddie was still mostly playing souped-up "Frankenstrat" guitars that were hot-rodded in the truest sense: jimmied for a weekend run in the mud, not carefully polished to look good in a magazine. Even when officially sponsored by Kramer Guitars starting in 1984—making Kramer the top-selling guitar of 1985—Eddie continued to use his old guitars under some subterfuge, sticking Kramer necks on the old Charvel Strat bodies for appearance's sake. He used other fine touches to his technique—like boiling his strings to break them in quicker, or lightly sanding the parts of the guitar where stage sweat tended to make the surface slick.

At the end of 1982, Kramer swapped out the whammy bars in its guitars, ditching the old Rockinger units in favor of the Van Halen–supported Floyd Rose tremolo. Floyd Rose had patented a number of improvements to guitar whammies that required licenses and royalties in all units sold, and Eddie had been integral in the development of the system, testing and finessing the system from prototype to polished product. "I've never asked Floyd for anything for my help," Eddie told *Musician*, feeling he deserved more than a thank-you after tens of thousands of Rose-licensed tremolos had been sold. "I was very involved in development on that thing. I don't care what he says. He kind of threw me a bone, but I'm a bit ticked."

A 1982 *Los Angeles Examiner* article contained shocking allegations that the band had gotten mellower backstage, and that Eddie had begun spending more time alone with his guitar behind the little red door marked "Tuning," slinking out occasionally long enough to grab a sandwich and a bottle of Blue Nun.

There were gritted teeth some nights as the others became less enthused about Roth's backstage three-panty operas. His credo remained as ever: "What you see onstage with Van Halen is probably what you'll find underneath the stage. And what you see backstage is probably what you're going to find upstairs in the hotel." He proclaimed that vigorous parties were the nightly payoff for a life increasingly spent in the back of limousines and radio station hospitality rooms.

Dave's entourage expanded to include Danny Rodgers and Jimmy Briscoe, two little people with a big wardrobe, waist-high circus clowns recently escaped from the Ringling Bros. Their tough-guy outfits poked fun at the growing security around the band, and they played a major part of the permanent ongoing photo op Roth called normal. "When you look out of your bedroom door and a midget goes by in a bath towel, you know you're not in life insurance," he told the London *Times*. "I believe in leaving the door open and letting everyone take a look. A fantasy is no fun unless everybody shares it."

So when *Life* magazine arrived in Detroit to photograph the band in September, Roth insisted that the band wives stay at home. He claimed the constantly bickering married couples were a distraction. The others complained that Roth was overdoing Van Halen's party-boy image. In any case, at least one high-profile wife, Valerie Bertinelli, had her feelings hurt. The rifts in the band widened, yet the gambit worked: *Life* wrote that "the most ferocious rock band on the road in America today" was performing "joyful rituals of excess," while readers gorged on photos of Roth examining a pair of panties thrown onstage and nearly having his snakeskin spandex ripped off by an open-mouthed admirer.

Van Halen's *Life* photo spread appeared in the same issue as a sad report on primates at a run-down animal farm. Wrote one disgusted reader afterward, "I found myself contemplating who the animals really were—the gorillas or the Van Halen rock band. It is my hope that Van Halen and others like them are soon the endangered species."

The fans could have used a little protection from the band after Dave streamlined his system for ordering sex at shows. The security team had drawn up a grid to help them identify troublemakers, dividing the floor of the concert hall into regions, so bouncers on headsets could quickly point out someone who needed attention: "Aerosmith shirt, hunting knife, sector C-5."

Roth subverted this system for his own lascivious reasons, distributing laminated backstage passes to the security staff, each marked with their initials, then from the stage calling out, "Blonde, pink top, sector A-4," pointing out the girls he wanted to see after the show. Whatever crew member's name Dave saw flapping around on his favorite girl's neck backstage at the end of the night would get a hundred-dollar bonus at breakfast the next morning. As far as intimacy went, it was a little like the invention of the drive-through window at McDonald's, but the morale of tour staff remained high.

David Letterman confronted Roth on this practice, expressing his disbelief at the apparent callousness toward sex. "Well, this is the

eighties, Dave," Roth said drolly. "We want to interact with the audience as closely as possible, because music is a sharing experience. I
feel that we can use technology to bring ourselves closer to each other."

When tickets went on sale in Las Vegas, at least two thousand fans
flew into a frenzy, causing more mayhem than the four members of the
band could manage. As the fans on line grew impatient, they began
pushing and fighting, smashing glass bottles, and eventually tearing
down a security fence and shoving a mobile trailer used as a box office
off its foundation. Some things were just simply worth fighting for.

Standards of decency were defined and defied community by community, however, and in October 1982, Worcester, Massachusetts,
celebrated the band with "Van Halen Day." "I'm dealing with all parts
of the body," Roth explained the band to TV's *Nightwatch*. "You pay
$8.50, and it's not enough to just hit up your ears. You gotta hit up your
ears, you gotta hit up your eyes, and then work your way down."

On the road with the lightweight band After the Fire in 1982, Van
Halen were routinely selling out 14,000- to 30,000-capacity venues
almost every night of the week, grossing nearly $100,000 on average.
The real money was in merchandise—if only 8,000 kids bought a $15
concert T-shirt, Van Halen were still leaving the venues with an extra
$100,000 per night in small bills.

As Roth described in his book *Crazy from the Heat*, this action drew
highly organized bootleggers who sold low-quality Pakistani shirts for
$5 outside the shows. The shirts had hilariously bad designs, they were
inked with a substance that immediately crumbled off like dried egg,
and they shrunk to infant-size if washed. Van Halen's merchandise
team went to war against the black marketeers, battling over turf in
arena parking lots across the country, with victory going to whichever
team had the most muscle, law enforcement clout, or extralegal allies
in their corner. They even copied the shirts, selling low-quality knock-
offs of their own, printed in Day-Glo colors with Roth's approval.

The tour romped into 1983, starting with a victory lap through
Venezuela, Brazil, Argentina, and Uruguay—well-planned warm locations to play during January. The band's decadence continued unabated,

with cases of booze, crates of beer, and untamed rivers of wild, willing fans. Fresh from military dictatorships in several stops, the South American rock scene was still a fly-by-night business, where unsavory characters were eager to take full advantage of freedom. Van Halen loved the adventure—they were recharging their own youthful enthusiasm, the wild spirit that dies when portioned out only in marketable pieces.

They were among the first Yankee marauders to leap off the pages of magazines onto South American stages. The gesture was appreciated, especially as golden-haired Roth rapped to crowds in Spanish, Eddie ripped through "Spanish Fly," and Alex's drum solo adopted Latin-inspired licks. "We sold 140,000 tickets and maybe 15,000 albums," Roth told *Faces*. "We had motorcades, escorts, we were treated like national heroes. Now I know how to fight for the right to do this the right way—to tour when we want to, in the right way."

"Turn off the goddamn bass amplifiers, will ya? Shut 'em down," Dave shouted in Buenos Aires before winging the four-minute Spanish version of "Oh, Argentina," accompanying himself on acoustic guitar. He unfurled a large Argentine flag before launching into "Ice Cream Man," and at that moment he probably could have been elected president.

While the tour continued, Eddie unfortunately lost the chance to produce a record for one of his influences, the British jazz fusion stylist Allan Holdsworth. Now a powerful protégé, Eddie had paved the way for Holdsworth's I.O.U. Band to sign with Warner Bros. He wanted to work with a player he had already declared a guitar hero's guitar hero. Unfortunately, Holdsworth grew tired of waiting for Van Halen and forged ahead with producer Ted Templeman. Eddie was disgruntled—especially since he wanted to play with guest vocalist Jack Bruce from Cream. But Holdsworth had underestimated the value of Eddie's fingers—he found himself back on an indie record label within a year.

When Van Halen retreated from South America at the end of February, Roth lingered below the equator for a few weeks of overachiever's holiday. Renting a rickety riverboat named the *Marcia*, he launched a six-week jungle expedition up the Amazon River with his best friend, Van Halen security chief "Big" Ed Anderson. They requested a visa from the

Brazilian government to visit protected Amazonian Indian tribes living in the densest rain forest near Peru. It was a reverse kind of missionary adventure—where Roth and Big Ed indoctrinated themselves in the ways of jungle survival. They hunted and fished in loincloths, and Roth got mosquito bites the size of golf balls. They happened upon a remote village where the locals threw a pinga and cachaça sugarcane alcohol party for their guests that Dave described as "Triple Christmas."

As Roth and Big Ed's boat sputtered into the heart of darkness, the villages along the river were warned of the advance of the Americans by shortwave radio. The entourage was hard to miss. At their final stop, they were welcomed with the desperate message: "Call home!" Some kind of catastrophe had happened that needed immediate attention back in the States.

As it turned out, Van Halen had been offered a million dollars to play a single show in front of half a million people, and they were freaking out because their singer was floating around a jungle out of contact. So Roth and Big Ed located a German geological expedition and were bivouacked out of the Amazon during a fierce rainstorm. They spent four more days traveling back to California. A week and a half later, after a brief hospital visit, Dave was cured of microbes, parasites, stings, dehydration, and was ready for Memorial Day.

———※※※———

US Festival '83 was a three-day confluence of music and new technology masterminded by multimillionaire benefactor Steve Wozniak, one of the two founders of Apple Computer. Wozniak had lost $5 million on US Festival '82, and he was looking to lose a few million more for the sake of a breakthrough cultural event that would draw hundreds of thousands of people to the San Bernardino Valley over the holiday weekend of May 28 through May 30.

Describing the event as a whole tour's worth of work for one show, Van Halen needed to put together video and radio programs as part of the agreed package. Preparations began while the band was still sweating out the arrival of all of its equipment and its lead singer from South America. To promote their lucrative appearance, unofficial band photographer Neil Zlozower re-created the classic Iwo Jima photo, with the four soldiers of Van Halen raising an American flag over a pile of dirt while David Lee Roth gripped his rifle and gazed off into the great unknown.

The paycheck for this gig would land Van Halen in the 1984 *Guinness Book of World Records*. The initial offer was for a scant million, but their contract called for a payday equal to or greater than any other band on the bill. When Wozniak offered David Bowie $1.5 million to appear the following day, Van Halen automatically got a $500,000 raise. If Eddie had taken his mother's advice and studied computers at DeVry, he wouldn't have earned as much in ten years as he brought home that evening. Roth joked that after paying for the production and giving the managers and agents their cut, he barely had enough money left to buy a dual-motor offshore racing yacht. Asked if he thought the band had been overpaid, Roth laughed and said, "Honey, I always sing like a million bucks!"

For their first show in over three months, Van Halen would play on Sunday—heavy metal day. The temperature reached ninety-five degrees by early afternoon on site at Glen Helen Regional Park by the time the music began. The $20 ticket also bought performances by Quiet Riot, Mötley Crüe, Ozzy Osbourne, Judas Priest, Triumph, and Scorpions. "I think the only way we really fit in was volume-wise," Eddie told *Guitar World*.

Quiet Riot and Mötley Crüe were still unknown L.A. club bands, while Ozzy Osbourne was finding his feet after the devastating loss of guitarist Randy Rhoads in an airplane accident. Judas Priest were a known quantity and delivered powerful, leather-clad British metal to the hot summer crowd. Triumph were the oddballs—a breather act, a mellow Canadian power trio whose best years were behind them. The adoring crowd loved them one and all—journalists reported that the applause at 1 P.M. for Quiet Riot was higher than for the headliners the previous day.

Creating a stupendous buildup, Scorpions played a well-choreographed and cataclysmic set, culminating in a human pigpile with the guitarists scraping their strings and squalling feedback for at least ten minutes. The German band brought the day to an explosive close. Before Van Halen could begin, however, announcements and proclamations for world peace on the stage ate up more than an hour. And while the band waited, naturally they partied.

The previous day, headliners the Clash had made much ado about their own $500,000 payday, scraping their consciences loudly while a band spokesman hilariously denounced fellow performers Sting, Stevie Nicks, and "Van Halen and *his* moron music." They petulantly agreed at the last minute to play, saying, "Van Halen will call us Commies if we don't." A later conversation between Eddie Van Halen and the Clash's Joe Strummer reputedly cleared the air, but there was a line drawn in the sand between them. As it was, many rival bands already felt like Van Halen used up all the oxygen in the room.

While everyone else choked on dust, Van Halen lived it up like pashas in their own private casbah—a tent city with arcade games, girls galore, champagne, and confetti. The contract rider included a hundred cases of beer, two cases of Jack Daniel's, and twenty-five pounds of M&M's—of course stipulating "no brown ones!" Requiring a staff and crew of over three dozen and a private security force numbering twenty, the Memorial Day invasion disintegrated into a never-ending quagmire of production demands and escalating costs.

Van Halen had always harnessed their nervous energy with the help of alcohol, and the anticipation being off the charts for US '83, so was the liquor intake. Roth barely finished a backstage interview with MTV's Mark Goodman: "I'm proud to say that after all these years of loud music, bright lights, and loud noise, I still don't need glasses—I drink right out of the bottle."

At the appointed hour, a special film of the backstage party beamed over the giant Diamondvision television screens. The three-minute fea-turette had been produced ahead of time in the Van Halen compound. It was a self-portrait caricature of the Van Halen reality, with Michael Anthony confusing a Space Invaders machine for a portable bar, Alex dodging a midget pulling a saddled sheep, Roth interrupted having sex on a piano, and Eddie popping party balloons with his cigarette. The cut back to reality was only slightly less surreal.

While giant VH logos flickered on the screens, Van Halen fired into "Romeo Delight." Eddie wore red-and-white overalls that matched his striped guitar, and Dave was sporting a sparkling purple housecoat, white gloves, and giant hair—all designed to dazzle back to the five hundreth row. They took a minute to get their bearings on the 435-foot stage. As their eyes adjusted to almost half a million screaming people, Eddie uncharacteristically flopped a couple notes. Roth lost his place halfway through the second verse and bellowed, "I forgot the fucking words!"

The band was explosive but unstable, with Dave occasionally weaving and distracted. He produced a harmonica during set-filler "The Full Bug" and gaffed the world's most torturous harp solo, then proceeded to invent a whole new set of lyrics. He staggered offstage bellowing, "I need a drink!" and the band vamped into a very active instrumental, a tune would later surface on *1984* as "Girl Gone Bad."

While giant television screens beamed the intimate details to fans encamped in the back of the crowd, nearly half a mile away, the band ran amok—force-feeding Jack Daniel's to a dwarf, twirling around the little guitar, and baiting the crowd's resentment of self-serious bands like the Clash.

Roth had reportedly been gobbed on repeatedly by a punk girl at a Clash show the previous year, and tonight he exacted his revenge— modifying one of his standard stage raps about whether he was really drinking whiskey from his ever-present bottle of Jack Daniel's. "The only people who drink iced tea out of Jack Daniel's bottles is the Clash, baby!" A weird insult, sure, but it didn't take much to turn the earth dogs in the audience against the British punk rockers.

Roth mocked the religious protesters handing out pamphlets outside the event, and then the banned "(Oh) Pretty Woman" video went up on the large screens, complete with crunchy synth opening "Intruder." Funnily enough, synth founding father Bob Moog had given a demonstration on the grounds the previous day.

The band bashed out an old favorite, Cream's "I'm So Glad," running into "Somebody Get Me a Doctor." At the end of the song, Eddie took a wicked knee dive and came up shredding. Taking a breather, Dave bebopped to the crowd. Out of the spotlight, Mike brought his bass tech,

Kevin Dugan, to the edge of the stage to survey the scene, sharing the moment with his valet. Shortly afterward, Dugan began wearing a T-shirt that read, "My two best friends are Jack Daniel's & Michael Anthony."

Mike accidentally unplugged his bass during his solo. When the cord popped out, he chucked his bass guitar into the air and let it drop with a 100,000-watt thud. The crowd adored the senseless destruction, which afterward remained part of his act for decades. "Since I've been dropping my bass, I can't believe the compliments I've been getting from people," he later said with a shrug.

Behind the band stood a wall of scores of speaker cabinets, while a pointed light spelled out the flying VH logo. If they were nervous performing before the pilgrims, it didn't look like it. If they were drunk, it wouldn't be a surprise. If they were having fun, it showed. They treated the crowd to the biggest backyard party of their lives.

The set lasted just under two hours. Meanwhile, heat, dehydration, lack of bathrooms, and metal fatigue thinned the crowd considerably before its end. "More people were arrested here today than the whole last year," Dave congratulated the crowd to uproarious approval. In fact, two people died. According to the *New York Times*, concertgoers were so fired up on their way home that they tore down the fences surrounding the event and rammed their cars into police cruisers. "They even hit a horse," a deputy said. The local sheriff told the press he hoped Van Halen would "never come back" to his county, a tin-plated recommendation for any outlaw.

The entire event was broadcast on the Westwood One radio network throughout the summer, and an edited television special with three Van Halen hits was featured on the fledgling premium cable channel Showtime. When the dust cleared, heavy metal day at the US Festival had cleared 375,000 paid admissions, and easily 25,000 more snuck into the site. That was twice as many tickets as the two other days of the festival—a statistic that proved hard rock had arrived. For all their bluster, it appeared the Clash weren't worth $500,000.

Back at Gazzari's on the Sunset Strip, a lengthy text message appeared on the marquee: "Congratulations, Van Halen, one and a half million a night isn't what I paid you eight years ago. I'm really proud of you."

Also in 1983, Eddie got a call from Brian May of Queen, who wanted some quick help on a recording session. The two had met during Van Halen's late-1970s UK tour with Black Sabbath, years after Van Halen had covered Queen in the clubs. Dubbed the Starfleet Project, May wanted to create a guitar-driven update of the theme to a sci-fi puppet show from British television. May would hold down a melodic rhythm guitar while Eddie provided high-end fireworks—a rare chance for Eddie to play in a dual-guitar setting.

Dabbling for a couple of days, the band nabbed two tracks and the seven-minute jam "Bluesbreaker," which they dedicated to Eric Clapton. Eddie told *Guitar* that during the recording he broke a string and continued playing out of tune. So when May sent the finished record to Clapton, Eddie was slightly mortified. Clapton was too, and reportedly pooh-poohed the song as very unblueslike. Eddie still used Clapton's solos as preconcert warm-ups, but when he met his idol in 1983, according to *Rolling Stone*, "He was so nervous that he got drunk and blew the whole thing."

The kudos from on high far outnumbered the complaints. Frank Zappa thanked Eddie for "reinventing the guitar," and Pete Townshend quipped to *Rolling Stone*, "That incredible virtuosity combined with that beautiful grin allows me to forgive him for letting David Lee Roth stand in front of him."

Eddie's guitar signified the brave new world. He owned the very concept of guitar in the 1980s as much as Les Paul when he added electricity to the instrument in the 1950s. Eddie could cherry-pick his favorite musical heavyweights for any kind of band or side project—yet he chose to remain loyal to his brother and boyhood friends, valuing the group spirit over the refined chops of the celebrated greats. There was one high-profile exception, although it only took him away from Van Halen for an afternoon.

One unbreakable pop dreadnought overshadowed the rise of hard rock in 1983—Michael Jackson's *Thriller*. Ultimately touted, perhaps correctly, as the best-selling album of all time, the utterly of-the-moment record reigned all music charts throughout 1983, stymieing Def Leppard's *Pyromania* in the number 2 spot, despite that album's selling six million copies.

Yet even Michael Jackson moonwalked under the electric hands of Eddie Van Halen, whose effortless guitar solo to the twice-Grammy-winning "Beat It" from *Thriller* was legendarily donated without payment. Maybe Eddie saw the chance to play for a new audience. Maybe he thought so little of Jackson that he didn't want a penny. Maybe he simply liked the song. "Everybody was out of town and I figured who's gonna know if I play on this kid's record?" Eddie said.

Using his battered red guitar and a hot-rodded Hartley Thompson amp borrowed from Allan Holdsworth, in under an hour he improvised a cavalcade of trademark finger tapping, whammy-bar dives, and legato touches for "Beat It." Afterward, Michael Jackson arrived and complimented Eddie's playing. Winking and nodding behind the door was Eddie's buddy Steve Lukather of Toto, who recorded the rhythm guitar and bass on the song.

"I really like that high fast stuff you do!" Jackson squealed to Eddie.

Embarrassed to ask for anything, Eddie shrugged, shook hands with producer Quincy Jones, and walked away from the session. "Maybe Michael will give me dance lessons someday," he told *Musician* afterward.

Roth claimed he learned of the collaboration for the first time in the parking lot of a 7-Eleven, where some Mexican girls were listening on a portable radio. Eddie's participation helped "Beat It" cross over to rock radio, and it became the single of the year. In a way, the pairing set the stage for what would soon be Van Halen's biggest album.

From convenience stores in Southern California to wooded English estates, the song reached people whose ears were only triggered by giant ripples. "The first time I heard Eddie Van Halen was on 'Beat It,'" former Led Zeppelin guitarist Jimmy Page told *Kerrang!* "I thought

'Christ, what's he doing?' I couldn't do what he does—and I've tried."

Eddie swore he was always barely in command of his own powers. "It's not really a talent, it's an obsession," he insisted repeatedly, as the world begged for his magic secrets. "I'm just a medium. Nothing I do is impossible. To me, music is about personal expression, anyway. It's not about how proficient you are." After he won the readers' poll for best guitarist in *Guitar Player* in 1983 for the fifth straight year, Eddie's name was permanently retired from the ballots.

By September 1983, vocals were done for the next album, but families and competing interests continued to slow the process down. Though they appeared frequently in the media, Eddie and Valerie remained homebodies, not socialites. Eddie could no longer be an anonymous presence, and hanging out in the Hollywood clubs was out of the question. The couple claimed their favorite tiny little dinner spot was Eddie's parents' house down in Pasadena. "I love it when Edward's home," Valerie told *Entertainment Tonight*, while the couple sat cozily on their couch, fireplace burning comically in the background. "Home sweet home is just very special."

On June 11, 1983, Alex was looking to learn what his brother liked about monogamy, marrying Valeri Kendall, a backstage lurker who had been a featured skater in Linda Blair's late-1970s skatesploitation flick *Roller Boogie*. Eddie was the best man at the wedding, lending support as his brother single-handedly doubled the world's population of women named Val Van Halen. Now Roth was the odd man out, the only bachelor of the group—though for how long remained anyone's guess.

Dave joined VJ Martha Quinn to ring in 1984 on MTV's Rock and Roll Ball, an ambitious production simulcast between New York and London. With one minute until midnight, they toasted the next Van Halen album as Roth proclaimed the night Van Halen's favorite holiday. He later told *Creem* that he had "this black chick and this white chick" in his bathtub singing "Why Do Fools Fall in Love?" at seven thirty the next morning. In contrast, Alex spent the night at Eddie's house, getting wasted and jamming. As giddy as the band's rise to this point had been, in the next twelve months they would all have many more reasons to celebrate.

KINGS OF ROCK

elayed by the US Festival, the process of making the next VH album grew into the longest yet. The record was the first produced at 5150, Eddie Van Halen's new home studio in the hills just beyond Hollywood. The name came from the California penal code for "involuntary confinement of a person for purposes of psychiatric evaluation," overheard by Eddie's right-hand man Donn Landee one night on his police scanner. In the years to come, 5150 would very appropriately become Eddie's rubber room.

Designed by Landee, the beta version of 5150 was a high-ceilinged sixteen-track studio suitable for recording, overdubbing, and simple mixing if needed. The recording room was roughly six hundred square feet, sound-insulated with fiberglass and rubber, with a booth on the north end so Eddie could face north like a compass needle while playing. A photo of Eddie and Alex's boyhood home in Holland hung in the kitchen. "This is my dream house," Eddie explained. "It's my house with a white picket fence."

For whatever reason, the construction on Eddie's property was passed off to city inspectors as a racquetball court—never mind that the soundproof walls were cinder blocks filled with concrete. A hitch arose in the form of a powerful AM antenna from a sports station broadcasting with 50,000 watts of power just a few miles away, potentially generating awful interference. To prevent Eddie picking up boxing matches and L.A. Rams games through his wireless guitars, the engineers wrapped a layer of grounded chicken-wire fencing around the entire 5150 facility, turning it into a high-tech shielded coop.

Eddie and Landee had already calibrated the board by producing the recordings from US Festival '83 for radio broadcast. Now the 5150 studio brought new possibilities to Van Halen. Their sound would become more processed and mellow, as their work schedule slowed to match the luxury of owning their own means of production. They got together when they felt like it, draining themselves of energy in short bursts and then splitting up for a couple weeks to recuperate and cut the grass.

"You should have seen what we did *1984* on," Eddie said, "a $6,000 piece of shit console that came out of United Western, an old green World War II thing with big old knobs and tubes. Donn rewired it to make it work."

Building 5150 gave Eddie a cocoon of his own making. He claimed he didn't even have a cassette player or a turntable in his house. He also professed to listening to more challenging music like jazz and punk for inspiration—even as David Lee Roth was heading the opposite direction, immersing himself in pop radio. "I think the only true rocker of the bunch is Al," Eddie told *Musician*. "He's the only one who listens to AC/DC and all that kind of stuff. Dave will walk in with a disco tape and I'll walk in with my progressive tapes and Mike walks in with his Disneyland stuff."

Dubbed an "$8.98 nirvana" by Roth, *1984* recombined the band's splintered interests. The seventy-second synthesizer landscape "1984" introduced the new era, an edit of a much longer electronic piece recorded at 5150 with Donn Landee. Along with whatever scraps of magnetic tape survived from "Sunday Afternoon in the Park" and "Invader" on the past two albums, Eddie was creating a sizable synth backlog in his library.

Ted Templeman and Roth planned to do Wilson Pickett's "In the

Midnight Hour" on *1984*, but ditched it after Eddie finally put up a vehement protest. "I'd rather fail with my own shit than succeed with someone else's," became the guitarist's new mantra.

Instead, the very first sessions at 5150 produced "Jump," a song that in raw form had already been rejected for *Diver Down* for one simple reason—Eddie played keyboards instead of guitar. "Eddie wrote this thing in synthesizer," Templeman told *Billboard*. "I really hadn't heard it for a long time, then he laid it down one night in the studio. It just killed me. It was perfect."

"We had intentionally stayed away from keyboards until then," Roth told *Classic Rock*, "because what instruments you used indicated which neighborhood you were part of. At the time it seemed important."

After all his years of lessons, Eddie's predilection for piano was nothing new. Even after catching hell at school for touching the precious Steinway, he often wrote songs on piano, then transcribed them for guitar. Such were the origins of "Hear About It Later" from *Fair Warning* and "And the Cradle Will Rock" from *Women and Children First*. But keyboards represented a rival musical style and society, and Van Halen were expected to lead the hard rock charge with guitars using as little circuitry as possible.

Eddie was either oblivious or headstrong. To him, the song sounded good. "Nothing can replace the guitar in my life," he told *Hit Parader*. "But I also love keyboards. I've always written a lot of our material on keyboards, it's just that in the past I'd reinterpret it on guitar. On this album I didn't do that. This only expands our sound."

Loyal hard rockers were horrified to see Eddie playing an electronic synthesizer for the first time in the video for "Jump." For the keyboard line, Eddie used an Oberheim OB-Xa, switching to a similar but newer Oberheim OB-8 in concert. Though he could have used sequenced or taped keyboards onstage, he played them live, with Michael Anthony taking over during Eddie's guitar solo. A whole new portion of the public loved the move: Recorded by the band in one take, according to Eddie, "Jump" became Van Halen's first number 1 hit single, topping the charts for five weeks.

Roth dedicated "Jump" to Benny Urquidez, the kickboxer who trained him three hours a day for months before the 1984 tour, even coaching him through an amateur fight. "Jump" was as good a philosophy as any, and Roth started using a lot of jump metaphors when talking about success, fame, and fortune: "I can teach you to jump up in five seconds—it takes years to learn how to land properly."

"Panama" was the singer's sexy ode to his 1951 Mercury lowrider, allegedly composed while he was lounging in the backseat being driven around Los Angeles. Through the car Roth met model Patricia "Apollonia" Kotero, a *Lowrider* cover girl and ex–L.A. Rams cheerleader. Her run with Roth was peachy—at least until she was ordered to break up with him by Prince while starring in his concept film *Purple Rain.*

While the band was laying down "Panama," the benefits of building 5150 were already paying dividends. Eddie recorded the revving engine sound effects by backing a Lamborghini up the driveway and pushing the blinking red button on his studio tape machine.

The video for "Panama" showed Dave swimming over the stage on a wire with a boom box on his shoulder, inner-city B-boy style. Eddie sat at the piano blowing smoke rings. Roth showed off the moves he'd picked up in strip clubs, doing a pole routine with himself in triplicate.

The clip also debuted a new trademark for Michael Anthony—a bass guitar shaped like a Jack Daniel's whiskey bottle, constructed from spare parts and some extra Kramer tuning pegs. Along with bass tech Kevin Dugan and pal Dave Jellison, Mike pieced the instrument together as an unofficial tribute to Van Halen's drink of choice—though Dugan had to be coaxed by Anthony to drink it. Michael later decided to build a high-quality version with the help of GMW Guitars in Glendora, California. The Jack Daniel's company offered to assist with the graphics in exchange for Mike's entry into their hall of fame; thus he became a Tennessee Squire. The whiskey-bottle bass became an icon, completely upstaging the giant orange-dotted popsicle-shaped "Davesicle" guitar that Roth used to play "Ice Cream Man" for several years.

For "Top Jimmy," Eddie showcased a Steve Ripley stereo guitar, one of fewer than ten made, which featured separate right-left panning for each string and a pair of built-in vibrato effects. It was a musical instrument with the technical abilities of a small aircraft. Based on "Top Jimmy" Koncek, a real-life character from Roth's nightlife, the song allowed Eddie to combine sweet harmonics with ridiculously fast rapid-fire blues licks in the vein of his former signature, "Goin' Home."

Alex credited the album's production squarely to Eddie and Donn Landee, even discounting his own participation. Eddie's home studio was truly their private Disneyland—the brothers and Landee recorded "Drop Dead Legs" during a late-night session and presented it to Roth, Anthony, and Templeman the following afternoon. Working this way, they could have released *1984* as a double album. But Templeman ordered Eddie to stop writing new material—there were already hundreds of half-finished songs on cassettes littering 5150.

Overall, Ted Templeman was pushed to the periphery during the recording of *1984*. The fights continued between him and Eddie, but now Templeman had to go home at night. Eddie was always on the clock. Among other deleted detours, Eddie finger-tapped a bass part to the explosive intro for "Hot for Teacher," a bubbling-over bottom-end bass track to set off the hyperactive drums and guitar. The option was scrapped because the band could never pull off a performance like that live. Michael Anthony was the band's anchor, not about to take off for the stars.

Opening with a monstrous fireworks display of Alex's double-bass drum technique, "Hot for Teacher" also showed Roth's off-the-cuff working method as a lyricist. A scratch track recorded live with the band showed that until the eleventh hour, he still hadn't settled on the words. "I missed so many classes, now my story can be told," he improvised. "Heard you missed me, baby, well, I'm *black*—I'm gonna sit right over here so I can concentrate."

"I was just improvising," Roth said. "Ted went, 'What do you have planned, Dave? You singing or what?' I said, 'No, in this one, we're all pretending to be in the classroom.'"

"A lot of the stuff is Dave's interpretation of life at that given moment," Eddie told *Guitar World*, admitting he often wasn't sure what Van Halen's lyrics meant.

The singer drew his lines from a mental word processor, editing and refining like a jailbird in solitary confinement composing his memoirs in his head. "I've never written down any lyrics, I usually just make it up in the studio," he admitted, stressing that the inflection was usually more important than the words.

While Van Halen were still bridling against formulaic song structures, the unusually sentimental "I'll Wait" was a pseudo-ballad about Roth's ideal woman—who at that moment happened to be a Calvin Klein underwear model taped to the screen of his hotel television. Though Roth and the others did not want another synth-laden track on the same album as "Jump," Eddie and Donn Landee were again adamant. Proving their point, "I'll Wait" propelled to number 13 on the *Billboard* singles charts.

Unlike *Diver Down*, which featured several one-take solos, all of the guitar solos on *1984* were overdubbed carefully, recorded during discrete sessions apart from the rest of the music. By now Eddie's solo bursts were attractions in themselves, dissected and critiqued by the cottage industry of fans, magazines, and aspirants created by his influence. Not that he was overthinking things—Eddie wrote "Girl Gone Bad" in a hotel room one night while Valerie was sleeping. So he wouldn't disturb her, he tiptoed into a closet and hummed the riff into his portable recorder for safekeeping.

Dipping into the old well that had served the band so reliably, Alex pushed for the return of "House of Pain." The club-days standard appeared on the Gene Simmons demo and elsewhere, resurfacing on *1984* with new lyrics and a more fluid arrangement—still, a typical bashed-out Van Halen album closer.

The album cover of *1984* featured a painting of a jaded baby New Year leaning on one elbow and smoking a cigarette. Dave claimed he handpicked the lettering font from the French graphic comic *Moebius*. The smoking cherub on the cover seemed like a quick-thinking blasphemy based on Black Sabbath's smoking, gambling angels from 1980's *Heaven and Hell*.

With three Top 20 singles and four videos in heavy rotation, Van

Halen discovered pop crossover in spades. Released in January and peaking at number 2, *1984* was quadruple platinum by October. It would eventually become the band's second album with Dave to top ten million in sales. This was the record where Roth earned the right to compare Van Halen to his frequent point of reference, McDonald's hamburgers. "Van Halen music ranks right up there with football and religion as something that will uplift you," he preached. Indeed, millions had been served.

Eddie called *1984* the first Van Halen record done the way he wanted. Sweeter still, Van Halen had ascended largely through its own efforts, producing appealing music videos and recording their own music in Eddie's backyard. The choppy waters of *Diver Down* were a memory. "The failure of our last record really wasn't our fault," Roth told *Hit Parader*. "If you want to find out why the album didn't do as well as it should, go ask our record company. There were a lot of people there at the time who were far more concerned with getting their daily allotment of cocaine than with promoting our album."

〰〰✦〰〰

MTV now reached over twenty-five million homes and had become a big wheel in the engine of the ever-spinning Van Halen promotional machine. Eddie and Dave even made a cameo appearance in the video for Frank Sinatra's "L.A. Is My Lady," from the singer's final studio album of the 1980s. While riding in a limo, Dave popped a videotape of vintage Sinatra clips into the backseat player, saying, "I got something new—it's the latest, it's the greatest, a little bit of Frank!"

Thanks to *1984*'s successful slew of music videos, in September 1984 the band scored at the first-ever MTV Video Music Awards. Now that the rock video form was important enough to warrant its own awards show, the band-directed clip for "Jump" took home honors for Best Group Video, Best Stage Performance in a Video, and Best Overall Performance in a Video. At the after-party a bouncer urged, "Watch your step" as Dave dipped under the velvet rope. "I always do," Roth replied.

Roth described the process of directing videos as an accidental art form—like watching television with the sound down and Black Sabbath or Wagner playing in the background. They claimed to have spent $600 and used one 16mm camera on "Jump"—as venerated progressive rockers Yes were embarrassed to learn when they requested a referral to whatever high-paid director had captured Van Halen's charm so intimately.

Roth still trashed Duran Duran and other MTV-favored synthesizer bands in *Billboard*, calling their music "a lot of icing." He told *Faces*, "It's no big sweat going up on that stage when you really can sing, or play an instrument. But if you don't have it, then it becomes tough . . . these new bands put in no effort at all. We used to think rock stars . . . were too coked out. But I don't think Duran Duran does coke, they're just all—milked out."

On top of the world, Roth was taking on all comers. In a *Creem* interview he wondered what kind of man writes songs about cars instead women, provoking a brief flare-up with solo singer Sammy Hagar, who called Roth a homosexual looking for a "relationship" with him and said Roth looked like a "woman in drag." Not above being dragged into a press war with a lesser luminary, Roth barked back through *Creem*, "Sammy definitely has a social problem—I think it's based on lack of education. And evidently he hasn't seen Van Halen lately or he wouldn't talk like he does."

Van Halen guessed the *1984* tour cost them around $100,000 a week to keep on the road—*Entertainment Tonight* claimed $500,000. The band used A and B stages, so that at the same time they were performing in Oklahoma City, the crew could already be erecting the framework for the following night's show in Wichita. The grand spectacle was a giant metal framework of lights for the band to frolic beneath, which unfolded little by little throughout the set, ultimately revealing a blinding array of lights in a "1984" pattern, turning every night into New Year's Eve.

After a quick trip to the tropics, Roth was ready for the road. Having exhausted every stripper routine he learned in Hollywood, he was kickboxing and running six miles a day to maintain his famous physique. "Everything I am, I was not born," he said. "I had to kick it into shape." He summoned monkey-style kung fu master Paulie Zink for a crash course in sword dancing, showcased in the "Panama" video. He also claimed to be learning Portuguese, Spanish, tap, dancing and bagpipes in his spare time—whatever it took to stay challenged and challenging.

"Being onstage is like being in the jungle," he told an interviewer. "You hear all the noise and the volume, and they're smoking in there, and people are throwing stuff up on stage, scarves and brassieres, and the keys to their house and car, and it's just a big mess—just like my hotel room, man. And it gets really hot, reaches about 110 degrees by the second song, and you're outta wind, and you're limping and you barely make it to the next song. And that's only the second song. You feel like an animal. It has great therapeutic value. I have a good time, that's why I got this job."

Van Halen and the conspirators at MTV colluded with dizzying power when MTV announced its "Lost Weekend with Van Halen" contest. The network soon received over a million postcard entries for a chance to spend three days with the band, doing everything that they did. The lottery couldn't have found a more perfect average Joe than twenty-year-old Kurt Jefferis, a department store loading dock employee from Phoenixville, Pennsylvania. Kurt had tossed half a dozen cards in the mail, before deciding to improve his odds and chuck another handful of entries in the post box—his winning card came from the second batch.

Kurt's catch was the American boyhood dream, 1984-style. His prizes included a VCR, a camcorder, an Atari game system, a private screening of *Footloose*, and a couple days spent tasting the life of Van Halen. Kurt's hometown newspaper ran the headline, "Would You Let Your Son Spend a Weekend with These Guys?" His mother quipped that she wished her boy had won a lost weekend with Perry Como instead.

For the blur of time from being picked up at his parents' house by limo and flown on a private jet to Detroit, Kurt Jefferis was like Charlie after winning the golden ticket to Willy Wonka's candy factory. He shotgunned beers with David Lee Roth, strapped on Eddie's striped red guitar, and endured the torments of the band's pint-size security staff—all for the vicarious thrills of viewers at home. At the end of the show, the band brought its pupil onstage, smashed a giant tray cake over his head, and soaked him with a dozen spurting bottles of champagne.

The band had been egging on audiences throughout the tour by pretending to film them with empty cameras, but that night the twelve thousand fans at Cobo Arena, intoxicated by the biggest rock band of the year and ignited by the obvious presence of MTV just as the network was beginning to break, were completely aware of the real cameras after weeks of build-up. When the house lights came up, the band could still see the shining white teeth screaming all the way to the back of the floor.

"If it's not some chick taking off her clothes, it's someone's hair getting torched because a sparkler lands on their head," Michael Anthony told *Bass Frontier*. "When I'm looking out at 50,000 faces, I'm watching as much of a show as they are."

Afterward, Van Halen whisked Jefferis past the backstage greeting line of music writers, local record store managers, and groupies hoping to rekindle encounters from 1979. The band gravitated toward the unassuming fan and doted on him, the realest guy in the room. Eddie blew smoke rings for him. They all sang "Happy Trails" together. At the end of the night, Dave started a massive food fight. "Everyone was involved," Jefferis told *The Inside*, "the band, Valerie, and the midget security guards. Mike and Valerie dumped potato salad on each other's heads. There was shit everywhere—broken plates and glass—it was amazing." Not fully aware of what they'd done, MTV had presented its first reality television show, and it was a smash success.

The entire tour felt like a celebration, and every single night was sold out to capacity. Eddie played a never-ending outpouring of crisp notes and riffs, teasing with short quotes from well-known songs. Mike was a constantly tumbling brick avalanche. Alex pounded on a humongous Ludwig kit covered in tiny square reflective mirrors, an environment built on six massive bass drums. Dave was now at his finest as ecstatic emcee, ringmaster of an unbelievable party. "We're a flame that burns for 24,000 people a night," he explained.

In New York, Roth had to be talked down from staging an expensive stunt at Madison Square Garden, releasing $10,000 in one-dollar bills from the rafters as a thank-you to fans. He called it "the Van Halen instant rebate." Even the ever-helpful Van Halen management team had to nix that idea, fearful of the legal repercussions of unleashing a money riot in the lawsuit capital of the world.

One interesting upshot of Van Halen's exploits in their ultra-prime was how the giant illusion of their lifestyle created a million dirty little white lies. Roth disallowing wives in Detroit and strategically tossing his room for the *Life* photo shoot, complete with panties hanging out of his cowboy boots, was part of the show. Van Halen had never lied about sex and drugs—in fact, they used their reputation to score more sex and drugs. But with three wives in tow and headaches galore, the party was more a spiritual creation on most nights than a sordid romp. As Roth often admitted, he didn't finish his onstage bottle of Jack Daniel's every single night.

Yet Dave was enjoying the bounty of being a man about town, and he promoted a big picture of Van Halen as endless sex, drugs, and rock and roll. Once unleashed, that imprint reproduced and multiplied everywhere and every day. Every time Van Halen's music touched someone, there was a chance for a rumor. Girls claimed they were paid to hang out with Roth. Letters came addressed from expectant mothers. A woman charged jewelry to his accounts on Rodeo Drive, and mailed invitations to their nonexistent wedding to two thousand of his closest friends. The punks talked about Roth showing up at their club in limos, picking up girls, and splitting—rarely mentioning how often he stuck around and got onstage to sing with the band.

Never mind that Roth did not actually have paternity insurance with Lloyd's of London—all anyone remembered was that he tried. As Van Halen's costume designer, Nancy Grossi, told *Life*, "All the girls ask me if David stuffs his crotch. He doesn't." Yet 50 percent of them would swear they heard that he did.

Even twenty years later, Ratt cover model and future Whitesnake wife Tawny Kitaen told *Blender*, "I dated Van Halen's manager, and we'd go to the Bahamas with David Lee Roth. If he had to travel with any narcotics, he'd shove it in my bag. We'd get in a car and drive David down Sunset Boulevard, looking for hookers, and then he'd bring 'em back to our house while I laid in my bedroom crying, 'I can't believe we have a hooker in the house!'"

Roth's pucker-faced, hip-grinding mating dances also invited speculation beginning around this time about whether he was bisexual. For certain, he was in touch with his feminine side, along with the feminine sides of half the female population of California. And he definitely danced outside the lines of Reagan-era Rambo masculinity. After all, he had come on the tail end of swishy 1970s glam rock stars like David Bowie, Mick Jagger, and Steven Tyler, frontmen whose sex appeal came smeared from the end of a lipstick tube.

"If you walk into a room and the room freezes, this is not a normal peer-group situation," Roth said. "When you achieve a certain level of success and popularity, people don't really want you to be regular, don't want you to be normal. I have to take care to circumnavigate being in that kind of situation."

Though as a rock star, he was a natural cultural enemy of punks, Roth began acting as unofficial top-secret sugar daddy for the Zero Club, a Hollywood after-hours bar and meet market operating beneath the auspices of a semilegitimate art space. There, Roth befriended underground figures like Tomata DuPlenty of L.A. punk legends the Screamers, Henry Rollins of Black Flag, and Mike Watt of the celebrated San Pedro punks the Minutemen. Rollins would later be instrumental in publishing Roth's autobiography, while the Minutemen's cover of "Ain't Talkin' 'Bout Love" would become a punk rock legend.

The Zero Club's resident bartender, Top Jimmy, was a white bluesman celebrated with his own song on *1984*. Roth reputedly caught Top Jimmy's Monday night act with the Rhythm Pigs at the raucous Cathay de Grande club sixty-four weeks in a row. The singer of the biggest hard rock band in the country was bingeing on inspiration, putting away the cardboard Rolls-Royces to walk alongside with some of the most creative—and poorest—people on earth.

After many nights prowling with these self-styled characters, Roth was showing unusual signs of introspection. "I sacrificed my education, my financial security, and my social background for something only one in a billion people get to do. From the beginning, I bet it all. Now the big voice comes from the sky and says the entry fee will be my family life. They take that right off the bat, because I have to live on the road."

One Day at a Time went off the air after nine seasons in May 1984, leaving Valerie with a Golden Globe Award and time to raise a family. As her schedule relaxed into more made-for-TV movies like *I Was a Mail Order Bride*, she noticed that Eddie's didn't—he still tinkered in the garage incessantly. "In the beginning when I met my wife, it was difficult," Eddie told *Musician*. "She didn't understand this thing that I had. It was huge, it was my life."

"I know his mistresses," Valerie said, "and they aren't people. My only threats are the electric guitar and the piano."

With the 5150 studio operating out of his house, Eddie could easily jump into projects during rare days at home. He recorded two songs, including an instrumental keyboard piece, for Valerie's movie *The Seduction of Gina*, a made-for-TV movie tackling gambling addiction. The director had pushed for more music from him, but Eddie felt uncomfortable surrendering tapes to a movie he hadn't seen. So in the middle of preparing Van Halen's new album, Eddie and Donn Landee took frequent trips to monitor how his music was used. Eddie felt like a novice, and he wanted to make sure everything was right.

With Landee's help, Eddie also composed background music for the teen comedy *The Wild Life*, starring Christopher Penn, Eric Stoltz, and Lea Thompson. He had been on the short list two years earlier to contribute music to the hit film that launched the eighties teen comedy explosion, *Fast Times at Ridgemont High*, and *The Wild Life* was a loose sequel also written by Cameron Crowe. Poor communication between the movie producers and the Van Halen camp thwarted Eddie's participation in *Fast Times*. Instead curly-haired California rocker Sammy Hagar penned the title track. But Van Halen were too great a part of the indelible fabric of high school culture to ignore completely. Crowe had gone undercover posing as a high school student to write the book that his movie was based on. For authenticity's sake, he made sure Van Halen bookended the screenplay: fast-talking slimeball Damone is introduced as someone who scalps Van Halen tickets, and surf hero Jeff Spicoli ends the movie a hero. After saving Brooke Shields's life on the beach, he spends the money hiring Van Halen to perform for his birthday.

In July 1984, Eddie made good on a previous promise and appeared live with the Jacksons' "Victory" tour in Dallas to tap out his now-infamous solo for "Beat It." Eddie hopped around, lost in the shuffle of choreographed dancers, electronic drums, and keyboard backing, until Michael Jackson shouted, "You got it, Eddie! Eddie!" and the guest ripped into a blazing twelve-second run. The great communion of techno-soul and high-tech rock arrived—finger-tapping guitar and Jackson's slippery moonwalk were two great exciters colliding from separate sides of the sun.

During the *1984* tour, Eddie began playing with an odd hinged panel attached to the back of his guitar. Like a folding stool, the contraption let him finger-tap with both hands on a flat horizontal surface, making his guitar more like a piano. With outside encouragement, he eventually patented the eccentric folding guitar tool, perhaps wary after all the innovations of his that had gone unpaid in the past ten years. But he remained skeptical that the idea would be marketable to anyone but himself.

Eddie's superstar status had gone through the stratosphere. His appearance at the 1985 NAMM (National Association of Music Merchants) convention caused a near riot. Meanwhile, fans were stealing his mail, and they eventually stole his entire mailbox. Eddie denied rumors he was working on a solo album, claiming that Van Halen offered him complete freedom and artistic satisfaction.

"I'm partially brainwashed by the whole aspect of the business," Ed told *Guitar World*. "What if I did something totally off the wall that I personally enjoyed, and people thought something weird about me? It's exposing a side of yourself that is very difficult to expect anyone to understand in the slightest way. I'd rather not expose myself or that type of music to any attack."

Yet trouble bubbled to the surface, as the success of the *1984* album and tour aggravated long-brewing ego problems. The band had become too big to fit on one stage. The nightly set was burdened with so many solo spots that Eddie later likened it to *The Tonight Show*— a disorienting whiz-bang of jokes, flashy guitar tricks, and crowd-pleasing antics. The musical freedom was advanced, bordering on over-indulgent. Eddie and Alex were jamming so long onstage that Michael Anthony often dropped out to let them explore.

Offstage, the personalities were starting to clash. "I'd stay up until six o'clock in the morning in the hotel room writing," Eddie told *Rolling Stone*. "Roth would bang on everybody's door at eight, nine in the morning, to get us to go roller skating or jogging. I'm going 'Fuck you, man, I just got to sleep," and he would be saying 'Well, man, you live wrong.'"

With Roth unmarried and still single-minded about the band, the others bridled under his constant supervision. Eddie complained of not being allowed to write longer "hypnotic" songs like Led Zeppelin, because Roth vetoed anything he couldn't dance to.

Van Halen had seriously neglected Britain and Europe since 1980, to the point that lesser marvels like Mötley Crüe, Def Leppard, and Bon Jovi were stealing their thunder across the Atlantic. To European hard rock fans the most recognized Roth wasn't Dave, but Ulrich Roth of Scorpions. Making a quick trip but getting the most from it, Van Halen signed on for the August 1984 Monsters of Rock concert before sixty-five thousand people at Castle Donington. Sharing the bill were Ozzy Osbourne, Gary Moore, Y&T, Accept, AC/DC, and Mötley Crüe.

No American band had ever headlined the venerable British metal event, including Van Halen who were in the unenviable spot of playing before AC/DC, whose crowds were loyal and grueling. They performed during the daylight, without the help of their vaunted lighting arsenal. Asked by the *Whistle Test* TV show how Van Halen felt going on before AC/DC, Alex joked, "We're taller."

The interviewers asked AC/DC what they thought of the Yanks. "They're more of a pop band than what we are," guitarist Angus Young answered. "We're more of a rock and roll band." After that assessment, nobody should have been surprised that when the gruff blokes in AC/DC lined up for an afternoon photo session, prima donna David Lee Roth suddenly appeared a few feet away with a boom box and began performing warm-up acrobatics. Roth could not contain his bravado. "There's liable to be a sense of competition at Castle Donington," he said with a grin. "It will be of the manner of who plays Edward's solo the best."

After camping in the mud for days, the notoriously unruly British festival crowd demanded constant entertainment. When overly bored or excited they hurled dirt clods and beer bottles filled with piss at the stage. With menacing black trash fires smoldering on the horizon and security struggling to keep overzealous fans off the stage, Van Halen responded by speeding up the tempo, overwhelming the Brits with an unusually kinetic display of power. Roth deftly high-stepped around thrown fruit, bottles, and rolls of toilet paper, and Michael Anthony killed on a striped Rickenbacker bass. Van Halen had something to prove to this country, and they delivered.

In the backstage corral, Hollywood homeboys Mötley Crüe made a big impression of their own kind. The new kings of the Sunset Strip were literally rising up to bite Van Halen. According to their bandleader Nikki Sixx, he was so drunk and coked up that as soon as he saw "squinty-eyed" Eddie Van Halen, he bared his teeth, lifted Eddie's shirt, and bit him on the stomach as a sign of affection.

"What's wrong with you?" Sixx gleefully recalled Valerie Bertinelli chastising him in the Mötley Crüe memoir *The Dirt*. "Biting my husband? You fucking freak!" Her yells only alerted the rest of Mötley Crüe to the feeding frenzy, according to Sixx—the band's singer promptly ran across the room and chomped into Eddie's hand.

Afterward, Roth seemed to be really beginning to view himself as Napoleon and all other bands the vanquished armies of Europe. "Mötley Crüe—I see them and I want to laugh," he told *Faces*. "All that rage—over what? A band like that is a quick fix." He belittled AC/DC's "pound, pound, get down, I'm gonna fuck your brains out victimization style."

Off camera, however, the band was fraying. Even generally easy-going bassist Michael Anthony was completely turning off to Roth, whose glittering star seemed to him like a faraway planet. He dreaded sharing the stage each night with someone he felt was a stranger. "I always thought, this guy's putting on a show for me now, too?"

Roth started traveling on his own tour bus, absorbing himself in magazines and books when not entertaining guests. He admitted his world was completely different than the Van Halens'. "There was always tension between me and Edward," he rationalized. "But there's always tension with me and everyone!"

Not helping matters, Eddie later admitted he was doing "a lot of blow" and drinking heavily to cope with the constant pressures of his popularity. He had more money than he knew what to do with, and a good buzz was his just reward for the headaches he had to deal with.

Though Roth was not a candidate to win an award from Nancy Reagan, he had a healthy distrust of hard drugs. "Never did heroin, never took pills, downers, or speed," he told *Rolling Stone*. "They kill your creativity and your spirit. Anyway, what's worse than drink and cocaine together is greed. Greed breeds egoism and sloth."

Reflecting on the hazards of his trade, Alex admitted to *Modern Drummer* that he suffered 15 to 20 percent hearing loss in both ears, which explained why he seemed standoffish to people meeting him for the first time. Seated nightly between walls of loudspeakers that would make airport baggage handlers cry for mercy, he explained how he often felt "noise drunk" mingling backstage after a show: "You don't hear any more highs, and you kind of feel alienated when you finish playing."

Turning a corner in his life, Alex was already onto his second marriage. His first trip with marital bliss had lasted only two months, and ended in ugly circumstances that brought tears to Eddie's eyes for a year afterward. This time Alex was more careful, and more serious—the newlywed Kelly Van Halen was a fresh-faced model from Canada who had worked on the legendary *SCTV* sketch comedy show.

The *1984* tour ended on September 2, 1984, in Nuremberg, Germany, former capital of the Holy Roman Empire and site of the war trials in the late 1940s that put a giant period on the end of the advance of the Nazi military machine. As if history was hammering home omens of disaster, the gig took place on a former zeppelin field from the era of the *Hindenburg*. When Van Halen left the stage that night, they returned home with vastly different plans, unaware that they might never play together again.

"We were in the middle of this thing, and it was getting bigger and bigger," Alex told *The Inside*. "Individually, we were so far apart that it was like night and day. We were never together, although it looked like we were from the public's standpoint. That's why in 1984 it was very natural for it to fall apart. We saw it coming, even though when it actually materialized it was a surprise. It was a complex deal. When you're in the middle of it, you don't have time to question or analyze anything—you simply go for it."

ROAD TO NOWHERE

The year 1984 seemed to sustain forever for Van Halen. The band had racked up a career total of more than twelve million albums in domestic sales, half of them during that calendar year. The arrival of the compact disc ensured that a good percentage of those albums would be repurchased in the coming years in the digital format. Then 1985 came calling like a hard, cold slap.

The band members had smelled one another's stage sweat, bad breath, and dirty socks for over ten years. When Eddie turned thirty in January, the angry young men were officially no longer young—just angry. "Van Halen has four personalities," David Lee Roth told MTV, "and they seem to be getting more different."

To the delight of fans and the chagrin of his band, Roth revealed plans to record a solo album. The announcement made the rest of Van Halen very nervous—though they desperately needed a break from their extroverted singer for a while, they let him run off to do his own thing with a great deal of skepticism about what was happening within the band.

Michael Anthony fell over himself laughing when he heard Roth was planning to release a cover of the Beach Boys' "California Girls." But that was exactly the idea, to make America giggle.

"I think it's something he's always wanted to do," Eddie told *Guitar World*. "Put it this way—it's something I've always wanted to do, and haven't done. I guess, in a funny way, it explains Dave as a vocalist and lyricist."

Appearing at MTV's New Year's Eve show with new bodyguards—a pair of female bodybuilders—Dave rang in the New Year with the video for "California Girls," the first video from his solo EP, *Crazy from the Heat*. Robert Plant of Led Zeppelin had just stepped out in a similar way with the R&B-themed Honeydrippers *Volume One* EP. Likewise, British soul singer Robert Palmer had recently teamed with members of Duran Duran in Power Station. There was a feeling in the air that the most substantial rock singers could check in and check out of MTV video projects without marring their lifelong reputations.

"I think it's the perfect time for me to do this," Roth told *Creem*. "I mean it feels right. You know, use my hand darling, I won't look."

In the vein of "Ice Cream Man" and "Happy Trails," Roth recorded four other covers for the first record under his name, all a bit unusual: the Lovin' Spoonful's "Coconut Grove," Louis Prima's Tin Pan Alley medley of "Just a Gigolo"/"I Ain't Got Nobody," and the jazz standard "Easy Street." His arsenal of sidemen on the record was impressive—Beach Boy Carl Wilson sang backups on "California Girls," and towering white-haired saxophonist/organist Edgar Winter of "Frankenstein" fame hammered keyboards.

The material certainly didn't clash with Van Halen—in fact, they had rejected "Just a Gigolo" for *1984*. All the songs were at least twenty years old, hailing from a bygone era—"Gigolo" was a hit in 1929. Roth also went out of his way to make sure producer Ted Templeman didn't put guitars in the mix, afraid of confusing the fans. The EP was fun adult music about sex and love, still captivating to a teen audience in the hands of this winsome new interpreter.

Some of these lines, Roth had been delivering to the bedroom mirror since he was in elementary school, and they harkened to something

much older. "Al Jolson is the classic showbiz model," he explained to
Penthouse. "The white gloves—drop to one knee—the Knickerbocker
break—the flatspin—smile! No dead space. I can't stand dead space
onstage. I've got a surgically implanted disco beat. My show has to be
130 beats a minute or better."

The record was assembled in a month and recorded in five days at
the Power Station in New York. Roth walked to the studio every day,
taking in the action of the city streets. Equally important was the production of the music videos. "Just a Gigolo" lampooned the living
history of MTV to date. Roth cavorted through an imaginary backstage
video world, shoving Billy Idol into his electric sci-fi stage props and
sending Boy George into a schoolgirl tizzy. He was beating video satirist
Weird Al Yankovic at his own game and pre-dating the smart-aleck *Pee-
Wee's Playhouse*. He was mocking MTV even as he became its greatest
product. "I wrote and directed those videos," he said. "Those are Bur-
lesque. Those are Vaudeville. I learned it from watching shows back in
the '60s, and from going to the Crazy Horse Saloon in Paris in the
1970s."

Roth was David Letterman's first guest of 1985, and while the two
self-deprecating Hoosiers sparred comically, Roth denied he would
soon leave Van Halen. "I've got strong tribal instincts, and we'll be
going to the studio sometime in the next month to start arguing again."
He claimed Van Halen would release a new album in 1985, and he
gagged about why Van Halen had never done anything like *Crazy from
the Heat*. When in doubt, blame the drummer: "In Van Halen we kept
trying to have a concept, but Alex kept forgetting the concept."

Van Halen were rehearsing for their next album, trying out tracks
"Summer Nights," "Get Up," and "Eat Thy Neighbor." They toyed with
the idea of releasing a live album, a chance to showcase unreleased
material. Yet progress was tough. Roth was becoming increasingly
unavailable, constantly off doing interviews about *Crazy from the Heat*.
After three months, they were making little progress.

The uncertainty started to spread into other important areas. The
band let go manager Noel Monk, who had wrangled them since early

1978, encouraging their crazy stunts and leaving no whim unsatisfied, considering no request too irrational. They couldn't agree on renewal terms for his contract, and suddenly he was gone. "Noel Monk was Dave's goddamn puppet," Eddie griped to *Guitar World*. That didn't stop Monk from suing Roth in L.A. County Superior Court the following year.

The spring of 1985 found Roth frequently stalling for time, partially because he felt uncomfortable proceeding without a manager. He also wanted Van Halen to postpone the next album and work as his backing band on a movie. The others were just pissed off. Rehearsals became unproductive, as Roth complained that the new songs were too sad and melancholy. He claimed Eddie had already broken the band covenant, putting soundtrack projects and outside guest spots ahead of Van Halen's seventh album.

In March, Roth claimed the Van Halen brothers presented him with a future career path based on minimal touring. "Well guys, it's been nice knowing you," Roth told the crew in the parking lot after a lethal spat. He left the studio and never came back.

Then in April 1985, Van Halen claimed they gave Roth an ultimatum, feeling that his solo career had brought progress on the new album to a standstill. Roth seemed preoccupied with turning *Crazy from the Heat* into a cinematic star vehicle; it was a zany adventure film along the lines of the Beatles' *A Hard Day's Night*, the Osmonds' *Goin' Coconuts*, and *Some Like It Hot*. Dave was finally on the verge of becoming Errol Flynn, Johnny Weismuller, Bugs Bunny, and Marilyn Monroe.

But Van Halen were not interested in being his backing band, or his backup plan. Eddie's report on his last conversation with the singer involved driving over for a sitdown at the Pasadena mansion Roth had bought from his parents and shared with his sister Lisa—the same building where Van Halen had practiced for years. "Maybe when I'm done with my movie, we can get back together," Eddie recalled Roth saying.

"I ain't waiting on your ass!" Eddie snapped. "So long, and good luck."

When Dave broke from Van Halen, with him went a major part of Van Halen's support system, including designers, truck drivers, merchandisers, stagehands, and creative director Pete Angelus, who had been working with Roth on the movie script. To illustrate how the Van Halen organization was gutted by the divorce, Angelus had been the sound engineer at Gazzari's. He had joined the adventure early and had done everything from lighting design to stage production to drawing storyboards for the band's videos. Van Halen's support system was ravaged. They dissolved their in-house merchandise arm, Van Halen Productions, and in the future simply licensed their name to professional manufacturers of memorabilia. The party seemed to be over.

The *Crazy from the Heat* EP went platinum in June 1985, a promising augur of future success. "Just a Gigolo"/"I Ain't Got Nobody" rose to number 12 on the singles chart. Roth appeared to have judged his massive appeal correctly and enjoyed being the undistracted center of undivided attention from an adoring public. After all, he had given thousands of high kicks and primal screams for the greater glory of the Van Halen family name for over a decade. Fostering jealousy and tension from his main meal ticket, "California Girls" became a Top 10 single.

For Roth, the urge to excel must have been enormous. He had proven all the high school guidance counselors wrong. He was successful beyond his wildest dreams. The sky was the limit. Yet he was still stuck with the same guys who knew him ten years ago, when he couldn't get a date because he was too talkative, always *on*, scaring away the local girls. Now he could have anyone he wanted.

"He treated everybody like a little lower than him," Eddie said shortly after Roth left, "including us in the band." And so the five-time guitarist of the year, the older brother, and the world's largest collector of Mickey Mouse watches applied the brakes on their glamour machine, and Roth went flying out of Van Halen, mouth first.

Curiously, even Ted Templeman, one of the band's closest colleagues, claimed he never saw the split coming. "I never saw any of it," he told *Rolling Stone*. "We were in there for seven years, we never had any fights—what was it? They told me they used to fight it all out in the basement before they got to me. So what the fuck's the matter? So does everybody else!"

Now billing themselves as the Picasso Brothers—part art, part pizza delivery—Roth and Pete Angelus plotted Roth's ascension to Hollywood stardom, pitching a project about the zany adventures of a fictional larger-than-life rock star, a ninety-minute explosion like the "California Girls" video done coast to coast. They sold the story successfully to CBS Films, and the road ahead for their deal was a short run of green lights.

"I think I can do just about anything as long as it's within my character's frame of reference," Roth told the *San Francisco Chronicle*. "Everything you've seen is part of me. We may have blown it out of proportion so it fits on your TV screen better, but I want to go on and do something bigger than that."

Roth had already done a boffo job of scripting the look, attitude, and public perception of Van Halen. Now he promised a rocking, whacked-out rebirth of the attention-addled stream-of-consciousness comedy that had made *Monty Python's Flying Circus* a household name in dorm rooms.

Off to a flying start, Roth and Angelus posted an open casting call for their *Crazy from the Heat* movie, seeking actresses and personalities with the following requirements: "If you are a woman, and you think you have an unusual character face and a beautiful body, or if you have an unusually beautiful face and character body, or any combination thereof, you're perfect."

Having narrowed down the field to virtually any woman alive, Dave's TV party commenced. "Let's find our women on the street, because that's where I found my music," he told Joan Rivers on *The Tonight Show*. "It's funny, nobody's ever entrusted a zillion-dollar project before to a couple of schnooks like us, Pete Angelus and myself." Their script was finished and shooting was scheduled to begin in January 1986.

Roth appeared at the wrap party for *Pee-Wee's Big Adventure* making a big noise that he had bet his producer he could make it to the MTV Video Music Awards in New York three days later in his red Mercury lowrider. With fanfare, he headed east, and then ducked into the first desert airport outside of L.A. The night of the awards, Roth wiped some dirt on his face and drove up well rested to the awards ceremony, where he stole the show—a variation on the bait-and-switch parachute stunt Van Halen had pulled in Oakland years earlier.

Up for several MTV Video Awards that night, Roth didn't win any. He partied with the Go-Gos, while Don Henley and "We Are the World" by USA for Africa notched award after award on the feel-good vote. Roth claimed Michael Jackson called him soon after to say he was "furious when you didn't win an award"—begging the question of what Michael Jackson looked like furious.

Roth appeared on *The Tonight Show* in late 1985, breaking the news that he had just ended a relationship with a girl. "When you fall out of a major love affair," he told Joan Rivers, "that's God's way of saying it's time to buckle down and make a lot of money." He cast his line out for Princess Stephanie of Monaco, admiring her broad shoulders— he was the "It" boy, he could marry royalty.

Then the unthinkable happened—or more like the typical Hollywood bullshit. Following a shakeup of the brass at CBS Films, Roth was left without a lifeline. He went from a $10 million budget to not having a deal, as the studio shuttered its doors. His only appearance on the silver screen in 1985 was in claymation form during a dream sequence in the John Cusack teen film *Better Off Dead*, where a heavy metal hamburger based on Roth and Eddie Van Halen holds court over a deep fryer full of bikini-clad French fries.

Roth sued CBS Films the following summer for $25 million, claiming breach of contract over their sudden disinterest in *Crazy from the Heat*. Ultimately, he missed the brass ring—he couldn't litigate himself onto a movie theater marquee—but Van Halen hadn't been signed on the first try, either.

Afterward, Roth dismissed Van Halen's claims that he left to be a movie star as "a lot of B.S. It's a lot of excuses that are being peddled because these guys couldn't get off their butt and make a record. We sat out in front of that backyard studio, in front of 5150, because Mr. Fingers couldn't get out of bed for four days in a row. And Mr. Sticks was out driving across the country with his new wife, and he wasn't on time either. And I wanted to make a record."

Millions of divorced kids listening to Van Halen in 1985 had just accepted that Mom and Dad weren't going to get back together, and now they were expected to deal with David Lee Roth leaving Van Halen. Against all advice, these playboy musicians were now role models. For many, without David Lee Roth there could be no Van Halen. Sour comments coming from both camps after the split didn't help. Like the end of every love story, both parties tried to minimize their attraction and the intensity of their relationship. In this case, twenty million interested fans were caught in the middle of the breakup—and the fallout of their emotional stress was toxic.

PART II

TOP OF THE WORLD

THE HAGARLITHIC ERA, 1985–1996

- **October 13, 1947:** Sammy Hagar born in Monterey, California.
- **1973:** Sammy Hagar joins Montrose, records two albums, and tours heavily.
- **1976:** Sammy Hagar leaves Montrose, launches solo career.
- **September 1985:** Eddie Van Halen announces at Farm Aid that Sammy Hagar is Van Halen's new lead singer.
- **November 19, 1985:** Sammy Hagar's ninth studio album, *VOA*, becomes his first platinum-selling disc
- **March 24, 1986:** Release date of *5150*; first "Van Hagar" album sells triple platinum by October.
- **July 4, 1986:** Release of David Lee Roth's platinum solo debut, *Eat 'Em and Smile*.
- **December 1986:** Jan Van Halen dies.
- **May 24, 1988:** Release of *OU812*, followed shortly by Roth's *Skyscraper*.
- **Summer 1988:** Eddie attempts sobriety while Van Halen tours with Metallica, Scorpions, and Dokken.
- **February 1989:** Tone Lōc's "Wild Thing" reaches number 2, a rap single that samples Van Halen's "Jamie's Cryin.'"
- **April 22, 1990:** Van Halen performs at opening of Cabo Wabo Cantina in Mexico.
- **February 2, 1991:** Release of David Lee Roth's *A Little Ain't Enough*, his last gold record as a solo artist.
- **March 16, 1991:** Eddie's son Wolfgang Van Halen born.

June 17, 1991: Release of *For Unlawful Carnal Knowledge*, Van Halen's third-straight number 1 album.

January 1991: Eddie debuts the EVH Music Man guitar and the Peavey 5150 amplifier line.

February 23, 1993: Release of first official live album, *Right Here, Right Now*.

October 16, 1993: Van Halen's manager since 1985, Ed Leffler, dies.

March 14, 1994: Sammy Hagar releases solo collection, *Unboxed*.

October 2, 1994: Fresh from rehab, Eddie Van Halen announces he will never drink again.

January 24, 1995: Release of *Balance*, the fourth consecutive number 1 studio album.

April 7, 1995: Eddie arrested at Burbank Airport carrying a loaded gun.

April 26, 1995: Van Halen returns to Europe after eleven years, as an opening act for Bon Jovi.

Fall 1995: David Lee Roth appears in Reno and Las Vegas with a fourteen-piece band.

November 29, 1995: Sammy Hagar marries second wife, Kari.

June 1996: Eddie and Sammy fight during phone call; Sammy Hagar leaves Van Halen.

September 4, 1996: Original members of Van Halen appear together at MTV Video Music Award, leading to renewed quarrels.

August 7, 1996: *Van Halen* certified diamond for ten million sold.

October 22, 1996: Release of *Best of Volume I*, with two new songs featuring Roth; despite the recent split with the band, it is his first number 1 album.

IT'S THE END OF THE
WORLD AS WE KNOW IT
(AND I FEEL FINE)

ith his torso bent back and striped guitar in the air, Eddie Van Halen had become an electric guitar icon. David Lee Roth, on the other hand, had become something even bigger—a celebrity representing all things rock and roll. Before the search to replace the irreplaceable could begin, Alex had to once again convince Eddie to continue with Van Halen. "During *Fair Warning* I wanted to quit," an exasperated Eddie told *Guitar World*, "but I stuck with it, and that's what burns my ass even more. If I would have quit then I wouldn't have spent an extra four years putting up with [Roth's] attitude."

Outside the band, the juicy sport of speculation began. Reports emerged that Van Halen would not replace Roth with any one contender but a constellation of stars. Eddie's collaborator Brian May from Queen offered his help. Phil Collins, Joe Cocker, Mike Rutherford, and Pete Townshend were all rumored to be lined up to work with the band, possibly sharing the limelight with several songs each on a glorified Eddie Van Halen solo project. Townshend wasn't free until the end of the year, however, and the band increasingly felt the need to put a more permanent band together as quickly as possible.

Also thrown in the rumor mill was Australian screamer Jimmy Barnes, a frequent INXS collaborator who had just left his band Cold Chisel. The band liked his unique voice, but "nothing really happened," according to Michael Anthony. Another candidate was twenty-year-old Eric Martin, who spoke with Eddie on the phone about Van Halen wanting a "soulful rock singer" in the vein of Paul Rodgers of Bad Company. Martin drove to Eddie's house and spent an afternoon waiting for him in 5150. He left without meeting the guitarist, and never worked up the nerve to return. "I chickened out, totally," he told Melodicrock.com.

After Eddie joined Patty Smyth onstage for two songs in Los Angeles, followed by two surprise appearances in Houston and Austin, Texas, her name also entered the mix. Smyth, a friend of Eddie and Valerie whose hard-edged Scandal scored a Top 10 hit in 1984 with "The Warrior," made music that was about as tough as rock radio sounded at the time, and replacing Roth with a leather-lunged woman would surely have been sweet comeuppance. Instead, Smyth married New York rocker Richard Hell in 1985 and became a mother.

In a show of support for Eddie from the music industry, in 1985 he was nominated for the first time for a Grammy for Best Instrumental Performance on "Jump." The record company was less nurturing. Anxious for the bounty of their prized animal, Warner Bros. asked Eddie for a solo album while the band deliberated over what to do next. Label boss Lenny Waronker also urged the band to change its name.

The solution came while Eddie was dealing with his daily errands. For some time, he had owned a couple Lamborghinis—cars that required more special care than his old $150 black 1959 Volvo. He was self-admittedly prone to spinning his fancy rides during late-night high-speed runs, causing the kind of wear and tear that he couldn't patch up quickly with chewing gum and a broken guitar string. He saw his mechanic often—elite import car specialist Claudio Zampolli, whose shop in Van Nuys, California, served celebrities with a taste for six-figure star vehicles.

Another regular fixture in Zampolli's showroom was Sammy Hagar, the so-called Red Rocker, a high-energy solo artist whose one bona fide hit was a social anthem for fast drivers, "I Can't Drive 55." Zampolli inadvertently brokered his biggest sale of the year when, after a chance meeting at the garage, he gave Hagar's number to Eddie and hinted that Sammy would love to hear from him. When Eddie phoned to talk about Van Halen, Hagar was in the kitchen with his wife, Betsy. Hagar later claimed he felt butterflies in his stomach, a weird premonition of destiny calling,

Butterflies became biting flies, however, when the two sides first tried to kick-start their courtship in a record company boardroom. As a coterie of managers, agents, and lawyers talked through the technicalities, any chemistry in the water was in danger of stagnating. During a cigarette break, the four musicians pulled one another aside and decided to play some music first and ask questions about the legalities later.

When Sammy met with Eddie and Alex, they tried out some ideas for "Summer Nights," one of the new songs they had already rehearsed with Roth. Engineer Donn Landee was on hand during the first jam sessions, and happily gave Hagar two thumbs up. After a few hours in 5150 the new band embraced one another—the Van Halen name would carry on.

Hagar had previously crossed paths with Van Halen several times. His early albums with Montrose were the testing ground for the production techniques of Ted Templeman and Landee, the team responsible for the first six Van Halen albums. The Hagar-penned "Make It Last" from the first Montrose album had been part of their set as a cover band in 1974. Van Halen had toured with Montrose, though only after Hagar's departure.

Hagar was in the process of reconfiguring his solo act when Van Halen called. The thirty-seven-year old singer had recently ventured into the economy-wattage supergroup HSAS with session guitarist Neal Schon of Journey, drummer Michael Shrieve of Santana, and bassist Kenny Aaronson of Foghat. During his lengthy career, Hagar had made a lot of friends—not just among musicians but among the A&R reps, tour managers, and promotion men who kept the music business in action.

"My only saving grace replacing a guy like Roth," Sammy said, "is that people know who I am."

<center>~~~~><~~~~</center>

The first California native to join the ultimate sunshine hard rock band Van Halen, Samuel Roy Hagar was born in coastal Monterey on October 13, 1947. With two older sisters and a brother, he was the baby of the family. Before Sammy reached high school, the Hagars moved to Fontana, California, a dusty lower-middle-class industrial flatland in San Bernardino County outside Los Angeles, best known as the birthplace of the Hells Angels.

Sammy's father, Robert, described as "alcoholic" and "scary violent" by family members, was a boxer who fought under the name Bobby Burns in the late 1930s. Initially known for his deadly punches, he ended his first eight fights with knockouts and fought Hall of Fame member Manuel Ortiz seven times. When the blows began taking their toll, however, Hagar became better known for his perseverance and stamina. The family always boasted that their father was never knocked down in a fight.

Robert left boxing briefly to fight in World War II, and his career never bounced back. He switched between bantamweight, featherweight, and lightweight divisions looking for spots on local fight cards, anything to bring home some cash. Eventually he boxed in the tough border-towns between California and Mexico where rules and regulations went out the window—along with the furniture and the losers. Sammy later compared his dad to Robert De Niro in *Raging Bull*—a violent, erratic, and dangerous man with a persecution complex.

When Sammy was five, his dad strapped gloves on him and sent him into the garage to trade punches with his older brother. The bloody noses continued for the next twelve years, until Sammy discovered his own voice. Quitting his father's footsteps after a few serious bouts, he took a cue from his new hero, Elvis Presley, and joined the local rock and roll scene in search of chicks and kicks.

In contrast to her headstrong, volatile husband, Gladys Hagar was a selfless caregiver. She slept with one ear open, ready to whisk her kids away when Daddy came home looking for a fight. She refused her youngest son drums, saying they were too expensive and too loud. When Sammy was eighteen, he asked her for a guitar to entertain his buddies down on the beach. "He wanted an instrument," Gladys said. "I was supporting the kids all by myself, and it wasn't easy. He said, 'I am gonna be determined, and I am gonna show you.'"

Sammy claimed he stole his first electric guitar off a music store wall, and began playing in bands like Skinny, Big Bang, Dustcloud, and the Justice Brothers. "My first band, we could only play one song, but we played it all day—'Miserlou' by Dick Dale." He became a journeyman on the local bar rock scene. Rare among his peers, however, Hagar was a virtual teetotaler who preferred outdoor activities to parties. "I was doing what everybody else was doing," Sammy told *Hit Parader*. "But because of seeing my father and how liquor took hold of him and ruined him, I turned off the booze quick." His father's descent was especially harrowing—according to Sammy he died at age forty-five in 1970 in the back of a police car, riding to the drunk tank after being scooped off the ground in a public park.

Sammy's big career break came in 1973, when former Van Morrison sideman Ronnie Montrose recruited him to sing for the band that bore his name. Hagar lasted with Montrose for two albums, penning the hard rock hit "Bad Motor Scooter" and cowriting "Rock Candy," "Paper Money," and "Space Station No. 5." Sammy flew the coop for a solo career in 1975, but the first song he ever wrote, "Bad Motor Scooter" remained a Montrose standard.

Hagar was always enthusiastic and outgoing, more like a featured performer than a flunky singer. He claimed he was fired in part for talking to the audience too much. "I was the figurehead of Montrose," Sammy said in the early 1980s, "like David Lee Roth is in Van Halen.

I was the one getting my picture in the magazines like David. People wanted to interview me. Before, Ronnie did everything on his own, and then it infuriated him when I became the center of attention. I was naive—I was as excited as a little puppy."

His January 1976 solo debut, *Nine on a Ten Scale*, failed to produce a radio hit, so Hagar built his career one night at a time, bonding with fans on a likable eye-to-eye level. Drawing on a boxer's idea of personal promotion, he first billed himself as Sammy Wild, and later the Red Rocker. He didn't experience the kind of immediate success that could make him think he had a magnetic personality—he won his audience with his positive attitude and by working for them with every pluck of his guitar strings. "I feel more like a worker than a star," Hagar said, frequently comparing his nightly job to mopping floors. "That's how I was raised."

Hagar rocked without much rage—he was energetic, but not usually angry or snotty. Yet his competitive approach to music continued. "Question my talent and I'll probably kill you," he told *Hit Parader*. "I've seen every group in this business play live and I can honestly say that I put out more in concert than any other performer. I would say I'm in the top three in the world in terms of performing."

For one thing, Sammy liked to talk. His stage raps grew legendary—one audience address in the early eighties reportedly clocked in at twenty-seven minutes. Telling jokes, trying on clothes, and shooting off down-home political opinions, he was an animated young presence on the meat and potatoes rock circuit. He understood the regional nature of touring in the 1970s, and eventually played the down-and-dirty annual Texxas Jam at the Cotton Bowl in Dallas, and the Astrodome in Houston more than anyone. Ripening as a solo artist, Hagar discovered the Red Rocker persona after penning the track "Red" for his 1977 self-titled third album, commonly called *The Red Album*.

Married to his sweetheart, Betsy, early in his career, Hagar shunned the temptations of the road but offered a steady stream of blunt songs about sex. His lyrics were simple but honest, sometimes even corny.

He described his own vocabulary as "pretty bad." Depending on the ear of the beholder, songs like "Dick in the Dirt" would either speak straight to the heart or fall flat in empty clichés. He frequently cited "I Can't Drive 55" as his best experience putting rhymes together.

Despite his self-professed shortcomings, he also experienced success as a songwriter. Bette Midler belted out his song "Keep On Rockin'" in her 1979 movie *The Rose*. Then soap opera idol Rick Springfield turned Sammy's "I've Done Everything for You" into a Top 10 single in 1981. Though Hagar had nothing to do with leather and spikes, his upbeat "Heavy Metal" kicked off the soundtrack to the 1982 animated fantasy film *Heavy Metal*. His "Fast Times at Ridgemont High" theme also appeared in a lead spot on that movie soundtrack— a position the director had originally slotted for Van Halen.

Though down-to-earth about a lot of things, Hagar also had a loose-screw Californian side. In 1968 in Fontana, he claimed to have experienced the first of several visitations by space aliens. "Anyone who thinks we're the only ones here, despite the vastness of the entire universe, is fucking crazy," he told *Guitar World*. "I'm a firm believer. When I was about 19 or 20, they downloaded everything that was in my head. I don't know who the fuck they are, but I've narrowed them down to a people called the Nine, who are called that because they're from the ninth dimension." He named his music publishing company Nine Music after the space invaders he claimed were watching over him.

In 1981, Hagar left Capitol and signed with David Geffen's brand-new record company, Geffen Records. Cleaning up his act, he joined a reliable league of rockers like Billy Squier, Aldo Nova, the Greg Kihn Band, and Quarterflash—acts that seemed sensible compared to the outrages of heavy metal and the decadent alienation of new wave. FM radio was a business, not a social revolution, and it needed to rock steady to keep its advertisers happy. For guys like Hagar who could deliver tracks like "Rock 'N' Roll Weekend," there was plenty of money to be made.

With solo success came money for a fleet of beach cruisers, convertibles, and custom cars including a 1959 Ferrari Alpha 400i Spider and a 1955 Ford Thunderbird. But a black 1983 512 Boxer with a worn-out driver's seat leather inspired his widely recognized "I Can't Drive 55." While Eddie Van Halen frequently admitted to coming up with riffs while diddling with a guitar in front of the TV, Hagar got his inspiration while alone behind the wheel. "I always drove like a complete asshole," he added. "Cut people off, tailgate, you name it."

By the time he reached Van Halen, Sammy had an impressive three gold albums under his belt: *Standing Hampton*, *Three Lock Box*, and 1985's Ted Templeman–produced *VOA*—a patriotic potshot against the Soviet Union for boycotting the 1984 Olympics in Los Angeles. The Red Rocker was anything but a commie. The *VOA* album cover pictured "Uncle Sam" Hagar parachuting onto the White House lawn to help Ronald Reagan manage the constant nuisance of foreign powers. *People* recommended the album to "rock fans who don't demand a whole lot of subtlety."

Sammy was a rebel who obeyed the rules and flourished. Where many rock musicians detested the music business, he created cameos in several music videos for his A&R man at Geffen, the celebrated rock swami John Kalodner. By 1985, he was an utterly commercial creature who remained deeply convinced of his own integrity. Following the news of Sammy joining Van Halen, *VOA* went platinum at the end of 1985. "If I wasn't so dedicated to being true to myself, I could have been a platinum-selling artist five years ago," he declared to *Hit Parader*.

Before Van Halen and Hagar could make any moves, they still had to appease the moneymen. The merger of two platinum-selling entities was not as simple as slapping high fives at the rehearsal room. With millions of dollars now at stake, Hagar's label Geffen Records prepared to go to war against Warner Bros. Geffen had only won Hagar after a protracted legal battle to free him from Capitol. Now, after his last solo album had finally gone platinum after years of work, he was already looking to change alliances. Hagar still owed Geffen three albums on his contract, and label executives were afraid they would be getting bupkiss—at least until this jaunt with Van Halen was done.

Eddie, Alex, and Mike kidded that they would tour with Hagar as his backing act, but that joke pleased their label Warner Bros. none. Several hundred hours of negotiation later, Geffen accepted the promise of one more solo album from Hagar, along with a cut of the proceeds from the next Van Halen album.

Since Van Halen were still operating without management, Sammy introduced his manager of the past nine years, Ed Leffler, to the brothers, and Leffler was soon signed on to take care of Van Halen's business. This was an important alliance for Sammy to bring to the band, ensuring that in any future decision making he could count on having the brass understanding his point of view.

Eddie appeared onstage with Sammy's band in September 1985 at the first annual Farm Aid charity concert for American farmers. Organized by Willie Nelson and John Cougar Mellencamp as a homegrown response to the Live Aid relief effort for Africa earlier that year, Farm Aid raised millions. Doing their part, Eddie and Hagar romped through Led Zeppelin's "Rock and Roll." With Sammy all over the stage in yellow shoes and his headset microphone, Eddie tore up a guitar solo on a Frankenstrat. Their rendition of "Wild Thing" was cut from The Nashville Network broadcast after Hagar started joking about his dick. But after Eddie's solo, Sammy announced the big news to the throng— he was the new lead singer of Van Halen.

While Roth and Eddie shared little in common outside the band, Hagar and Eddie became buddies fast. Sammy soon bought a beachfront house in Malibu two doors down from Eddie. Almost immediately, the band began flaunting its good fortune. "We had a toothache for about eleven years," Alex Van Halen said about Roth, "and we finally went to the dentist and had it extracted, and got a crown with a gold cap."

Even happy-go-lucky Michael Anthony breathed an acrimonious sigh of relief. "I would dread having to do a photo session with Roth, because I worried about how he would think I looked when I got there," he told *Rolling Stone*. "I know Edward and Alex felt the same way, because Roth's saying 'You gotta dress this way. Go and buy some clothes. Why are you wearing that?'"

Though Hagar and Roth had traded insults in the press in the early 1980s, the two men appeared to preach similar if not compatible personal philosophies—everyone should follow their own path, listen to their own soul, and give not a damn what anyone else thinks. They clashed on musical styles, personal conduct, and fashion, but they both dressed themselves with bizarre gusto. Though not fond of Roth's glittering capes and feather boas, Sammy packed his wardrobe with sleeveless yellow jumpsuits covered with red straps that could have been designed by Ronald McDonald.

Unmistakably, the two men's concepts of self-fulfillment made Roth and Sammy polar opposites. Roth liked standing head and shoulders above everyone in the center of the room, serving as a shining example to make other people feel good. Hagar was completely different—a populist who communicated with crowds by showing how much he was just like them. The main question remained whether Van Halen's sense of humor, fury, and passion could remain intact with Hagar as vocalist.

While the world reserved judgment, Van Halen's former singer was not inclined to be charitable. He mocked his former bandmates in the press, helping to spark one of rock's greatest ongoing rivalries. "I don't know if there's a Van Halen without David Lee Roth," he declared immodestly, "but I know that nobody cares about Van Halen without David Lee Roth."

ROLL WITH IT

One week before Van Halen were due to begin recording their first album with Sammy Hagar, longtime producer Ted Templeman called with bad news. He remained committed to David Lee Roth, who was still a Warner Bros. artist, and scheduling conflicts between the two projects meant he wouldn't be able to record with Eddie, Alex, Mike, and Sammy. The news was not all bad—the producer and the wunderkind guitarist were wearing on each other's nerves anyway.

With Templeman out of the picture, Eddie decided to produce the next album himself with Donn Landee at the 5150 studio. But already troubled by the uncertainty surrounding the loss of Roth, Warner Bros. banged its iron fist and refused their boys full creative latitude. A search began for a producer from a top-shelf list of candidates, including Chic mastermind Nile Rodgers, Tina Turner's private synthmaster Rupert Hines, and Quincy Jones. The band chose Mick Jones, an acquaintance of Sammy's, whose radio candy while creative leader of Foreigner had sold millions. Pop metal like Def Leppard had seized the day from the lightweight rockers, but Foreigner's *Agent Provocateur* album still went double platinum in 1985.

Officially *5150* was made during four weeks between November 1985 and February 1986, though in truth Jones only needed to polish the tracks that Alex and Eddie had begun long before he arrived. The album cover artwork depicted Atlas, the Greek Titan who the band claimed spent 5,150 years holding the earth aloft on his shoulders. It was a fitting depiction of the work Van Halen still had ahead of them.

Hagar leered, "Hello, baaaby!" at the start of album opener "Good Enough," and the comparisons were off and running. While not an unknown quantity, the grinning "I Can't Drive 55" Hagar was an unlikely replacement for the larger-than-life Roth. Essentially the band had substituted the edgy, unattainable parade marshal with a versatile and approachable everyman.

The focus of *5150* was obviously on polish, not on kicking ass. Not by accident, "Good Enough" resembled the soundtrack music Eddie had done for *The Wild Life* and *The Seduction of Gina*—in fact, the song was developed from incidental music in *The Wild Life*. Eddie recorded his guitar track in a single take. As an introduction to a new band, *5150* was like being invited to the party of the year and arriving to find a few close friends and a warm welcome instead of a raging bash.

The new era of Van Halen began in force with "Why Can't This Be Love?" a midtempo pop song with a lively synth melody and some of Van Halen's most processed playing to date. Roth had largely curtailed keyboards in the band since before *Diver Down*. Now Eddie's objective number one was to shake off Diamond Dave's criticism and hit the keys. "There's no more governor telling me what I can't do!" Eddie yelped. He had been vindicated when the keyboard-driven "Jump" became the band's biggest hit. "Why Can't This Be Love?" also rose up the charts to become the hit of *5150*, reaching number 3.

"Get Up" offered some of Hagar's most obvious boxing lyrics over a double-time countrified stampede of Eddie's swerving guitar. Alex's speedy electronic drums sounded like a spitting robot, as sampled drums supplemented his trademark taut snare. Since early 1983, he had integrated hexagon-shaped Simmons electronic drum trigger pads in his kit—a sign of admiration for Bill Bruford, the seventies fusion and progressive rock basher who had already switched to electronic drums. Though they had the warmth of a microwave oven, they had the logistic advantage of being easier to route directly through the soundboard.

Hagar stated often that he had dropped his next solo album and tour when the call came from the band, yet he was careful not to impose himself immediately on the mighty Van Halen. The key to keeping the band's sound was letting Eddie write all the music, then melding the songs together organically by jamming on the ideas. Hagar brought lyrics and for the time being left his music at home. As always, the songs were credited as group compositions, though Eddie described Mike's input as spare: "He usually goes along with everybody else and doesn't have any strong preferences."

"Dreams," which would become Hagar's favorite song with Van Halen, was solid synth pop written with help from producer Mick Jones. Perhaps in response to its similarities to Kenny Loggins's "Danger Zone," the U.S. Navy's Blue Angels later edited a demonstration video of precision fighter jets to this song.

For the feel-good anthem "Summer Nights," Eddie used a headless Steinberger Trans Trem guitar—a radical redesign intended to bring the guitar into the future. Skeptical hard rock fans simply considered it a castrated guitar. Easing the transition for guitar fiends, he decorated it with trademark black-and-white stripes on a red background. The unique axe had another upside—when he parked his cigarette in the guitar neck, he could lean over and puff without losing an eye to a tuning peg.

Van Halen had expanded musically, adding more dimension than just riffs, rhythm, and Roth. The highly polished single "Best of Both Worlds" was a down-home rocker with a throbbing bass line and bluesy clenched-fist delivery from Hagar. Some of John Cougar Mellencamp seemed to have rubbed off on the Red Rocker at Farm Aid.

Hagar's lyrics for "Love Walks In," another keyboard-driven song, were the first in a series of alien-themed ballads. He wrote this one about the "little grey dudes" in the book *Aliens Among Us* by Ruth

Montgomery. "I think Edward Van Halen is an alien," he told MTV. "I don't know what planet he's from, but they all play guitar."

Van Halen were still growing. "You've got to realize that being in a band with two brothers can be tough once in a while," Hagar told *Guitar Player*. "These two guys think alike. Ed kicks something off, and Al goes gotcha, boom! Meanwhile I'm going, 'Hmm, what is this—a Dutch tune?'"

Yet Hagar deferred to Eddie in most cases, and that sensitivity led to an imbalance of overly sensitive songs on *5150*. The title track, however, was Eddie at his unrivaled best as a rock guitarist, and Sammy sounded relaxed and throaty—he wasn't shrieking at the top of his range. The fast, off-kilter riff leading into a racing guitar solo over rapid double-bass drumming could have surfaced on *1984* without seeming out of place.

Beginning with a jaunty guitar intro, "5150" was a brooding rocker with a shifting rhythm and melody in the verse that presaged by several years the coming of Pearl Jam. Eddie had concocted the song in a New York hotel earlier in 1986, while excited about visiting MTV with the new band. He must have been excited frequently throughout the year, because he was still writing way too much material. For instance, the rudiments of what became "316" were done in 1986, though they didn't surface again for five years.

The album closed with "Inside," a strange studio vamp played using horn samples on a Fairlight and bass sounds from an Emulator—the most expensive and realistic virtual instruments of the day. The strange synthetic funk rock was as typically eighties as music could be, a mixed plate of rock, pop, and funk that would have fit on a UTFO, Fishbone, or Vanity 6 album.

Overall, *5150* was sonically low-resolution compared to the big, booming rock of the past, but that was the point. Van Halen wanted to become a class act. Fans were polarized and paralyzed. The dashing, debonair leader of the pack been replaced by the easygoing neighbor from down the block. There were even reminders of the new singer's résumé hanging from the bedposts—the inner sleeve of *5150* contained a concession to Geffen Records telling Van Halen fans where to get Sammy Hagar solo albums.

Yet like a long-suffering abused wife with a doting new husband, Van Halen acted like they had found peace and happiness. The album wasn't Van Halen with a new singer—it truly was a band reborn. The band members now seemed offended by the whole idea of Roth, and they clucked their tongues at the indiscretions of their early success. "We're not out to prove anything," Eddie told MTV. "We're all musicians. There's no Vegas trip to it anymore." They had arrived where they wanted to be, while Roth didn't have any particular goal except to stay in motion.

The band's choice of singer was vindicated by the world at large when the "Van Hagar" lineup knocked Whitney Houston out of the top spot, and *5150* became Van Halen's first number 1 album, certified platinum just eight weeks after its late March release. "Why Can't This Be Love?" became a Top 10 single, and two other songs charted in the Top 40 without the benefit of music videos. The album soared on the high end of the *Billboard* chart for a year and three months.

"In a funny way, it doesn't feel like a new band," Hagar joked on TV. "It's really weird, it feels like we've been together a long time. I'm thinking about hopping around, joining Journey next, and then the Stones."

Van Halen now appealed to a whole new audience for whom Roth had always been too obnoxious. This mainstream pop demographic, more familiar with the band through its media notoriety than its music, were surprised to find a likable, smooth Van Halen that wouldn't get them into trouble with their teachers or coworkers. These were the kids who had sat in school on hot afternoons staring out the window at the corner, where as older Van Halen fans had skipped class and smoked cigarettes—probably while listening to "Runnin' with the Devil" on a cheap boom box.

The plan was to clearly define Van Halen beyond David Lee Roth. They got rid of their striped overalls and dressed in jeans and simple clothes, and they got sensible haircuts. They also delayed production on any music videos for *5150*—clearly Roth's medium of choice—

although practically speaking, with the loss of so many key people to the Roth camp, Van Halen's capacity to create videos was temporarily crippled. There wasn't time to film a clip for the first single, "Why Can't This Be Love?"—even the Alaska and Hawaii kickoff dates for the tour were scrapped while final mixing on the record was completed.

Though Roth had accused the brothers of dragging their feet and no longer wanting to travel, the *5150* tour ran over a hundred shows in 1986. Hours after the release of the album, Van Halen were onstage in Shreveport, Louisiana, before a crowd of ten thousand, introducing Sammy in a town where he had never played before or gotten any radio airplay. The fans were prepared with anti-Roth banners and T-shirts, lots of them picturing a red circle with a red line through Roth's name— a reference to Sammy's favorite symbol, a crossed-out 55 mph speed limit sign.

Sammy was not shy or even very diplomatic. Like a political operative at a campaign rally, he pressed the flesh and let the homespun Roth protest banners fly from the stage, adding his own commentary. The audience felt deserted, and he comforted them and was not above donning a shirt that read "Dave Who?" to get the point across.

Roth claimed to love the attention. "Sammy is my boy, he works for me," he boasted to Howard Stern. "He's my bitch, and when he says my name, we just sell that many more records. He reminds people of the glorious past even more."

As the rivalry intensified, the comparisons between Sammy and Dave began—and never really ended. "Every night, Sammy Hagar has to sing 'Jump,'" Roth fired away, "and I won't ever sing a Sammy Hagar song."

At Van Halen shows, Hagar began pulling concertgoers from the crowd to sing "Jump," patting the breathless fans on the back and saying something about how they did a better job than Roth—until the others in the band asked him to cool it. Throughout this escalating popularity war, Hagar and Roth had still never met. "I doubt he really wants to talk to me," Hagar told *Rolling Stone.* "I think he's got more against me than I got against him."

Van Halen's two-and-a-half-hour sets also included "Panama" and "Ain't Talkin' 'Bout Love." The new track "Best of Both Worlds" turned out to be a great foot-stomper, and by and large the new band rocked harder live than on the new album. A couple of nights, they teased the crowd by riffing on their favorite backstage warm-up, Robert Palmer's "Addicted to Love," mimicking dance moves from the famous music video.

The *5150* stage was a futuristic mini-city of angled metal ramps centered by Alex's dense cluster of drums. Sammy and Eddie met in the middle and jogged in place happily. Their chemistry was obvious and more wholesome than the volatile energy Roth packed with the band. The Hagar fit made practical sense. If not joyous, they truly looked and sounded happy.

Instead of aggressive lines and angles, Van Halen now came onstage dressed to party in comfort clothes that looked like beach-wear. Sammy sported an off-the-shoulder zebra-striped sweatshirt. His boxing training served him well for aerobic stamina. Nobody expected an aerial gymnast like Roth, but Hagar remained in constant motion, even jumping off the drum riser—definitely a graduate of the school of thought that the time for standing perfectly still onstage ended in 1969.

The set was light on old Van Halen, substituting Hagar's "I Can't Drive 55" for set pieces like "Ice Cream Man." With his own material, Hagar came to life onstage—"There's Only One Way to Rock" from his *Standing Hampton* album became a dynamic high point. "Whether or not you like 'I Can't Drive 55,'" Eddie said, "I think Sammy's fans would be disappointed if we didn't play it."

One major surprise was Sammy strapping on a red guitar for "Love Walks In," tackling the entire song complete with rudimentary noodling solo including finger tapping, while the world's preeminent guitar alien Eddie Van Halen happily pounded a synthesizer a few feet behind him.

Mike's bass solo preserved the band's wild animal spirit, pounding and rolling like a giant marble on the walls of the crystal castle stage. He grabbed a cheap copy bass, hurled it off a riser onto the stage, jumped up and down on it, hammered his arsenal of effects, then swiftly stepped out of the spotlight for a second to exchange the punching-bag bass for his real rig. The ingenuity of cheap showmanship still could not be stopped—and neither could Van Halen's image of indestructibility.

The band was still selling out concert halls nearly every night. When a music video became unavoidable, they simply produced a long-form live concert video, *Live Without a Net*, recorded in New Haven, Connecticut. The title came from one of Sammy's new nightly routines, singing "I Can't Drive 55" from a lighting rig fifty feet above the stage.

Hagar's trade was rocker—an all-purpose description used by newspapers like *USA Today* to describe any musician who chewed gum onstage. "Yeah, I'm a happy guy, and I refuse to be bummed out," Sammy told *Rolling Stone*. "I like being happy, and these guys have been unhappy for a long time. They're used to coming in, everybody pissed off, this guy yelling at that guy, everybody trying to hold each other back. It was a real mess towards the end. A lot of people might say, 'Well, isn't that what makes great bands?' No, that's what ruins great bands."

Good-naturedly posing for a Warner Bros. publicity photo wearing straitjackets, the band claimed convincingly that for the first time its members shared a common vision. No longer the combustible sum of competing parts, Van Halen were now a happy, harmonious unit. "It's just pure music," Eddie said with a smile, though he couldn't resist a few parting shots. "That to me is a little bit classier than ripping the kids off, doing some clown show. It's just more down to earth now."

Since Sammy joined the band, they'd called their good-old boy humor together "Bocephus mode." When Hank Williams Jr. got wind that they were using his nickname as a call to party, he invited Van Halen across the country line. Just as Van Halen got out from under the shadow of their old singer, Hank Jr. was finally growing beyond comparisons to his father. Van Halen came to the party in costume, appearing as Hank Jr.'s backup band in his video for "My Name Is Bocephus." Also along for the hayride: comedian Bobcat Goldthwaite, prop comic Gallagher and Dan Haggerty of *Grizzly Addams* fame. Just to fit in, Alex shaved his head bald before the shoot.

Ticking off Roth, Van Halen finally appeared for the first time on the cover of *Rolling Stone* in 1986, while he had to settle for the cover of *Spin*. As it became clear that all interviews for *5150* would include a healthy dose of vitriol toward him, Roth called a press conference in Toronto. "Just like any band, we had a career difference, and we decided to go our own ways. Two weeks later I'm reading in *Rolling Stone* about what an asshole I am, how poor little Eddie was forced to spend twelve years of his life living a lie, and here comes his wife to back it up. So I stayed quiet for six months, reading diatribe after diatribe. I don't think it's necessary to make a choice, but Van Halen demands it—for some bizarre, retarded reason. They demand the audience makes a choice. Well, I'll rise to the challenge. If we have to have a comparison, I eat you for breakfast, pal—I eat you and smile."

<hr>

After a brief series of wilderness adventures, Roth resurfaced with a new band of lethal players that could only be described as Van Halen killers. "Something that always thrilled me is getting into some situation where the outcome is unpredictable," David Lee Roth said. "I've always approached music with a sword in one hand, and a torch in the other."

The first recruit was bassist Billy Sheehan. He came aboard during the summer of 1985, and helped initiate guitarist Steve Vai and young jazz drummer Gregg Bissonette. "Though my dream was to play in Van Halen, I thought it was close enough and I agreed," Sheehan told Rotharmy.com.

For Roth to score Sheehan was a sure shot over the bow of the good ship Van Halen. Known as the "Eddie Van Halen of bass," Sheehan had introduced finger tapping to four-strings back in his Buffalo-based band Talas. They opened for Van Halen on the 1980 "Invasion" tour. "I saw Van Halen kick ass for about thirty shows," Sheehan said. "On the worst nights they were better than any band around." Sheehan and Eddie compared technique and talked shop. And though they never took it any further, they fantasized about Sheehan replacing Michael Anthony in Van Halen.

Looking for an equally dangerous guitarist, Dave contacted puffy-haired Billy Idol guitarist Steve Stevens, who declined. Sheehan and Roth then rooted out twenty-five-year-old Steve Vai, a former Frank Zappa sideman who had replaced Euro-metal guitar prodigy Yngwie Malmsteen in the band Alcatrazz. Roth met Vai at his favorite after-hours club Zero One, after the guitarist had finished secretly recording with ex–Sex Pistol John Lydon on the Public Image Ltd record *Album*.

Vai was a student of Joe Satriani, the Berkeley guitarist whose 1987 album *Surfing with the Alien* was among the first guitar instrumental albums to crack the *Billboard* Top 30, a feat that many compared to toppling Eddie Van Halen. Now all the younger gunslingers were over their awe and taking aim at King Edward's throne. If there was such a thing, Roth had hired "Evil Eddie," a faster, meaner player who took what Eddie did in the 1970s to a new place.

Drummer Gregg Bissonette came from the Maynard Ferguson big band, a jazz ensemble where his brother played the bass. He toured the world and recorded a live album with the group. "I figured if he can power 22 guys without an amplifier and still do his job," Roth told *Creem*, "he ought to be able to lead these two around, and carry me back home."

Roth trained his fledging troupe on old Van Halen material to gauge their chemistry, and then proceeded with songwriting. "I listened for potential," Roth explained. "And when I found the musicians I wanted, I decided that if they weren't walking around unattended, I would—in the great old American rock and roll tradition—simply steal them from another band." Even Eddie's longtime guitar tech Rudy Leiren came to assist Vai for one week during rehearsals.

Full of gravel-voiced sincerity, Roth courted the Canadian press with his sensibleness. "[Van Halen's] got nothing better to talk about than me. *I do*. I've got a beautiful band, man, and I've got a great future."

When asked about his relationship to the Van Halen brand, however, Roth was quick to defend the legacy. "Hellafied brand name, isn't it? It's just like Ajax. It's just like the guy who invented the package for Lucky Strikes cigarettes. They said he was done, he had one stroke of genius and he'd never have it again. He went on six years later to design the S-1 locomotive. So don't expect that after ten years of love and labor I'll just step outside of it."

If the *Crazy from the Heat* EP was a polite diversion from the high-energy rock of his day job, Roth's full-length solo debut, *Eat 'Em and Smile*, set its sights straight on Van Halen's home base. Released in July 1986, the album declared tribal warfare—and now that Van Hagar had gone the pop route, Roth offered fans the irresponsible hard rock they craved. The record quickly rose to number 4 and went platinum in September, vindicating the frontman's decision to fly the coop.

"Are you ready for the new sensation?" he crowed at the start of "Yankee Rose." "Guess who's back in circulation!" His voice sounded coarser and wilder, while the music began in a frenzy and climbed higher. "Yankee Rose" cracked the Top 20 and rolled out the carpet for Roth's solo career.

The Roth-Vai songwriting team penned the feisty "Elephant Gun" and "Bump and Grind." "Shy Boy" was a hectic metal showcase written by Sheehan's prior band Talas. As opposed to the steady, throbbing bottom end Michael Anthony created for Van Halen, Sheehan rode his bass alongside Vai like a second lead guitar player, putting the music's energy all the way up front. Roth's concept was all active ingredients.

Roth revived his movie aspirations for the music video for the sublime summer pop song "Goin' Crazy." During an ultra-bright intro sequence nearly as long as the song itself, he buried himself in an enormous fat suit complete with bulbous neck, bad necktie, and rhinestone belt buckle. He became a vulgar five-hundred-pound record company executive—a fair indication of the poor regard he held for the people he worked with in the music business.

Ever the old-time entertainer at heart, Roth brought the vibrating pop metal orgy to a grinding halt with an album-closing cover of Frank Sinatra's "That's Life"—a welcome respite for listeners out of breath by the finish line. The record was all Roth, all the time—his pepped-up ensemble had recapped his entire career in just over thirty minutes, managing to play and say twice as much as any mortal hard rock band.

An unusual Spanish-language version of the album appeared, titled *Sonrisa Salvaje* ("Wild Smile"). At the urging of Sheehan, Roth took the time to translate and sing all ten songs, a cosmopolitan move that set him apart from the run-of-the-mill hairbangers in L.A. While the world was not yet ready for bilingual cock rock, Roth did swing an invitation to perform at the Miss Mexico pageant, where he lip-synched two songs from *Crazy from the Heat* beachside for an audience of girls in bikinis— nice work if you can get it.

Eat 'Em and Smile led to a long tour of over a hundred shows with Cinderella in tow throughout 1986, shifting to Tesla in early 1987. Steve Vai later reckoned that his guitar chops were at a career high during the tour. Along with an expanded array of costumes and sword dances, Roth wielded a massive inflated microphone with his name printed down the side, wagging it from hip level. Flaunting his bravado and libido, he remained aware that the public expected more from him as a solo artist than the gyrations of a naughty sex god.

Interviewed by *Penthouse*, Roth sounded wistful for the open-minded sexual sophistication of the 1970s. The girls he was hitting between the legs weren't connecting with him as often between the temples—they had become too young and too predictable. The age of the sexually experienced and adventurous professional groupie was over. "What's in the room next door now are college girls, working girls, secretaries, nurses, assistants. It's not really like New York after-hours anymore—as much as I might like it to be." He joked about suffering "choice fatigue" and ended up back at the hotel alone many nights.

Then again, fatigue was inevitable when the Polaroids from his scrapbook featured sights like a backward-leaning naked girl being used as a coffee table, a lit cigarette in her vagina. Sheehan recalled dozens of women jumping into the shower with the band after one show. "Anyone that was backstage knew what it was about and was a willing participant," he reported to Rotharmy.com.

Regardless, Dave was learning that life was downsized outside the charmed world of Van Halen. He was working twice as hard for slightly smaller returns. On the other hand, he was officially in charge now, earning a bigger piece of the pie and spared the aggravation of constantly arguing with the Van Halen brothers. He had jumped ship and all the safety that entailed, and he remained head and shoulders above all the other glam metal pirates in the water.

Potshots continued to fly like confetti between the Roth and Van Halen camps. Eddie Van Halen sounded less than impressed with *Eat 'Em and Smile*, calling Roth's solo group a "pasted together junior Van Halen." Roth harped on Sammy's age, and he called Eddie "a wonderful guitar player" but "a shitty human being." He declared, "Van Halen had disintegrated into a spiteful bunch of bleary-eyed, argumentative procrastinating individuals."

"I think the Van Halens forgot where they came from," he complained. "They keep saying they were a Volkswagen with me, and now with their new singer they're a Porsche. A Porsche—that's all they talk about these days. And that's exactly what they went for—they went out and made the kind of music that will get you that kind of fancy car. I'll always have a lot more fun in the backseat of my Volkswagen, baby."

NOTHING'S SHOCKING

After taking *5150* to triple platinum, Van Halen were war-torn and battle-weary. Surviving the first foray while still fighting Roth had been exhausting. Eddie's face looked puffy, and Alex was shorn bald—as if his hair had disappeared because of worry. "I said a few things in anger that I should apologize for," Eddie told *Rolling Stone*. "But I cried. I was bummed. I slagged him in the press because I was pissed and I was hurt. The thing was Dave is a very creative guy, and working with him was no problem. It was living with the guy."

The latest blows weren't easy to push to the background. During the 1986 tour, manager Ed Leffler had been hospitalized in Texas after being assaulted in a hotel elevator. Worse, Valerie Bertinelli suffered a miscarriage that threatened her marriage to Eddie. "It wasn't the easiest thing to deal with," she told interviewer Debby Bull in 1987. "But nobody knew I was pregnant, so nobody knew I had a miscarriage. I'd like to have four kids. Ed says he wants a full band."

Though she professed total love for her guitar player, lengthy absences and continual drinking constantly tested the couple. She admitted to a women's magazine that the marriage needed work. "He doesn't abuse me, but he hurts himself," she told *Redbook*. "He's got a problem I'm not happy with, but I bring stability to his life."

The year 1986 ended sadly for Van Halen, as Alex and Eddie's father, Jan, died in December from complications stemming from alcoholism. He was in his late sixties. The brothers holed up in the 5150 studio at Eddie's house for ten hours playing music together. David Lee Roth called to express his sorrow.

One of Jan's last wishes was that Alex and Eddie would stop drinking before they destroyed their bodies as he had done. In a seismic shift in priorities, Van Halen's most unfettered party animal, billed by Sammy as "the greatest rock and roll drummer in the world—drunk or sober," Alex Van Halen climbed on the wagon in April 1987. The brother who had stayed out all night in high school while Eddie stayed home and practiced guitar was now tackling sobriety. The band's wild-life image mattered little compared to the members' continued health and vitality. Van Halen would have to carry on with a drummer who no longer got drunk at sushi restaurants, climbed up on the table, stepped on a sake glass, and fell onto the searing hibachi grill. That Alex was a creature of history.

Though the elder Van Halen brother was well on his way to staying clean, Jan Van Halen's request proved more difficult for Eddie. As Sammy was learning, the hell-bent "Bocephus mode" was really a permanent affliction. "At first Sammy thought Alex and I were drinking because we were so excited to have a singer, that we were celebrating," Eddie told the *Seattle Post-Intelligencer*. "Then he realized that that's the way we were every day. I think he was a little scared."

Expensive visits to rehab were not helping, either. After all, Jan Van Halen had taught Eddie to drink and smoke as a twelve-year-old boy. "I tried to quit it for him," Eddie told *Rolling Stone*. "I tried to do it for my wife. I tried to do it for my brother. And it didn't do any good for me. After I got out of Betty Ford, I immediately went on a drinking binge, and I got a fucking drunk-driving ticket on my motorcycle."

In February 1987, Eddie revealed a new close-cropped haircut on *Saturday Night Live*. He appeared in a skit with his wife parodying their home life, and also finger-tapped and whammy-bar-dived his way through a bluesy rave-up alongside G. E. Smith and the SNL band. The stodgy backing players and Eddie's preppy sport jacket and hair brought to mind Michael J. Fox miming to Eddie's guitar tracks in the 1950s sock hop in *Back to the Future*—a conservative step back to the good old days of rock and roll.

Meanwhile, Sammy Hagar went head-to-head with Roth as a solo act, fulfilling his Geffen contract with a self-titled album in 1987, produced by and featuring bass guitar by Eddie Van Halen. *Sammy Hagar* peaked at number 14—and was soon retitled *I Never Said Goodbye* by the winning viewer of an MTV contest designed to juice interest in the album. The single "Give to Live" cracked the American Top 40, and "Eagles Fly" fluttered at the lowest altitude of the Top 100. Though it met with unimpressive reviews, the album went gold.

What had seemed like a concession to Geffen now looked like a smart move on Hagar's part—the leverage of a separate identity outside Van Halen. "It's hard to say exactly why I'd want to make another one because I get the chance to do anything I want with Van Halen," Sammy said. "But there might be a time when I've got something that isn't quite right for the band, and then if I get a few more songs together, I'll have the makings of another solo album."

While Sammy enjoyed his freedom, Van Halen took a break during which Eddie claimed to put down the guitar for nearly a year, focusing on piano and keyboard. He emerged in early 1987 just to play bass on "Winner Takes It All," a toss-off song written by Giorgio Moroder and sung by Sammy for the soundtrack of *Over the Top*—a corny remake of *Rocky*, starring Sylvester Stallone as a golden-hearted truck driver striving to become the world's greatest semiprofessional arm wrestler.

The movie was not a cinematic milestone, but newly minted A-list rock star Hagar was invited to arm-wrestle Stallone in the music video for the song. The ex-boxer had fought his way to the top of the music business. "I really didn't know anything about these guys," Hagar said of his decision to join Van Halen. "In my solo career I was doing fine.

Things were going really well. I worked a long time to get where I was, and to just go back and start over again. I didn't know. But after we played music together, there wasn't any question. Artistically, it was the thing to do."

⟨⟨⟨⟨⟩⟩⟩⟩

Production for the next Van Halen album was hurried, as the band was late to snap back into the rhythm of working. Reassured by the success of *5150*, the band confidently proceeded without a producer, overseeing the recording themselves and crediting nobody on the album. Throughout most of the creation, the title intended for this album was *Bone*. Sammy spotted *OU812* stenciled on the side of a truck, and adopted the license-plate joke as a title—a kind of ultra-casual answer and taunt to David Lee Roth's *Eat 'Em and Smile*.

This was a Van Halen you could bring home to meet Mom and Dad. Instead of sneaking a joint and a bottle of Ripple wine behind the school gym, *OU812* was an album of prom themes—complete with pangs of lost innocence, lives at the crossroads, and dealing with heavy decisions. The hints of grit and darkness gave substance to the radio-friendly rock, without clouding up chances of airplay. The band also took a somber approach to graphic design, using a black-and-white portrait for the album cover, while the back jacket depicted a monkey contemplating a human skull—a riddle conceived by Alex Van Halen.

After the synthetic *5150*, the more natural production of *OU812* was welcome. Synthesizers and digital drums still ruled the day, but they were allowed to breathe in the real world. Strangely, the guitar was largely subdued and the bass guitar was almost nowhere to be found—as if the band was trying to hide its animal impulses. "I probably didn't even have to play on that album," Mike later told *The Inside*. "Because of the production, you could barely hear any bass."

Opening with a pulsing electronics, "Mine All Mine" was an ominous synth-rock track built up from sequenced keyboards. The lyrics put Hagar through ten hard days. "I beat myself up, hurt myself, punished myself, practically threw things through windows, trying to write the lyrics," he told writer Martin Popoff. "I rewrote that song lyrically seven times, ripping papers up, drinking tequila all night one night to where I had the worst hangover in the world and I couldn't even go into the studio. And I'm not like that. I don't hurt myself very often. So Donn Landee and I locked ourselves in the studio and I sang the lyrics, and the whole time he had his head down on the console because he was trying to give me some space. When I finished, he jumped up with fuckin' eyes bugging out of his head and said 'that's the coolest song you ever wrote.'"

The teen romance theme "When It's Love" was the first song completed, written before Sammy even arrived at the studio to start work. The Van Halen brothers played him their tape when they picked him up at the airport, and by the time they arrived at 5150 the lyrics were done. Eddie unwrapped his full arsenal of Roland, Oberheim, and Yamaha synths on this one, even running MIDI cable into a Steinway grand piano. The schmaltzy single went to number 5, and sales of contraceptive sponges among teenage girls very likely reached a new peak.

The first appearance of full guitars on *OU812*, "A.F.U. (Naturally Wired)" became the band's opener on tour. Tidily bundling Sammy's soaring yell, Eddie's harmonics, and Alex's chopped-up big rock drums, the track was mostly midtempo with fast parts and lots of open space—an excellent chance for technicians to adjust the lighting and sound.

The inspiration for "Cabo Wabo" came to Sammy near his vacation house in Cabo San Lucas, Mexico, while he was watching a wobbling drunk attempting to walk through a chain-link fence. At the time, the song was best known for being the first time Eddie used a wah pedal. In a few years, it would be hard to imagine "Cabo Wabo" as anything but a promotional Halenmercial for Sammy's forthcoming south-of-the-border party empire.

"Source of Infection," a tipsy tribute to James Brown, rekindled the untethered spirit of early Van Halen. Sammy had suggested calling the album *Source of Infection*, but Alex found it offensive. The idea was shot down immediately.

Though the idea for "Sucker in a 3 Piece" dated to before Sammy's time in the band, the song sounded a lot like the steady sex and potatoes rock that was the Red Rocker's claim to fame.

Van Halen assumed the coast was clear to resume playing covers, gracing *OU812* with a juke joint version of Little Feat's "A Apolitical Blues." Donn Landee had engineered the original, so he copied the setup for the recording using just two mics in 5150. The band recorded live, and Eddie added piano parts later.

Eddie seemed for the first time to be writing dirty blues songs, something he had always avoided in the past. "Finish What Ya Started" was another country rock song in the Mellencamp vein with a roadhouse feel, benefiting from unusual fingerpicking and a peppy arrangement. Eddie hit on the riff late one night after all the music they needed for the album was already done. He shouted from his balcony in Malibu to Sammy's house two doors down. Sammy rose from bed and found Eddie outside beckoning him, a guitar over his shoulder and cigarette in mouth.

"So he had a good song and I had the tequila," Hagar told writer Martin Popoff. "And Eddie smokes, so he couldn't come in. I don't allow people to smoke in my house. We're sitting outside on the porch, and I took my acoustic guitar and we wrote right on the spot 'Finish What Ya Started.' I didn't have the lyrics quite done yet but I went back upstairs after we finished. About four in the morning and I'm laying there going in my head to myself 'Come on baby, finish what you started.' Because fuck, the guy got me all wound up, and I'm sitting here in bed with the song running through my head and I jumped up and wrote those lyrics."

The chemistry and camaraderie of the Van Hagar lineup were paying off. In the stripped-down black-and-white video for the song, Sammy whooped it up with the others on a big hollow-body electric guitar. "Finish What Ya Started" peaked at number 13 in *Billboard*, making a grand total of four Top 40 singles on the album.

Dedicated to the memory of Jan Van Halen, *OU812* was released

May 24, 1988, and became the second album in a row to hit number 1. Within eight weeks, it went double platinum, proving that the success of the Hagar-era Van Halen was not a onetime fluke. Their material had changed radically, but they remained an important band. Though the moment could be fleeting, for the time being Van Halen was a family.

~~~~~~~~

Roth kept up the pressure, as his second solo album went platinum just weeks after release. The cover of *Skyscraper* showed him all alone in his element, dangling from the side of a mountain. To promote the record and bring his climbing hobby to a more convenient locale, Roth arranged for the crew who built Disneyland's Matterhorn to create a mini-mountain on the roof of Tower Records on Sunset Boulevard. He climbed around the rocks on top of the store while fans cheered from the parking lot and cars stuck in traffic swerved to avoid awestruck pedestrians.

While *Eat 'Em and Smile* had been a boisterous off-the-cuff outpouring of ideas, the construction of *Skyscraper* became much more labored. Steve Vai moved into a co-producer capacity when overdubs and effects grids became overwhelming. Billy Sheehan called the album "kind of contrived and well-thought out—too well-thought out." Dissatisfied with the band's music, he left to form Mr. Big with guitar shredder Paul Gilbert, and was replaced in Roth's band by the drummer's brother, Matt Bissonette.

Skyscraper had its moments of made-for-TV perfection, like Roth's rants on "The Bottom Line" laced with heavy guitar trills, and "Perfect Timing" with its Michael Anthony–like backing vocals. The record was still all Roth, but except for the wistful and reflective "Damn Good," it lacked heart. "Stand Up" was nothing but a mindless aerobics exercise, a parody of eighties synth pop.

The standout on this album of would-be TV themes was "Just Like Paradise." On this near-perfect rock confection, Roth wisely planted his boots and hung loose for the ride. The single climbed to number 6, helping *Skyscraper* raise up the album charts to the same position. For the "Just Like Paradise" video, a crew captured Roth climbing on vertical rock at Yosemite, while Vai contorted over a three-necked heart-shaped guitar on a soundstage. Inspired, the producers of a new TV teen drama called *Beverly Hills 90210* tried unsuccessfully to license "Paradise" as their theme song.

As expected, the *Skyscraper* tour was happily excessive. Continuing the mountaineering theme, Roth rappelled from the lighting rigging in his rock-climbing outfit. He also flew across the stage every night on a surf-board suspended from the rafters. "If you have money, you can buy a laser effect," he explained. "When we do tricks, we don't hire some designer for $100,000. It's as simple as when I used to go see *Peter Pan* onstage when I was a kid, when we'd get home my sister would hang a board in the room, and I'd strap myself into it, and slam forward into the future."

He was now traveling with enough uniforms in his wardrobe to out-fit a small militia. "That goes back to when I was eleven years old in the Boy Scouts—that was the first uniform they forced me to wear." He was also photographed in a frilly, colorful pair of skimpy pants sewn together from women's underwear thrown onstage during his shows—Roth had been hoarding every scarf, bandanna, and dirty underthing thrown onstage since the early 1980s. In fact, he later revealed that he often kept in touch for many years with the women he met on tour. Through their marriages and divorces he kindled the flames—a gentlemanly side to the infamous cad.

If Hagar was reticent to sing old Roth material with Van Halen, Roth himself was only too happy to deliver the goods, laying claim to the most heated material from the back catalog, like "Ain't Talkin' 'Bout Love," "On Fire," and "Hot for Teacher." He remained a one-man challenge not just to his former band, but also to the legions of also-rans then populating the airwaves. "If you can't do it on stage with one white light bulb at the end of a fifteen-foot cord, and a T-shirt, a pair of jeans, a borrowed guitar, and a crummy amplifier—then you can't do it at all. That's where it's all gotta come from. Everything else is icing."

Roth had the good sense to bring Poison on the road with him—

lightweight hair metal with box-office draw but not a hope in hell of upstaging the master. "I feel like a shining example, but I'm not sure of what," Roth said to *Creem* about his influence on L.A. glam. "I think the key is to steal from more than one influence, though. Van Halen's computer program wasn't written by any one programmer."

Roth was losing his patience with the rock scene, and his ebbing interest showed. Seeking fulfillment outside the VIP area, he went scrambling up hills with rock-climbing clubs around the world while on tour. Instead of waiting in the hotel until showtime, he tucked his hair under a hat and walked the streets in search of adventure. He would drag along some of the crew to go biking or walking until they were lost beyond all hope in a strange city, then call the front desk of their hotel demanding an immediate rescue.

Roth returned to England's venerated Monsters of Rock festival at Castle Donington, where Van Halen had sparred with AC/DC four years earlier. Joining more aggressive acts like Iron Maiden, Megadeth, and the sleazy new lords of the Sunset Strip, Guns N' Roses, Roth's colorful plumage looked like a good hunting target for the British press. First, a security scuffle erupted onstage when Roth's guards pushed a grounds security man away from the microphone. Unfortunately, two fans had been crushed during Guns N' Roses' set earlier that day, and the festival guard was desperately trying to tell the crowd to take a step back before anyone else was hurt.

Roth came away looking like the ultimate callow American. At the time, the British rock press was extremely influential in the United States, rightfully taking credit for breaking every major band from Twisted Sister to Mötley Crüe to Metallica. Falling in their bad graces had repercussions—they could dictate who moved ahead and who needed to retire. There was life beyond MTV in the big wide world.

Shortly afterward, the Roth camp tangled with opening act Great White following a show at London's Hammersmith Odeon. Directing the tour, Pete Angelus kicked the unlucky Great White off the remaining dates. Then guitarist Vai left Roth after the tour, joining the more mature, levelheaded hard rockers Whitesnake.

Roth had another platinum record on his wall, but while he was literally at his commercial peak his mind seemed to be up in the thin mountain air. While in Japan, Roth appeared in a series of rarefied television spots for Toshiba-Japan, dancing on the wing of a plane and twirling for high-end electronics under the "Quality & Fitness" brand concept. The spots isolated Roth as an airbrushed version of himself, trying to stay one step ahead of reality, striving for a starring role in the popular imagination.

After *OU812* went platinum in eight weeks, Roth shrugged off the widening gap in album sales, reminding journalists that he didn't have to split his earnings four ways. He was taking on larger-than-life dimensions in the Van Halen universe. The band hadn't contacted him, and they professed to have not heard his new album. They had built him up as a punching bag and a scapegoat, but now wanted to steer clear. "I haven't talked to him," Eddie grumbled.

Roth had nothing but contempt for his replacement, calling Hagar a "mediocre talent" on Howard Stern's radio show. "Sammy would sell the property rights to his butthole to get fame, because he was a complete failure until Van Halen came along." Dave compared Van Halen to a men's lodge and slagged their change in sound. "It's a nice quiet domestic upper-middle-class kind of rock and roll existence, and I don't want any part of that."

———※※※※※———

With two number 1 albums, Hagar had earned the right not to sing "Jump," a song he felt "had Roth written all over it." In its place, Van Halen's music had indeed become less visceral. They were now so musically acceptable that Billy Joel contacted Eddie in 1988, asking if the boy wizard would produce his next album, *Storm Front*. Drinking excessively, disorganized, and overwhelmed by Van Halen's plans for a major summer tour, Eddie turned down the piano man.

Reigning over a nation of heavy metal one-hit wonders, Van Halen marshaled the troops for a grand tour of the kingdom. During the summer of 1988, they licensed the "Monsters of Rock" trademark from the European company that hosted the annual events at Castle Donington. Packaging a big festival the likes of which the United States hadn't seen since the seventies, Van Halen would be headlining over Scorpions, Dokken, Kingdom Come, and newcomers Metallica.

Van Halen were elder statesmen. Though considered leaders of eighties metal, they hatched during the tail end of the era of Black Sabbath and Led Zeppelin. Van Halen had actually competed with those legends in the late 1970s. "A lot of these guys today like Bon Jovi are eight years younger than me," Michael Anthony told *Rolling Stone*. "It doesn't make me feel old—but it kinda does."

Once he quit drinking, Alex Van Halen remained sober. But after flunking Betty Ford, the only thing that temporarily stopped Eddie was a tropical sickness contracted near the Turtle Island luxury resort where he and Valerie went to celebrate their seventh wedding anniversary. While fighting a 105-degree fever and recovering for over a month, he developed a new appreciation for health. He admitted he had been half-cocked for over a decade, cracking beers open before eating breakfast. "It feels like something's missing, but if my brother can do it, I should be able to do it."

Not helpful was touring for months with bands like Metallica, a band that riotously nicknamed itself "Alcoholica." To help keep himself on the straight and narrow, Eddie gingerly suggested a new backstage rider request not to have alcohol available. The band insisted it was still a wild and crazy bunch of guys. "I guess you could say as far Van Halen calming down," Mike told *Rolling Stone*, "we've calmed down to everybody else's party level!"

Calmed down or not, the biggest rock event of the summer inevitably drew fire from religious groups decrying rock's depravity. The lyrics to "Black and Blue" and "Sucker in a 3 Piece"—both typically raunchy and single-minded Sammy compositions—were read on *Good Morning America*. The would-be censors raised an interesting point—why Van Halen would go to the trouble to make music designed to rock the masses and then dent their commercial appeal with blatantly artless songs about fucking.

From its first night in East Troy, Michigan, the tour faced the full brunt of PMRC-inspired antirock forces all summer. The PMRC—Parents' Music Resource Center—had its origins as a group of political wives in Washington, D.C., that had initiated public hearings on rock lyrics in 1985, leading to Parental Advisory Warning stickers on objectionable music. From a certain skewed viewpoint, the giant green dinosaur mascot on Monsters of Rock tour merchandise was misinterpreted as a satanic demon. In Foxboro, Massachusetts, on June 12, Van Halen won a legal action brought by concerned parents' groups that would have canceled the concert. The band agreed to trim the nine-hour event to six hours, a stressful solution to a needless hassle.

At the L.A. Coliseum soon after Metallica ripped up the stage with its thrashing assault on a corrupt society, Van Halen played "When It's Love" for the first time. They had waited a long time, but they finally had their first official power ballad worthy of ten thousand spent Bic lighters. "There were about 90,000 people there, doing the swaying arm thing," Alex told *Guitar*. "During the ride out at the end everybody lit matches and were singing along. The whole building was shaking, because it has a very deep, clean sub-bass that rattled everything."

Around that time, Michael Anthony added an offstage synthesizer to his elaborate bass solo that he triggered using foot pedals. His routine wasn't so much an expression of musical virtuosity as a chance to fill the physical bowl of the arena with gut-ripping low-end tonal sweeps. Eddie's solo dazzled the eyes and the brain, but Mike's showcase could terrorize a crowd with its sheer powerful force.

Monsters of Rock was ultimately a modest moneymaker, and its main cultural importance was showing how incredibly popular Metallica had become, going platinum without the help of MTV or rock radio, and rivaling Van Halen in T-shirt sales. Cashing in on the massive popularity of hard rock they had pioneered in the 1970s and dominated in the 1980s, Van Halen embraced "When It's Love" and moved onward. Their heavy metal days were behind them.

To complete the *OU812* tour cycle, Van Halen hired the infinitely tamer opening act Private Life, a female-fronted light rock band that

Eddie was producing. Even the stodgy *New York Times*, though incorrectly citing Eddie's style as needing "an arsenal of effects," noted the band straining to balance its bad-boy origins with the new "goody-goody" material ushered in by Sammy. "Its newer directions aren't encouraging," the review concluded.

A fitting harbinger of the times was the digital compact disc, which outsold vinyl albums for the first time in 1988. Eddie Van Halen had learned to play Eric Clapton licks by slowing down Cream albums to 16 rpm. The CD format was a fixed-speed delivery system, putting an end to slowing down, scratching, skipping, or stacking. The album art was smaller and more sterile. Groups began to eschew hot recording spots like Sunset Sound Recorders in favor of digital boards. There was much less room for teenagers to roll joints on a CD jewel case than they'd had on an LP jacket. The hang-loose, forgiving freak scene that spawned Van Halen was gone, replaced by the modern-day metal machinations of righteously angry and precise Metallica and Megadeth on one hand, and technologically enhanced pop schmaltz on the other.

After a run of shows in Japan, the *OU812* tour wrapped in Hawaii in early 1989. Sammy told Alex he wanted time off, and the band obliged, laying low from February 1989 until March 1990. During that downtime, Eddie built up his 5150 studio, doubling the room of his racquetball court–size facility, replacing the main mixing board, and at the far end of the recording floor adding an isolated drum room in his brother's honor. When he was finished, the facility also featured a small video-game and pinball arcade. For shuttling the yards between his home with Valerie and 5150, he bought a golf cart and had it customized with his trademark guitar stripes.

Eddie performed at a tribute to Les Paul, the elderly pioneer of electric guitar and multitrack recording. When MTV launched its *Unplugged* series in 1989, the network invited Van Halen to perform acoustic versions of their hits, but the band had no interest—they stated that they meant for their songs to be heard with feedback and distortion intact. Eddie's free time led him quickly back to music, and he commenced plans for a new house apart from 5150 that would be his domestic nest with Valerie and their hopefully soon to be expanded family.

Around this time Los Angeles mayor Tom Bradley called Eddie to ask about his home studio. Eddie was worried, because 5150 was still officially zoned as a racquetball court, not a recording studio. Not calling to enforce the zoning law, the mayor simply wanted to hold Eddie up as an example—the Hollywood Association of Recording Professionals wanted the city to crack down on home studios, claiming their owners were renting them out and hurting traditional sound production rooms. Eddie's studio proved otherwise. "I don't want people recording here, putting a mojo on the vibe," Eddie said. "I like keeping it to myself." For his celebrity testimony in this political squabble, he was given the proper zoning variance to legally make music at his house, already one of the most successful studios in Southern California.

Then on April 22, 1990, Van Halen performed at the opening of their Cabo Wabo Cantina, a bar and restaurant in Cabo San Lucas, Mexico. Looking to plant some of their earnings in a warm coastal party spot, the band had joined manager Ed Leffler and a Mexican investor, sinking $1 million into construction. MTV dedicated "Viva Van Halen Saturday" to the event, broadcasting a full day of campy vacation footage of the extremely sunburned band cavorting on the beach, eating tacos, and riding ATVs through the city marketplace, leading up to their late-night barefoot performance to a packed house of contest winners and vacationing guitar heroine Lita Ford.

Their move to the coastal town turned out to be prescient. All during the 1990s, while decrying the illegal Mexican immigration problem, thousands of Americans poured into Baja California in search of cheap coastal property, warm, beautiful weather, and an endless fiesta fueled by beer and tacos. Seeking nothing more than an investment that sounded fun, the band bought in on the ground floor.

Diversifying his line, Sammy also launched Red Rocker Hyperactive clothing in 1990 at the Action Sports Retailer convention in San Diego, introducing a whopping fifty items of endorsed apparel based on his stage gear, including blue jeans, sweats, and what he called "loose and crazy clothes." At the time he was heavily into biking around Mill Valley, California, and he also produced a line of Red Rocker mountain bikes manufactured by Fisher.

Van Halen's vacation was starting to look like retirement. Stepping onto the neatly trimmed fairway, Eddie golfed in his first of many fundraisers at the First Annual World Music Invitational Pro-Am Celebrity Golf Tournament in Dallas. At the same time, he entered the 1990s with the distinction of being *Guitar World*'s "Player of the Decade" for the 1980s—not only was the honor appropriate, it was essentially unchallenged, but it came with significant pressure to be just as meaningful in the 1990s.

LOVELESS

Van Halen regrouped in March 1990 to begin to grapple with the new decade. During the three years since they had recorded an album, popular music had registered tectonic shifts. In a strange harbinger of changing tastes, Van Halen indirectly scored a number 2 single in early 1989 and a subsequent number 1 album via slush-mouthed rapper Tone Lōc's "Wild Thing," a springy party anthem built entirely on a looped sample of "Jamie's Cryin'," licensed almost as an afterthought for a flat fee in the free-for-all pioneer days of digital sampling.

Protected by their layers of platinum, and weighted by maturity, Van Halen fought against inertia by recording a rowdy rock record titled *For Unlawful Carnal Knowledge*. After years of working with Eddie and building the 5150 studio from lumber and blueprints to hit factory, producer Donn Landee was out of the picture. Surprisingly, the band was back in touch with Ted Templeman, the guiding hand of Van Halen's early albums. He agreed to hone Sammy's vocals and supervise the mixdown. Though Templeman's role as producer was very limited, the aim was clearly to make a "definitive" document of the band that at least slightly acknowledged its beginnings.

To break in the new drum room in 5150, the band brought in engineer Andy Johns, the ears responsible for eighties liquid sugar like Cinderella's *Night Songs*, Autograph's *Loud and Clear*, and albums by Giuffria and House of Lords. Before glam metal, Johns had also produced rock milestones like Television's *Marquee Moon* and Derek and the Dominoes' *Crossroads*. From Alex's perspective, Johns possessed the only qualification that really mattered—he had engineered John Bonham's monstrous drums on Led Zeppelin's *II*, *III*, *IV*, and *Physical Graffiti*.

While Johns and Alex swapped stories and micromanaged the drum set-up, placing upwards of twenty-two mics on his kit, Eddie threw two $100 Shure SM-57 microphones in front of his amps. He already knew the sweet spots by heart—one mic in the center and the other slightly angled beside. He still used essentially the same equipment he had since the first album. So he wouldn't have to wear headphones while Alex banged away in the isolated drum room, he often recorded his parts from behind the mixing console. The two rigged a closed-circuit TV camera so they could see each other while recording.

In Alex's opinion, Van Halen's rhythm section was not the drums and the bassist, but him and his brother. "If you notice on all the records, it is really the drum and guitar that create the turbulence, the movement," he said. "Mike just carries the bottom down there, providing the subsonic qualities. Because Ed's guitar is very fat, and what Ed plays is very intricate, there's a lot of stuff to play off of. Sometimes I accent with that, sometimes against it. Interestingly enough, he's also very rhythmically attuned—everything's more intertwined."

As recording progressed, the band gathered for a couple hours each day at 5150 behind Eddie's house to listen to his new riffs, play video games, and jam on new ideas until they became songs. Beginning with "Judgement Day," the majority of each track was complete before work started on the next, creating an eclectic compilation effect.

Johns also schooled Eddie in how to really run the board at 5150—in the past, Donn Landee had always done it for him. "Eddie has this part of his brain which you would call semi-genius," Johns said. "He recognizes things very quickly that would take you or I some time to ponder on, or someone would have to show us, or we would have to go to school."

Eddie played the intro to album opener "Poundcake" using the sound his guitar picked up from a Makita power drill. "My maintenance guy in 5150 was replacing a piece of gear," Eddie explained. "He picked up the drill, and my guitar happened to be on—it sounded cool, but it was a total accident." Thinking like a showman, Eddie later decorated the power tool with red and white stripes and took it on the road.

True to the theme of its title, *F.U.C.K.* reveled in sexual innuendo and Sammy's skirt-chasing lyrics. The red-light raunch of "Spanked," an ode to 1-900 phone sex, wanked with the naughty slink of Tina Turner's debauched 1984 hit "Private Dancer." Eddie introduced a six-string Danelectro bass on the song, which he played with an EBow, a finger-size battery-powered device that produced glowing guitar sounds rich with overtones.

For sure, the creative energy that Eddie had dissipated on the past two albums across synthesizer, recording, production, and arrangement was now harnessed more in service of playing electric guitar. Though Eddie's head went deeper into crafting the album's sound with guitar overdubs, he bristled at suggestions that Michael Anthony did not play the bass parts. Flashing on his wit, however, Eddie quashed speculation about a solo album by quipping that every Van Halen recording already was a solo album.

Eddie compared himself to Joe Perry of Aerosmith, a "vibe" player who relied on feel more than flash, but Eddie's work on *Unlawful* was anything but subdued. His style was now institutionalized, and without abandoning his many signatures, he often teetered on the outer boundaries of his comfort zone. Loosely adapted from a 1977 original titled "Show No Mercy," the intro tones of "Runaround" rang like something by U2, while "Pleasure Dome" revealed a smooth atmospheric guitar over galloping drums.

Eddie frequently described his solos as falling down the stairs, hoping to land on his feet. The tremolo dives of "In 'n' Out" were exactly that kind of adventure, tuned to a progression that would not have been out of place on *Women and Children First*. On that song, Hagar's lyrics even seemed thoughtful, as he outlined a blue-collar lament about how the little man gets screwed at both ends, paying to be born and paying to be buried. Though this was certainly a familiar barroom lament, Hagar offered in his own survival philosophy: If you can't avoid getting the shaft, go with the flow and work the game to your advantage. If you can't change the world, you can at least skim a little change off the top.

"Right Now" was a piano ballad inspired by Andy Johns's former client Joe Cocker, though Hagar's wails sounded more wistful than tortured. Eddie had actually written the song before Sammy joined Van Halen, and the piano stabs that herald the song appeared in his *Wild Life* teen comedy soundtrack. Beneath the main dramatic theme lurked an eerie piano riff that pulled the airhead qualities of the song back down to reality. Another callback from earlier songwriting, "Top of the World" was originally written in 1984, with a stairstep guitar riff that answered the closing notes of "Jump."

Otherwise, *F.U.C.K.* did not draw heavily from old unused material. When the album was complete, at least four songs were tossed back in the bucket, including "Numb to the Touch" and "Lost in the Ether," possibly to resurface in some later form.

Despite Eddie's gestures to sobriety after his father's death, the *F.U.C.K.* sessions were marked by the frequent *pffft* of beer cans opening—at least half a case a day. "My problem is that I go to the office to drink," Eddie told *Guitar World*. "It's completely ass-backwards. And the only reason I keep doing it is because it still works, believe it or not. It just breaks down the inhibitions. And I'm too inhibited, ordinarily—I get real nervous."

The album took over a year to produce, and by the end of the sessions Sammy was just stopping by in his trademark Ferrari to pick up dupes of the day's mixes. "We were a little bit lazy," Sammy told MelodicRock.com. "We had so much success and we were having such a good time. Fucking Eddie and I were out buying new cars everyday and racing them down Pacific Coast Highway, you know, having a good time and not wanting to go into the studio and work as much."

Released on June 17, 1991, *For Unlawful Carnal Knowledge* again landed in the top album spot, defying trends that saw most of the younger-generation Hollywood hard rock bands falling like victims of an epidemic. Van Halen's third consecutive number 1 album in a row, it remained on the charts for well over a year, despite uncertainty over whether more family-oriented retail chains would carry the album because of its lewd title. Stores like Wal-Mart refused to stock albums bearing Parental Advisory stickers for foul language—let alone a CD whose title itself was a four-letter word.

Immediately, the band was served with a $2 million lawsuit by the devoutly Christian McNutt family of Tulsa, Oklahoma, whose telephone number was supposedly pictured scrawled on a chalkboard at 5150 inside *F.U.C.K.* The digits had belonged to a friend of Eddie's, a poor sap who joined harangued victims of late-night rock and roll prank calls like Sam Hagar of Bakersfield, California, David L. Roth of Atlanta, and unlucky recipients of "867-5309" worldwide.

While on the clock, the band's lawyers also filed a lawsuit against NC-17 rappers 2 Live Crew, who brazenly sampled "Ain't Talkin' 'Bout Love" for a riff in "The Fuck Shop" on their As *Nasty as They Wanna Be* magnum opus. Van Halen weren't too old to understand the nature of rap sampling—they had been using samples and sequences themselves for almost a decade—but after Tone Lōc bum-rushed the security gates, it was time to get paid.

Musician magazine contributor Matt Resnicoff earned a dubious dishonor by penning a skeptical and faintly insulting article that challenged Eddie's insularity, lack of self-reflection, and complacency as a musician. Eddie shut off the tape recorder several times during the interview, bristling at Resnicoff's questions. "You would like to see me probably explore different avenues," Ed said defiantly. "Well, I'm not into it. I'll explore whatever avenue I want to explore at the time."

When the unfavorable article appeared, Van Halen manager Ed Leffler—nicknamed "the Club"—responded with Old World muscle, phoning Resnicoff to decry the "cheap shot article" and threaten, "I'm gonna hurt you. . . . You're a no-good motherfuckin' kike." To his credit, Resnicoff did eventually put his money where his mouth was, quitting music journalism to pursue a career as a professional guitarist.

Van Halen's boosters remained many and powerful. The brass at MTV were still practically married to the band, continuing to support *F.U.C.K.* as if nurturing one of their own, particularly the zeitgeist-licking clip for "Right Now." After a decade, Van Halen was one of the last bands from the MTV class of 1984 still going strong.

"Top of the World" pecked the Top 40 charts and along with "Poundcake" and "Runaround" reached the number 1 spot on the Mainstream Rock chart. The album's other single, "Right Now," only reached number 55 in *Billboard*, but its outdoor appeal was immediately apparent at sporting events, where it quickly gained a spot in the jock rock hall of fame. Though one of the tamer tracks on the album, its dark piano tones were one of several notable troubled undercurrents on *F.U.C.K.* that would define Van Halen's output in the nineties.

Ultimately the album became Hagar's favorite with the band, with *5150* a close second. *F.U.C.K.* was the hardest rock he'd recorded with Van Halen, probably what Roth-era fans would have preferred at the outset in 1986. At times it resembled the best possible Sammy Hagar solo record imaginable. Though sounding more vivid, Van Halen did seem to be entering a holding pattern—but nobody was going to complain about circling at number 1.

Several weeks before *F.U.C.K.* was due, Eddie and Valerie released their first collaboration, Wolfgang William Van Halen, born two weeks late on March 16, 1991. Eddie inserted the quiet interlude "316" for his infant son, named after the boy's birthday. Now a typical new father, rising multiple times during the night to placate the crying baby, Eddie made fun of his party-all-night reputation. "I'm legitimately burnt instead of just being fucked-up burnt," he told *Guitar Player*.

Still flying solo, David Lee Roth claimed to have toyed with marriage, and expressed interest in having children. But so far he was still more interested in nurturing a gigolo image. "I'm a very family-oriented type of guy," he quipped. "I've personally started three or four since January."

In 1991, he mustered the energy to produce his first album since 1988's *Skyscraper*. He spent nearly five months in Vancouver, Canada, recording *A Little Ain't Enough* with producer Bob Rock, fresh from recording the Metallica black album, soon to rise to stratospheric heights. During his stay up north, Roth rented the top floor of the $15 a night Nelson Palace Hotel—a seedy locale complete with downstairs strip club. "I don't think a sleazy lifestyle is any kind of distraction, it's the rule," he boasted.

Roth remained the ultimate marketing man, going to greater lengths to remain a topic of discussion. The video for the title track pictured him cavorting in a pink custom Jeep with thirty-six-inch wheels. An old favorite ride was also preseed into action—the vintage red lowrider from Van Halen's "Panama" video. He believed in his versatile bag of treats and refused to change the wrapper like so many trend-jumping pop stars on the tail end of success. "I'm generally happy," he quipped. "I'm just never content. People say I live in my own little world—well, at least they know me there."

Still, something was up—his latest album was rife with end-of-the-road allusions and imagery. "Last Call" was an attempt at a cash cow, an evergreen for every bar to play at closing time. Vocally, the track felt like the final fading moments of a long party that had raged with full force back on *1984*'s "Top Jimmy." Other songs like "Tell the Truth" and "Lady Luck" frequently dwelled on loneliness and farewells.

Roth was one of the first to arrive fifteen years before, and now he looked to be one of the last to leave the Hollywood glam rock shindig, revving out to the sunset in a fruity pink Jeep like an old gunfighter after the law came to town. When the *Las Vegas Mercury* asked if he was shocked when spandex fell from favor in the late eighties, he set them straight. "It takes an extremely masculine man to look sexy in a pair of pink bicycle shorts."

His 1991 record *A Little Ain't Enough* featured prodigy Jason Becker on guitar in place of Steve Vai. Tragically, Becker was diagnosed with Lou Gehrig's disease one week after joining forces with Roth. Now Roth again needed to rebuild his band with new guitarists before he could tour. He compared the process to the constantly changing roster of an NFL team, but he could no longer afford to hemorrhage big league cash.

On the live front, Roth still flimflammed and bamboozled the crowd with a characteristic mile-a-minute pitch. His inflatable microphone grew a few feet longer and sprouted a shiny saddle so Roth could ride it around the stage like a bucking bronco. The band's drum set was now positioned delicately above the garter line between a pair of forty-foot drop-dead inflatable legs, while fishnet stockings big enough to catch a white whale dipped tantalizingly into giant cherry red pumps on either side of the amplifiers.

After fifteen years under the bright lights, Roth's routine was showing wear and tear. His extensive 1991 co-headlining tour with Cinderella played to arenas that were half full on average. Unlike five years earlier when he took Poison on the road, now a glam metal support act was just dead weight. The tour moved westward, and after a few nights pulling 16 percent capacity in Grand Rapids, Michigan, and 24 percent in Bonner, Kansas, the remainder of the shows were called off.

The album cracked the *Billboard* Top 20 and mustered a gold award. But the loss of the 1980s seemed to be hitting Roth harder than Van Halen. Ten years earlier, after his first six platinum albums, he had spoken of a Roman centurion whose job was to stand next to Julius Caesar to whisper, "All glory is fleeting." Now he needed to hear that message.

There was one sure way back upstairs—jumping back into Van Halen. Roth sounded wistful for the camaraderie of his former band, perhaps hopeful for a return. "If we could get it on track here, we could make history," he said. "Barring any act of death or Ferrari, who knows what will happen?"

Roth appeared on Howard Stern's radio show in July 1992, offering his pitch to be reinstated in Van Halen. Perhaps sensing some weakness behind the band's protests of continued happiness, he unleashed his cruelest torrent of anti-Sammy abuse yet. "Sammy is a mindless little bridge troll. Everything that comes out of his mouth is word barf. It's the lowest common denominator. It's music for children. Jimi Hendrix never made music for children. The fourteen-year-olds may have loved it, but the Beatles never made music for twelve-year-olds."

Roth claimed that Ed Leffler, who he called "Sammy's manager," was blocking all communication, even calling Dave to shout at him that nobody got through to the band unless without his say-so. "The first time Edward graduated Betty Ford I tried to call, and then the second time I tried to call, and then the third time I tried again," Roth claimed.

He also denied that he left Van Halen to pursue a movie career. "The reason I left Van Halen was they were completely stoned all the time," he told Stern. "How do you make music with someone who is completely stoned or copping a buzz on a regular basis?"

When Eddie heard the news, he scoffed at Roth's claims of unanswered phone calls. He wanted no part of any reconciliation. "I've had the same phone number since 1980—there haven't been any messages. For anybody to think he's coming back is just ridiculous! It was a divorce—and who wants to relive that?"

Van Halen's song remained the same. "Roth is really more of a comedian," Alex told *The Inside*. "Basically, he jumped around a lot. Roth went sideways as fame affected him. He thought he was bigger than life and that he was the shit. Watching it happen was actually very sad. You're very connected with the people you play with, and you've got to remain centered. He forgot to remember that."

Behind the scenes, Roth was carefully reassessing his situation, first by putting three thousand miles between himself and the endless silicone and spray-on tans of Southern California. He moved to New York City, where he had first tasted culture and counterculture under the arm of his nightclub owner uncle Manny. "I'm somebody who sees art, color, pathos, and passion in just about everything," he said. "I'm surrounded by that in New York. Everywhere you go it's a conglomeration."

For a brief time, he maintained a low profile, rock-climbing incognito up the Hudson River in New Paltz, New York. He also managed a treacherous six-week wintertime ascent on a 22,000-foot Himalayan mountain range that made his day job seem almost dangerously unimportant. He prepared for the climb for a year and a half, yet he slipped several times,

lucky to live to tell the tale. Afterward, not only did Roth no longer
sweat the small stuff, he seemed not to be bothered by his musical career
at all. "When I'm gone, I take the Stanley Kubrick approach, and I'm
truly gone," he promised. "I can't compose under a microscope."

Roth's star may have been waning, but as they say in showbiz, he
could still get arrested. Fending for himself, he was busted in April
1993 while buying a five-dollar bag of pot in Washington Square Park,
sections of which were then an open-air drug market in New York City.
Two dozen others were caught in the sweep with him, mostly college stu-
dents from New York University dorms that ring the park.

The news came as a shock, mainly because the public assumed a former singer of Van Halen would have a much better pot connection.
Gossip columns suspected a ploy for attention. "The fine was $35," Roth
countered. "In New York, the fine for letting your dog crap on the sidewalk is $100. If I wanted publicity, I'd have crapped on the sidewalk."

In 1991, Kramer Guitars declared bankruptcy after losing a royalty lawsuit brought by Floyd Rose. Anticipating the collapse, Eddie gave birth
to another baby when after twenty-one prototypes, his new partner
Ernie Ball Music Man unveiled the new EVH Music Man signature guitar. Compared to his slapdash Frankenstrats, this was a more refined
instrument suiting Eddie's regal position. Production was limited to little more than a thousand per year, with each one handcrafted to
consistently high quality.

The new gear featured two completely different pickups and a bass-
wood body with a hard, resonant maple top. The design combined
elements of the Fender Telecaster and the Gibson Les Paul, and aimed
for sustain and tone quality over fuzzy brown distortion. This axe was
clearly the weapon of an older warrior, a far cry from the slipshod
kamikaze hand-built model Eddie now derided as a "piece of shit."
"When I first started out, to me the most important thing was how fast
you could play and what a technician you could be," he told *Guitar*. "It's

all changed. My priorities have changed . . . I think I'm much more conscious of the overall end result as opposed to just being me."

The elite new guitar helped temper Eddie's manic outbursts. On *F.U.C.K.*, the band had tuned to conventional E notes, whereas in the past he either tuned a quarter step down or let the tuning stay wherever the guitar found itself. Eddie—who inspired a generation of players to tear out their neck pickups in favor of the attack of the bridge pickup— played most of the album with the mellower front pickup of his Music Man. "The main thing I look for is a sweet, warm sound that isn't like someone chuckin' razor blades at you," he explained.

Along with a new guitar sponsorship came a new amplifier—the Peavey 5150 line. He spooked the engineers during the design process with his "magical" ears and touch. "When Eddie came to us, he sent us his Marshall and his Soldano and other things and told us what he wanted," Peavey product manager Tony Pasko told WolfgangGuitars .com. "A lot of his amps had something wrong with them and they were always broken as he was always tweaking them, changing transistors, adding juice gooses or what have you. And to us they sounded crappy. Then Eddie would visit and he would play through them and it was like, wow that sounds pretty good. And the point was—it was just Eddie."

Unlike Eddie's new genteel guitar, the 5150 amp was a step in a dirtier direction. It offered six gain stages in its circuitry, twice what a 1970s Marshall amp would carry, and while gain stages alone did not make the amp, these were awash in rich, tonal distortion. While a young, aggressive player could be forgiven for not even knowing the expensive EVH Music Man guitar existed, within ten years the 5150 amp would become standard at heavy rock, hardcore punk, and extreme metal shows.

Eddie branched out as a musician around this time, experimenting with different playing styles as well as technical innovations. His circle of jam pals was expanding too, beyond Steve Lukather, with whom Eddie had performed a set of Hendrix and Cream covers earlier that year in a group called Phuxnot. Collaborating with a former new wave rival, Eddie also played rhythm guitar on Thomas Dolby's 1992 outing *Astronauts & Heretics*. To promote his new signature guitar, Eddie appeared at the NAMM music retail convention jamming in a booth with future Deep Purple guitarist Steve Morse and British country guitarist Albert Lee—two disciplined heavy hitters who kept the free-floating Eddie in check.

Eddie shared the stage with George Harrison and David Crosby on December 14, 1992, for a performance of "A Little Help from My Friends," at a benefit concert for the family of late Toto drummer Jeff Porcaro. Eddie the wunderkind was now officially rock aristocracy, nearly fifteen years after winning his first player of the year award. He spread his vitality around, plugging in with supporting act Alice in Chains during their hit "Man in a Box"—surprising guitarist Jerry Cantrell, who thought a soundman had messed up and put a delay on his guitar.

Hoping to shake loose some fresh insight from the band, *Guitar* assigned Sammy to interview Eddie for the magazine. While the pair was installed in the lobby of the Bel Air Hotel, rehashing their love of Jeff Beck and Eric Clapton, comedian Al Franken strolled past. Sammy egged him to asked the world's greatest guitarist a question, so Franken asked which finger Eddie would choose to lose if forced to slice one off. "Probably the pinkie on my right hand," Eddie replied, a rare disarming moment.

Though Eddie admitted he hadn't bought a new record since Peter Gabriel's *So* in 1986, he couldn't help but see that a new era had arrived in full force by 1992. Metallica, U2, Nirvana, Pearl Jam, the Red Hot Chili Peppers, and Guns N' Roses all registered Top 20 *Billboard* albums for the year. The numbers didn't lie—the introduction of Soundscan meant that record sales were now counted at the cash register by actual units, not by the previous system of cronyism that had kept many dinosaurs on life support. Alternative, country, heavy metal, and R&B albums shot to the top, while music industry pet projects like 1991 chart toppers Wilson Phillips and Michael Bolton were walloped.

Van Halen's hand remained strong. Metallica had benefited from joining them on the 1988 Monsters of Rock tour. The Red Hot Chili

Peppers were like Van Halen through a funhouse mirror—cocky lords of Hollywood with a flamboyant lead singer, a virtuoso bass guitarist, and a colorful wardrobe straight out of David Lee Roth's fantasies. Most of the new breed of hard rock bands still took major cues from young Van Halen's music, visual style, and reckless approach.

In September 1992, Van Halen cleaned up at the MTV Video Music Awards, as "Right Now" brought home top honors for editing and direction, as well as Video of the Year. Surely some forces of history were grumbling, as Nirvana's phenomenal "Smells Like Teen Spirit" clip was passed over. Funnily enough, Nirvana leader Kurt Cobain reported that the first-ever rock concert he attended, in 1983, had been to see Sammy Hagar and Quarterflash—and he had worn an oversized concert T-shirt for a week.

Van Halen still represented the American dream, but the dream was in crisis. Rock bands were no longer expected to smile. Politically, the mood was edgy, as a recessionary economy and signs of war in the Middle East left music fans wanting something more than tits-and-ass lyrics. Not to say that Van Halen didn't reach their share of intelligentsia. After Eddie commented modestly on MTV in 1992 that playing guitar the way he did wasn't as hard as brain surgery, neurosurgeon Jim Schumacher from Massachusetts General Hospital in Boston got in touch to offer one day of brain surgery training in exchange for guitar lessons.

Van Halen had thus far skated through the storm, but the question remained how the band would adapt to the new realities—whether they would notice and react, go by way of the dinosaur, or simply continue to hover untouchable in their own perpetual success. They often dismissed grunge and rap as updated versions of the punk and disco they had blown past on their initial rise to glory. Yet their true direction in the 1990s remained murky. "A lot of times we reminisce about the clubs we used to play," Mike said, suggesting a desire to go back to basics. "Those were the good days. It's kinda neat playing in a little room."

According to David Lee Roth, Alex Van Halen had always blocked live recordings because Led Zeppelin had never done a live record, just a lackluster soundtrack to their concert film. Now in February 1993, one of the greatest live acts in rock and roll released its first live album, *Right Here, Right Now*. "It's kind of like a greatest hits, but it's not," Alex explained. "It's kind of like a live album, but it is," Sammy joked. The first official answer to hundreds of bootleg releases captured a typical Sammy-era live set in its prime. Included among two dozen tracks running over two hours were four Roth-era songs, the individual solo spots, plus a crowd-pleasing cover of the Who's "Won't Get Fooled Again" with Eddie playing the keyboard part on guitar.

Spurred by the radio broadcast they produced for Westwood One, Van Halen started work on the live album by themselves. After a month, however, Alex and Eddie reached "terminal mixing capacity." They lured Andy Johns back to 5150 one last time to mix and make sense of miles of disorganized tape from remote truck recordings. He reached back as far as the 1986 and 1988 tours for good performances of a handful of songs. Once assembled, the live album peaked at number 5, and went double platinum by September. One of the families whose disaster-stricken home was pictured on the cover threatened legal action but quickly settled out of court.

Michael Anthony's wish to play clubs was granted when the band booked a March 3 gig at a familiar venue—the Whisky a Go Go in West Hollywood. The show was touted as a fifteenth anniversary gig, dating to their signing with Warner Bros. Van Halen had played dozens of dates there in 1976 and 1977, the final year of their stint as a club band. Now prior to launching its 1993 *Right Here, Right Now* tour, the band put up 250 tickets at $20 each. More than three thousand fans waited for a spot, and when the ticket sales location was announced, a massive footrace began down Sunset Boulevard, stopping traffic and drawing six dozen policemen to the scene. Tickets sold out in fifteen minutes, and the band filmed the mob scene for its live video for "Dreams" from *Right Here, Right Now*.

During an interview video Van Halen filmed at 5150 to promote the live album, Alex half-jokingly spoke his mind to Sammy. "I have a philosophy—it's safety of the past. You know why? There's safety in the past, because it cannot be changed. There's comfort." Whether intended as a joke or not, Van Halen were growing more comfortable with putting their past on display.

Venturing to Europe in March 1993 for the first time in nine years, the *Right Here, Right Now* tour was launched in Munich, Germany, not far from Nuremburg where the *1984* tour had ended. They had never been to Europe with Sammy before, and gained an unexpected publicity bump from fifty-six-year-old international superstar singer Nana Mouskouri, earner of 250 gold and platinum records around the world. "I just love Van Halen and David Lee Roth, or hard rock," she said.

After seeing his fist-pumping stage presence, Continental crowds blamed the über-American Sammy for keeping Van Halen away from Europe for so long—especially in Holland, where a thirteen-year absence had strained family ties.

Back in the United States, Van Halen picked up erstwhile Mötley Crüe singer Vince Neil as an opening act. This former David Lee Roth clone now had a successful solo act while his former band carried on with a new lead singer. In the Mötley Crüe biography *The Dirt*, Neil fondly recalled bonding with Sammy through kamikaze shots before Neil's set and margaritas before Van Halen's. "He ended up with the short end of the deal," Neil said with laugh, "because he was always wasted before he hit the stage."

Van Halen successfully created the extramusical importance they had sought with the Monsters of Rock tour but in an entirely different way. They organized a drive for fans to bring canned food to concerts to be donated to needy families through USA Harvest. Joining a different kind of major-label feeding frenzy, Warner Bros. donated six tons of chicken in Van Halen's name.

Though they were traveling in jets and limos, Van Halen were transcending the trends by remaining normal guys, a band of the people. Stunned concertgoers after an August show in Texas saw Eddie Van Halen laughingly going from car to car in the post-concert traffic jam, looking to thumb a ride back to Houston—his limo was parked by the side of the road with smoke coming from under the hood.

Nodding to Generation X, Sammy grew a goatee and Michael Anthony sported a "Mosh" T-shirt when the 1993 tour ended in Costa Mesa, California in August. During "Finish What Ya Started," the band members' wives came onstage at the last show dressed like Playboy bunnies.

Eddie Van Halen met Kurt Cobain later that year, and appeared unimpressed by the new breed of rock star. Eddie stumbled into Nirvana's dressing room backstage on December 30, 1993, at the Great Western Forum in Inglewood, California, and began badgering towering bassist Krist Novoselic, insisting he was so tall he should play basketball. Then Eddie naturally offered the newest sensation their mark of arrival—he wanted to join Nirvana onstage for a jam. "We don't jam, we're not that kind of band," Cobain said. "Besides, we don't have any extra guitars."

Eddie jerked a thumb at Nirvana's second guitarist, Pat Smear of the legendary L.A. punk band the Germs. "Let me play the Mexican's guitar," Eddie suggested. "What is he, is he Mexican? Is he black?"

Then Eddie began sniffing a deodorant bar, leaving white residue on his face. The others in the room didn't see a shy, half-Indonesian Dutch immigrant whose life had been spent half in seclusion with a guitar—they only saw a drunken celebrity acting like a huge asshole.

"It was horrible! I was just shocked," said Smear, who counted Eddie as an idol. "I was thinking, 'God, Eddie Van Halen hates me!'"

Pestered by Eddie's drunkenness and offended by slurs directed at his bandmate, Cobain suggested Eddie go onstage by himself and play "Eruption" after they finished their encore—the kind of smartass insult that slides right over the head of square elders, especially impaired rock stars.

It was not the first time a Van Halen brother's lack of inhibition backstage had come across like patent racism. In the late 1980s, Alex met Living Colour guitarist Vernon Reid after a show, and promptly insulted him by saying he couldn't understand why a black man would even want to play guitar.

"Feeling pretty ghetto," Reid told the *New York Observer*, he nonetheless summoned the nerve to upbraid Alex, saying "Why don't you go ask your brother? He's a real musician." Eddie and Sammy had just praised Reid in the pages of *Rolling Stone* weeks earlier.

By 1993, Van Halen were cool and cutting-edge only in the most corporate ways imaginable. Their "Right Now" TV spots for Crystal Pepsi, for example, marketed the colorless, caffeine-free cola as "the clear alternative." *Saturday Night Live* mocked the ads with "Crystal Gravy" parodies, promising salvation through translucent meat sauce. Though certainly a massive payday for Van Halen, shilling for a failed soda pop was not painting a path to a promising creative future.

Less than four months after meeting Eddie, Kurt Cobain was dead. "I don't think things are any worse than when I was young," Eddie told *Rolling Stone*. "I think there are certain bands that even complain about making music. Hey, if it's a problem, don't do it. As much as I loved the music Kurt Cobain made, and as sad as it is that he's not with us any more, I can't help thinking that if what you're doing caused you to kill yourself, I would have stopped doing it. It ain't worth it. Stay at home and make music in your bedroom for yourself."

More and more, that seemed to be exactly the direction Eddie was headed. Van Halen started to float adrift after their manager, Ed Leffler, died at age fifty-seven on October 16, 1993, two quick months after being diagnosed with thyroid cancer. "He was more of a friend and a father figure to all of us than he was a manager," Eddie said. The loss affected the brothers gravely, with Eddie later reporting that he hit an emotional rock bottom.

"To me, death's always looking at you," Hagar said matter-of-factly. Ever the pragmatist, he resumed business quickly, organizing a promotional schedule for his *Unboxed* solo collection that had him away from Van Halen just three months after Leffler's death. The timing strained the band's relationships.

For the short term, Van Halen began managing themselves, putting more stress on a group that was tired and emotionally drained. For the first time in nearly twenty years, Alex and Eddie were personally faced with the deluge of phone calls from booking agents, golf magazines, and TV producers asking if they would like to appear on cooking shows and celebrity food fights. Their affairs quickly became a shambles. With every piece of bad news, the pressure on the band increased. "When Ed Leffler died, the band that we created in 1986 died with it," Sammy later said regretfully.

MELON COLLIE AND THE
INFINITE SADNESS

David Lee Roth's March 1994 album *Your Filthy Little Mouth* came calling like a colorful circus barker but left with a whisper. Feeling the metal fatigue, Roth teamed with funk producer Nile Rodgers, mastermind behind disco hits by Chic, Diana Ross, Madonna, Mick Jagger, David Bowie, and others. Mr. "Le Freak" himself, Rodgers had originally signed up to do the music for Roth's ill-fated movie, and seven years later they were consummating the plan.

The album took the boldest tangent of any Roth solo outing yet. Relying heavily on a horn section and big bass lines, Roth was now a tour guide through an underbelly of night scenes—similar to what David Johansen from the New York Dolls did when he greased his hair and became life of the party Buster Poindexter. Not oblivious to the changing winds of musical fashion, Roth hoped to either outsmart the trendsetters or avoid the issue altogether through his strength of character.

"Everybody's Got the Monkey" was an improvement on the silly fun that slipped through his grasp on *Skyscraper*. Roth's voice had regained its throaty purr, and the big rock sound was fully flushed.

Jumping in and out of genres like an impatient channel-switcher, he also dabbled in country-western music with "Cheatin' Heart Café," a duet with Travis Tritt. "No Big 'Ting" nodded to dancehall reggae.

Covering Willie Nelson's piano blues "Night Life," a short-haired and moody Roth took a melancholy stroll through the big city, from slick rainy sidewalks to subway train, no company except a cigarette. The grainy black-and-white music video could have done for lost souls what "California Girls" did for bikinis, except that virtually nobody saw it. Roth was becoming a tree falling alone in the wilderness.

None of these dalliances alone should have sunk his career. Roth had gotten away with stylistic murder many times. *Crazy from the Heat* finally came out on CD in 1992, and remained one of the most popular left-hand turns in popular music history. Roth was versatile to the core, going all the way back to "Ice Cream Man."

But as Van Halen proved with "When It's Love" and "Right Now," big audiences didn't want torch songs; they wanted power ballads.

Roth's latest hotshot guitar player was Terry Kilgore, who had played in rival bands to Van Halen in the club days. "I think a lot of people were rough on him because he was trying to make a transition," Kilgore told *The Inside*. "You try to change from what you are, and people don't accept it. I think he should have left his hair long and gone out and done the same thing, but he didn't want to do that anymore. Dave wanted to expand his musical horizons."

Though Roth had been trying too hard since day one, this time he actually sounded like he was trying too hard. Something was missing. Maybe it was too painfully simple—when he cut his hair, he lost his creative license. He forgot his own golden rule: "Rock and roll is nothing but shoes and haircuts."

Mouth debuted at number 78 in *Billboard*, then dropped off the chart after two weeks. The album was his last for Warner Bros. More cracks formed in Roth's foundation in January 1994, when an earthquake rattled his Pasadena mansion, leaving it without heat. Insurers paid

$350,000, and Roth came after them a year later with a $5 million lawsuit.

While Roth was in New York City working on *Mouth*, Valerie Bertinelli happened to be visiting Manhattan on a press trip. One afternoon she and her husband went shopping. "Without really thinking about it, we walked right past him," Eddie recalled. "Valerie called out to him, and he turned around and kept walking. I turned around and walked a half a block back. At the time he was working with Nile Rodgers on his record. I shook Dave's hand, and he just looked at me in shock, and didn't say a word." Whenever Roth's life went off script, he froze.

Shortly afterward, Alex weighed in on Roth's continued long-distance overtures toward rejoining Van Halen. "I simply find it strange," he said. "Here's a guy that quits a band, and then when his so-called solo thing falls apart, tried to wedge his way back in. It's like, 'Sorry about fucking your old lady, but I need a job, man.'"

After meeting with practically every big-league rock manager, Van Halen settled on Ray Danniels and SRO Management to replace Ed Leffler. Besides a history with progressive rock forefathers Rush dating to the late 1970s, Danniels's primary advantage was he was married to the sister of Alex Van Halen's Canadian actress wife, Kelly, making him Alex's brother-in-law.

"What Ed Leffler was to me, Ray has been to Alex," Hagar told *Billboard*. "If Alex wasn't sure about some deal that came down, he would always call Ray for his sounding board. Ray was already there for Al, but after Ed died, Alex started turning to Ray more and more."

Danniels was hired against the wishes of Hagar, who insisted on signing a separate management deal. The two men clashed from the start. "The second Ray Danniels came into the picture, everything changed," Hagar told the magazine *The Road*. "They'd do anything, because it's all about the money, which is crazy, because Eddie doesn't need money."

With Leffler at the helm Sammy had been the main conduit between management and the band. Now the singer was hearing about business decisions through Alex or Eddie. The dynamics changed, and so did the balance of power. "At the point I came in, Michael Anthony was very gracious," Danniels told *Hits*. "Everything seemed okay. But Sam was distant and made it clear that he had his own guy with Ed Leffler, who had managed him prior to joining Van Halen. He felt a loss of control."

Danniels began renegotiating the band's contract with Warner Bros., getting more money that came with certain strings attached—like a number of greatest-hits releases. These were pivotal points in how the band set its priorities, and the outcome would soon have a terrible effect on Van Halen's stability.

Eddie returned to rehab in late spring 1994, and marked the change by shearing his raggedy hair into a boxy crew cut. "I was waking up every morning with the true alcoholic shakes and the dry heaves," he told radio DJ Razz. "That was happening for a few years, actually. I would have to drink a few beers just to feel normal. I just couldn't handle it anymore. I shaved my head because I was so pissed off and frustrated with myself, I grabbed my Norelco shaver and did a butcher job. Valerie freaked, obviously. But the result is great for both of us. That was the beginning of a new me."

Sammy later added a few sensitive details about the night Eddie cut his hair—that Eddie was locked outside, completely wasted, and Valerie wouldn't let him in the house. "Let's get this straight," Sammy told *The Road*. "While I was in the band, Eddie was not sober." Valerie Van Halen admitted she was getting sick of fetching drinks and aspirin. "Fourteen years living with an alcoholic is my limit," she threatened.

By this point, Alex Van Halen had already been sober for eight years. "I had my demons," Alex said. "The toughest part was not being able to celebrate with everybody after gigs. Alcohol is funny. It's socially acceptable and it's part of partying, but it can turn on a dime and get its hooks into you. Then it's time to pull out."

Van Halen's singer agreed. "Ed and Al woke up in the morning, started drinking and, at the worst times, passed out two or three times during the day," Hagar remembered. "They had to quit, because they didn't have any brakes."

Rather than push sobriety on his younger brother, Alex assured Eddie that the day would come when he would know it was really time to stop. "It used to be, the musicians are here, whip out the stuff. It was true, but things are changing," he said.

Throughout this turmoil, Sammy was in the process of dissolving his marriage to wife, Betsy, after twenty-three years. The couple had two sons and had built their life together from the start of Sammy's days as a professional musician. Beyond the emotional toll, the split was expensive—until Sammy discovered a fast way to ease his financial crunch. Geffen Records was interested in releasing a collection of Sammy's greatest solo hits. Ed Leffler had previously kept Geffen at bay, but after the death of the manager, they approached Sammy again.

Hagar was only obligated to okay the package and to appear for a short time to promote the release. However, he negotiated a higher advance by recording two new songs, "High Hopes" and "Buying My Way into Heaven," which he claimed had already been rejected by Van Halen. "The reason I did include two new songs on *Unboxed* was for the money," he confessed in *Guitar World*. "I got Geffen to pay me exactly the amount of money I owed my wife for our divorce settlement. I paid her off with all the money I received for that album and didn't make a dime off it."

The album's title appealed to a music retailer's sense of humor by poking fun at the endless bloated box-set collections on the market, many of them just a greatest hits CD with an expanded booklet. The CD cover recalled Hagar's distant past as a fighter—and he still remained an avid fight fan, following women's boxing, attending prizefights, palling around with Ray "Boom Boom" Mancini. Reminiscing about his days as a quick jabber, he admitted, "I like to see a man get the shit beat out him!"

Unboxed popped as high as number 51 on the back of evergreen material like "Heavy Metal" and "I Can't Drive 55." During a brief promotional tour, Hagar appeared on *Late Night with David Letterman* in March 1994, playing a red model of Eddie's signature guitar. He allegedly canceled an appearance on *The Tonight Show*, however, after Van Halen refused to allow Michael Anthony to join him onstage. The band was still in mourning for Ed Leffler while its singer was out on the chat circuit, and Eddie resented seeing Sammy on TV every night.

The appearance of *Unboxed* started new battles within Van Halen. Eddie sounded clearly unhappy talking about Sammy's "loony fucking solo career," as memories resurfaced of another lead singer testing the waters with a solo record before abandoning Van Halen. Sammy, however, viewed each call for band discipline as an attempt to stifle his personal freedom, and he shook off suggestions to slow down.

Van Halen turned down an offer to headline the twenty-fifth anniversary of the Woodstock Festival in August alongside Green Day, Metallica, Nine Inch Nails, Aerosmith, and Bob Dylan. Their only live show during 1994 was the April launch party for Eddie's Celebrity Golf Challenge, at the Hard Rock Café in Los Angeles. The band members took requests from a crowd of peers and friends like Dweezil Zappa, while guests like guitarists Jeff Beck and Steve Lukather joined them for a well-lubricated set of rock standards.

Following a troubled summer, Eddie entered rehab yet again, while the tabloids and TV news show *Hard Copy* stirred up rumors about an infidelity causing trouble to his marriage. Desperate to set things right, on October 2, 1994, Eddie took a big step forward and announced to the world at large that he was giving up drinking permanently.

<hr />

Coming four years after *F.U.C.K.*, Van Halen's fourth studio album with Hagar arrived during a crisis juncture. No longer soaring freely across the floorboards, the band had become a cumbersome beast—an institution bound by tradition, big business, and otherworldly expectations. Yet written and recorded in just five months, *Balance* was the musical departure that its predecessor was not.

Van Halen's tenth album was more emotionally shadowy than its autopiloted and horny predecessor. Van Halen were fighting to hold themselves together, while still struggling to forge a new signature sound. The album continued to show the band's maturity, combining the reborn rock power of *F.U.C.K.* with the sadness hinted at during *OU812*. There were fewer overdubs and more guitar riffs, and if Van Halen seemed a little long in the tooth, they also showed their fangs.

The record was nearly named *Seventh Seal*, before the band settled on the calmer approach of *Balance*. "We were going through some inner band turmoil and disagreements," Alex told *Metal Edge*. "Things got really out of kilter, but when we got into the studio and played . . . it's like things were back into balance."

After preproduction at 5150, the band headed to Bryan Adams's Warehouse Studio to Vancouver, Canada, for three weeks with producer Bruce Fairbairn. They worked eight-hour days starting around noon, recording vocals at Adams's house and studio. Hoping to catch an immediacy missing since the relatively carefree days of *Diver Down*, Fairbairn usually held Eddie to the first or second take of a solo. He assured the still self-critical Edward that bursts of inspiration still beat polished perfection every time.

If the hard mood of *F.U.C.K.* showed the band's cloudy moments, "The Seventh Seal" was a full thunderstorm, named after an Ingmar Bergman film about a medieval crusader who returns home to find his homeland ridden with plague. Complete with chanting monks and dangling metal bells, the song unveiled a vast, open, U2-like guitar wall that propelled through the darkest terrain Van Halen had ever tackled. The guitars were giant and methodical, with the rhythm galloping like Led Zeppelin's "Achilles Last Stand."

The mystical overtones originated in part from Eddie's newfound sobriety. His therapist since 1992—when Eddie still came to her sessions drunk—was Sat-Kaur Khalsa, a Sikh woman. She pushed the notorious drinker to let go of his beer-can safety raft and swim like mad toward his spiritual shore. "She had me do all kinds of crazy breathing exercises, then had me relax with my eyes closed and try to go to that place where I am after a six-pack," he told *Rolling Stone*. "Because all the booze really did was lower my inhibitions. In actuality, it was blocking the light." After viewing cigarettes, beer, and his guitar as a holy trinity for twenty years, Eddie tried songwriting sober and churned out three songs in one thirty-minute blast of desperate absolution.

All too quickly, *Balance* moved squarely into maudlin Sammy territory with "Can't Stop Lovin' You," a divorce ballad on par with Cher's "If I Could Turn Back Time" or John Waite's "Missing You." The song was Sammy's attempt to assume his ex-wife's point of view—that she was still madly in love with him. The band fared better when it poured its anger into hectic rock like "Aftershock," an emotionally straining fist-shaker complete with a borrowed Metallica lick. The tune was one of several songs where Eddie unplugged his Peavey 5150 amp and put two mics on his recently rebuilt old Marshall Super Lead.

Following the honky-tonk rocker "Big Fat Money" came "Strung Out," eighty-eight seconds of avant-garde piano terror documenting an episode from ten years earlier. While renting film composer Marvin Hamlisch's beach house in the early eighties, Edward had investigated the sonic properties of a Yamaha grand piano with the delicate use of hammer, saw, AA batteries, and silverware. The recording of scrapes and snapping strings cost over $10,000 in keyboard repair alone, and was culled from six hours of raw tape—potentially the most edgy Van Halen bootleg never released.

The material on *Balance* reflected a lot of sorrow—like the syrupy piano ballad "Not Enough," featuring strings and Michael Anthony's first encounter with a fretless bass. Eddie still lived on site at 5150, and Alex's house was two miles away. The pair operated as they always had, throwing themselves into their work as they dealt with the death of Leffler, Eddie's drinking, and a new crisis—Alex's recent separation from his wife of ten years, Kelly, the mother of his young son, Aric.

Outside the Van Halen family, Michael Anthony now had two daughters himself, and like Sammy he was less able to drop whatever he was doing with his family when the brothers called. This divide carried over into the studio, where Alex described increasing tension in the air. Sammy did not seem to enjoy being there. "Sammy would only come in between three and five," engineer Mike Plotnikoff told *The Inside*, "and he had dinner reservations at six, so you had to get what you could of him in that amount of time, and that was it. I think that was why Eddie and Sammy weren't getting along."

The first of two back-to-back instrumentals, "Doin' Time" was Alex's first album solo, concocted from drums and effects during one day alone in 5150. The sweeping vamp "Baluchitherium," named after an extinct fifteen-ton land mammal, actually had recorded vocals until producer Bruce Fairbairn suggested they be nixed. Sammy felt the song was too melodic, so his replacement singer was Eddie's Dalmatian, Sherman—Eddie taped a hot dog to the microphone to keep the dog interested and howling.

"Don't Tell Me (What Love Can Do)" was a melodic hard rocker that put Hagar's well-practiced screams on a pedestal—supported by Eddie's finger-step guitars, Alex's pounding pace, and Michael's golden backing vocals. "The whole slant of that song was one of universal love," Alex told the *Album Network*, "that it can cure all and fix all, and the planet will be alright. Well you hear so many people talking about, but I don't want to hear it. Show me. I'm sick and tired of people telling me this shit." The album closed with "Feelin'," another magnificent minor-key rock epic with a string section and heartrending vocal performance unlike anything Sammy had previously brought to Van Halen. The track brought a solid ending to a stormy record—and would soon prove to be a resounding finale for the Van Hagar era. Afterward, the band put aside four complete songs that only needed vocals and called the album done.

Another crucial relationship for the band appeared to be on the rocks, when MTV passed on the video for "Amsterdam"—shot on location that January during Van Halen's first return to the city in nine years. After a decade of world premieres, lost weekends, New Year's parties, and special accommodations, Van Halen were shocked to be spurned. But the channel was moving on. Music was no longer its priority—least of all not middle-aged rock music. "That was bullshit," Hagar complained to *The Inside*. "They said that the drug connotations kept them from playing it. That's a pile of crap, because they've got rap bands singing about anything they want."

Sammy's smoked-out sentiments didn't pass muster with Eddie and

Alex either, who felt the song did their birthplace a disservice. Sammy refused to budge, pushing his vision of the Dutch capital of "dope and pussy" over the memories of the Van Halen family homeland.

Released in January 1995, *Balance* became Van Halen's fourth consecutive number 1 studio album. It went platinum by March, shuttering sideline claptrap about whether a hard rock band could survive in the mid-1990s. The *Balance* so-called "Ambulance" tour began in March with a sickly spring cough, as flu-stricken Sammy Hagar struggled to make dates. Eddie's knees wobbled the first night in Pensacola, Florida, as he looked out over a capacity crowd of over nine thousand fans and prepared to play sober for virtually the first time in his career. He found that he liked being aware of the audience and enjoyed the process of coming out of his shell.

The updated stage show was elaborate—and expensive. Bringing living room comfort to a country of couch potatoes, Van Halen commandeered the same giant Jumbotron screens that hung over Times Square, becoming the first act besides Barbra Streisand to use them in arenas. One of the stranger video effects was a projection of Sammy Hagar's face on a giant dollar bill.

The band also hired a high-tech Autopilot system so that lights would automatically follow the musicians using infrared and ultrasonic cues. They were the second band, after ZZ Top, to adopt the system—a quantum leap ahead of the lighting stomp pedals Michael Anthony had brought with him from Snake when he joined Van Halen twenty years earlier.

A total of seven stage cameras brought the sweaty details of every performance to the back rows, just like at a sporting event. With short hair, work shirts with name patches, and ripped blue jeans, Van Halen now looked like a bunch of guys who had just finished hanging drywall in the basement and decided to jam a few Top 40 tunes.

Sammy's ailing throat forced the band to cancel a night in Orlando, Florida, and then three shows in California in early April. Some nights his vocal outages became a boon for fans, like when the band broke from its preordained routine for a ten-minute jam on the longed-for "Ain't Talkin' 'Bout Love." Some nights, Eddie would pop into the intros for old unheard ghosts like "Mean Street," "Romeo Delight," and even "Runnin' with the Devil." He seemed to be chafing at the bit to play original Van Halen classics despite Sammy's reluctance. Fans definitely wanted to hear them—those first six albums continued to garner multiplatinum sales—and crowds screamed while Eddie teased them.

The still-inscrutable Alex appeared to be taking bizarre drummer behavior to new heights, performing with a Freddie Mercury walrus mustache and a neck brace. The neck support was not just a weird wardrobe choice, however—Alex had ruptured three vertebrae while hoisting his son onto his shoulders. Eddie mentioned a childhood treehouse accident and a teenage spill, earlier injuries whose effects had accumulated with time.

Eddie continued leaping high, but his moves were increasingly curtailed by a throbbing pain in his hip. Thinking he had taken a bad swivel on the golf course, he underwent CT scans and MRIs. He was diagnosed with an avascular necrosis—a loss of blood supply to his joint that had made the ball joint of his hip collapse. Doctors recommended surgery immediately. Instead, he bought a cane and continued with the tour. "I'm hobbling, yeah," Eddie said. "It's from years of hopping around onstage and drinking, not feeling what I'm doing to myself. I'm almost seven months sober now, so the pain is a lot worse."

Then on April 7, 1995, the Oakland show was canceled after Eddie was arrested at Burbank Airport for boarding a plane with a loaded .25 caliber pistol. "First commercial flight after an eternity of charters," he said with a shrug, explaining that the gun had become a constant companion after years of stalkers and psychodrama. Eddie went to court, paid a $1,000 fine and was handed a year's probation. They also destroyed his gun. He had been detained about ninety minutes while the cops deliberated over whether the guitarist was a terrorist. "One of the cops was like Barney Fife," he said, "a real young guy with one bullet in his gun. Thank God Andy Griffith showed up later on. The Barney Fife was telling me to come clean before he did a check on me. Glad Andy Griffith showed up."

As the tour continued, Valerie remained a supportive presence, popping in with four-year-old Wolfgang in tow to announce the latest findings she'd dug up as a mole digging through Van Halen's various AOL chat rooms. One day, while the family was driving together, Van Halen's "Hot for Teacher" came on the radio. "I said 'Wolfie, that's Daddy,'" Eddie laughingly told the *Albany Times-Union*. "He said, 'It sounds like Daddy playing guitar, but who's that singing? That doesn't sound like Sammy.'"

Alex shaved his impressive facial hair, but his drum solo still included a routine of him playing alongside a prerecorded video of himself on the giant screens—still wearing what looked like a paste-on Groucho moustache. That quirk in the otherwise seamless shows gave a glimpse into the perverse humor of Alex's world. He displayed his superiority wordlessly, banging out hailstorms of Latin-style percussion on the world's loudest drums.

A $10,000 big-screen nature video for "Eagles Fly"—a ballad from Hagar's 1987 *I Never Said Goodbye* album—became a nightly set piece. Sammy started slowly playing guitar by himself, and then the band joined him to create the big finish. "You throw another guitar player out there and Eddie's not used to that," Sammy told *Guitar*. "When I start playing I mean it, and he feels that. I say, 'Come on, motherfucker, you can kick my ass but you're going to have to kick it good.' It makes him play, and I like that aspect."

Cutting back on his ritual pre-show bourbon, Michael Anthony began incorporating Bach finger-stepping phrases into his lengthy bass solo. He now had a Tabasco bass in his arsenal, but like the Jack Daniel's instrument, the copyright holders got wind and ruined the innocent spirit of the tribute. Tabasco asked him for the bass to hang near their headquarters at the Hard Rock Café in New Orleans. They paid for Mike to build a new one, but to his chagrin the graphics weren't as inspired the second time around. He remained the most easygoing member of the band, always flashing his 1977 smile. "I calm down once I'm onstage," Mike told *Guitar*. "Audiences are different. It's almost like meeting somebody famous for the first time—you start out nervous and then calm down."

A new addition, former Night Ranger, Montrose, and Sammy Hagar band keyboardist Alan Fitzgerald, lurked in a dark tent off to the side of the stage, triggering prerecorded samples of special effects like strings, gongs, and bells. He also cued the keyboard lines for "Jump" and "Right Now" so Edward would be free to play guitar.

Though still a formidable live act, the band seemed listless. Sammy's vocals often floated to the background rather than penetrating—although the loyal crowds sang along most of the words anyway. Introducing "Not Enough" in Toronto, he stood on a soapbox. "This song deals with a relationship situation. It's about true unconditional love, which is the only time you ever feel love. Us guys are kinda dumb sometimes, we always want our women to prove to us how much they love us so we can open up and show our love to them. You can only feel love when you give it, you can't feel love when you take it."

Sammy couldn't be faulted for sharing some personal insight, but Van Halen's audience hardly expected the world's foremost sires of hard cock arena rock to lecture them about sensitivity. It was a little too late for Van Halen—especially after the *F.U.C.K.* album had strapped its male sexuality to the front of a locomotive and rammed it home. No longer right here, right now, Sammy seemed wrong place, wrong time.

The band continued collecting food for USA Harvest, asking for fans to bring canned food to concerts. Donations far surpassed the contributions from 1993, totaling over 360,000 cans. The Presidential Points of Light Foundation had celebrated the charity in 1994. Now for their ongoing efforts Van Halen were invited to the White House by President Clinton. Against all advice, they declined. "I don't dig the guy," Hagar told *The Inside*. "I didn't vote for the guy and I certainly wouldn't vote for him again. The only thing I'll say good about Clinton is that I like what he's doing to the cigarette companies. No one's ever fought those people before. "

Showing the politics of a hardscrabble self-made millionaire—not shared by many musicians besides Sammy's pal Ted Nugent—the Red

Rocker spurned Clinton while donating thousands over the years to archconservative ex-surfer California congressman Dana Rohrabacher. Sammy had always admired Ronald Reagan, a rarity among California celebrities, and wore his patriotism on his album sleeves. "We actually gave them an option," Hagar said about the Clinton White House. "We told them that if they donated one million pounds of food to USA Harvest, we'd go. If Van Halen fans can donate damn near one million pounds, then White House can, as well. So I'm glad we didn't go. I don't like to back somebody I don't like."

A contentious string of summer dates opening for Bon Jovi in Europe did little to lighten the mood. As opposed to the years of untouchable success they'd experienced in the United States, Van Halen were becoming a nonentity across the Atlantic, performing fewer than twenty dates in the past ten years. When they appeared with Roth on German and Italian television during their early years, the gaudy high kicks and smiling faces had impressed the dour Continental rock audiences, but in recent years Van Halen suffered for its lack of loyalty to the European rock community.

During the European trek with Bon Jovi, Alex was shocked when a fan asked after a concert if they had any other records besides *Balance*. "The tour is a rock and roll band and a bunch of posers together," he told a German paper. "We indeed play the same venues Bon Jovi plays, but we simply wanted to play in front of as many people as possible. The sad thing about it is that he, Bon Jovi, tries to get some credibility out of it."

Hoping to make their return to Europe a low-stress adventure, Van Halen only made problems for themselves. "That was pretty much a mess," Mike later agreed. "We came away with a big following, but trying to handle Mr. Bon Jovi became a bit stressful after a while. He even complained to our manager that we wouldn't come out after our set and watch his band play."

Dutch audiences especially wondered why Van Halen were opening for Bon Jovi. During a promotional tour in January, the band arranged to borrow instruments to play a supposedly secret club show for the Dutch 5150 fan club. Word leaked, and three thousand fans waited in the cold and snow for hours hoping to catch a glimpse of Holland's greatest rock export since Golden Earring, sympathetically singing "Happy Birthday" to Eddie on his fortieth birthday. The gig was broadcast live over national radio, renewing interest in the band due to the warm intensity of the performance. Yet the May 1995 open-air appearance with Bon Jovi in Eddie's birthplace of Nijmegen was plagued by problems, not of the least of which was Sammy's numbskull wardrobe choice of an Ajax soccer jersey. Representing the effete rival team from Amsterdam, Sammy's gesture was about as welcome as a Chicago Bears jersey would be in Green Bay, Wisconsin.

Back in the States, the remaining dates had their share of highlights. In Minneapolis, a coterie of bald, chanting monks wearing red gowns, hailing from Gyuto Tantric University, opened the show with the hypnotic drones leading to "The Seventh Seal." The Toronto show was recorded for a pay-per-view performance. To reward their crew for putting up with movie cameras, lights, and the extra labor, the band rented a boat and took their hardworking road dogs for a cruise around Lake Ontario.

In Denver, the crew began setting up as usual for an outdoor show. The forecast called for snow, in September—and for once, the weatherman was correct. The band performed through a pounding snowstorm, trading snowballs with the audience. Hagar slipped and fell on his ass. By the time they were done, nine inches of white stuff covered the city. Then on October 6, Van Halen were inducted into Hollywood's Rock Walk, for their "significant contribution to the evolution of Rock and Roll as a universal art form."

Yet in the view of many observers, management was milking Van Halen, forcing them to continue to work when they needed time apart and rest—especially Alex who was injured and wearing a neckbrace. At a New York show, hard blues guitarist Leslie West came onstage for an encore performance of his band Mountain's "Mississippi Queen." Afterward, he commented on the strange atmosphere backstage, with the band obviously separated into two camps: Van Halens and non–Van Halens. With the tension in the band, Hagar indeed favored the company of Michael Anthony, still the least burdened band member.

Sammy blamed some of his throat problems on Edward's persistent cigarettes, so he and Michael were now sharing nonsmoking dressing rooms and limousines.

Sammy knew how to relax. For his birthday the weekend of October 9, he and Mike, with old bandmate David Lauser, headed eight hundred miles south of San Diego to Cabo San Lucas. As Los Tres Gusanos (the Three Worms), the trio traditionally performed at the Cabo Wabo Cantina every year during events like Sammy's birthday, New Year's Eve, and the club's anniversary in May. Van Halen had only performed at the club's opening and second anniversary party, a ninety-minute club set that included ZZ Top and Led Zeppelin covers.

The Cabo Wabo nightclub was actually keeping Sammy busy. Manager David Haliburton had quit at the beginning of 1995, and the new partner renovated and brought in more money. As business improved, Sammy's brother, Bob, moved south to develop the menu and keep an eye on the place. The Van Halen brothers had sold their interest in the club, and they resented this distraction as much as they did Sammy's solo career.

Even as the brothers lost interest in the nightspot, Sammy was growing more dedicated. In October 1994, he had invited a coterie of rockers including Stephen Stills, Lars Ulrich of Metallica, Matt Sorum of Guns N' Roses, and Jerry Cantrell of Alice in Chains to pump up the reputation of Cabo San Lucas. Still splitting his time between Malibu and Maui during the long periods between Van Halen tours, Sammy was increasingly drawn to his fledgling empire in Mexico. "Even Americans turn into good people when they're down there," he said with a laugh.

The band finished its tour with two dates in Hawaii in early November 1995. Hagar married his girlfriend, model Kari Karte, on November 29. The pair had met while Van Halen were on tour. He invited her along with him and Eddie to judge a bikini contest in a bar, and then flew her to the band's next show. Their ceremony was on Mount Tamalpais in Marin County, California, above Hagar's home in Mill Valley north of the Golden Gate Bridge. His friend Whoopi Goldberg was present, along with Eddie, Alex, Mike, and all of their wives.

Hagar admitted he didn't listen to rock music anymore: "Around our house, we listen to a label called Windham Hill, out of Mill Valley, California. They have a *Winter Solstice* and a *Summer Solstice*—the greatest records you've ever heard. You put those fuckers on and it's like being stoned off your ass without smoking anything!"

‹‹‹‹‹‹‹›››››

David Lee Roth recorded voice-overs for a disembodied brain in a Nintendo Game Boy ad campaign, then capped off the year with an enterprise designed to put him out to pasture like a true show man. He launched a casino revue at Caesars Palace Tahoe, which led to a showroom gig at Bally's in October, and finally arrived at the MGM Grand casino in Las Vegas the final week of December. Since he was a campy connoisseur of dancers with feather boas, and a lifelong admirer of Frank Sinatra, the move made perfect sense.

Backed by a hot-tempered fourteen-piece orchestra from Miami called the Blues Bustin' Mambo Slammers, Roth appeared in short hair and a white suit holding court over a stage filled with colorful dancers. Recalling the where-are-they-now segment in Van Halen's 1984 "Hot for Teacher" video—presenting Alex as an ob-gyn, Edward a ward of a mental asylum, and Mike a sumo wrestler—Dave seemed closest on mark to the prediction he would become a flashy TV game show host.

Dave's Vegas act opened with James Brown's "Living in America" and tore into Boz Scagg's "Lido Shuffle." When fans roared for Van Halen songs, Roth trod the line between showing them love and calling them out as hecklers. He was no Tony Bennett, but lack of a great voice was never a liability on the Strip. He had chutzpah and pizzazz—and most importantly seminude showgirls—plus melanin-challenged old-school Texas blues keyboard wizard Edgar Winter on his side.

Dave reprised his most suave moments, like "Just a Gigolo," "California Girls," and Sinatra's "That's Life," and he rearranged "Jump" for big band. He reportedly spent $100,000 producing a video for "Ice Cream

Man" to promote the show. Between songs, he updated the Rat Pack's Sin City swagger for the 1990s, injecting plenty of marijuana references and O. J. Simpson trial gags and dangling his mic from groin level over the girls in the front row. "Careful ladies," he purred, "he spits when he's miffed."

"That is the greatest thing I've ever seen in show business," Jay Leno gushed sincerely after Roth performed his act on *The Tonight Show*. Seated beside fellow seventies motormouth Robin Williams for a Leno interview filled with jabs at Van Halen and Michael Jackson, Roth laced the conversation with pot references, hyping his new Vegas act by joking, "The waitress refreshed my bongwater."

Frustratingly, Roth was again a square peg in a round hole. After all, "Living in America" wasn't a song of triumph—it was the theme song of the pampered champ Apollo Creed in *Rocky IV*, performed moments before he was pummeled to a pulp. Roth had misjudged the willingness of his audience to jump with him into the unknown. The fans wanted his catlike reflexes and primal roar, not decrepit borscht belt jokes like, "As my old grandpa Joe, a Russian immigrant who died at the age of a hundred and two would say, 'May you die in bed at the age of a hundred and twenty-eight, stabbed to death at the hands of a jealous lover.'"

With Vegas and the Hard Rock Hotel and Casino on the verge of transition, Roth came to town two steps too soon. While Frank Sinatra still lived, there was no room for Dave to wiggle into Vegas, carrying the baggage of Henny Youngman and half the tummlers of the Catskills. "I went down to the Hard Rock Café, man, and it was all updated. They had gambling chips with rock stars on them—Jimi Hendrix on the $25 chip, Eric Clapton on the $50 chip, and I'm on the bagel chip!"

Following the failed sideways move to the Las Vegas Strip, Roth's musical career reached flameout stage. Yet as he frequently advised Van Halen fans, echoing Eddie's stance against cover songs, "It's far better to fall flat on your face for your own effort than to die bending over backwards for someone else." Soon after leaving Vegas, he received a call from Warner Bros. to let him know Van Halen were putting together a greatest-hits album using some songs from his days with the group.

ILL COMMUNICATION

The Chinese year of the rat, 1996, started okay for Van Halen. Four days into January, they learned that "The Seventh Seal" had been nominated for a Grammy for Best Hard Rock Performance. Then at the January 1996 NAMM convention, Eddie unveiled his new signature Peavey Wolfgang guitar—again an archtop like a Gibson Les Paul, morphed into the shape of a Fender Telecaster. Guitar players had seen Eddie's new Peavey when he appeared on David Letterman in late 1995. At the same NAMM event, Sammy Hagar and Washburn introduced the three electric-acoustic hybrid guitars in his Red Rocker line, plus a solid-body electric called the Cabo Wabo.

Eddie had ended his collaboration with Ernie Ball Music Man, citing production problems with the limited 1,000-per-year line. He had joked that the guitars were good enough that he could go into any store, take an EVH off the wall, and play it onstage that night—but finding the guitar in local stores was impossible. Waiting periods on orders for the small edition had climbed steadily, now reaching over a year for a guitar. So Eddie turned to his amp manufacturer, Peavey, the reliable Meridian, Mississippi, based workhorse with the capacity to mass-produce the model with a few adjustments. He patented and added a "D-Tuna" switch for quickly flopping the tuning to drop-D, relaxing the E string a whole tone while the other five strings remained locked tight in the nut. At $1,700, the Peavey would become more common than the pricier Music Man.

While planning to lay low after the strenuous *Balance* album and tour, the band bought time by working on a movie soundtrack for the tornado picture *Twister*. With *Balance* producer Bruce Fairbairn in tow, they began work on two new songs—the pensive and melodic "Humans Being," and an epic ballad called "Between Us Two." Though the fee they collected was high for a movie soundtrack, Van Halen could certainly afford to pass on the project if they had known the ultimate effect on the band. "Ray Danniels was always looking for ways to make his cut," Sammy told *The Road*. "The guys wanted to do it for some stupid reason."

The *Twister* project became its own kind of disaster, a whirling vortex of misplaced priorities and scheduling struggles that tossed the band members through the air and left them miles away from where they began. "We weren't supposed to work the first half of '96," the irritated newlywed Hagar told *Guitar World*. "Eddie was supposed to get his hip surgery done, Al was supposed to get the vertebrae in his neck fixed so that he wouldn't have to wear that neck brace all the time and look like a paraplegic, and I was having a baby with my wife."

Instead, days turned into weeks. No longer drunk and amiable, the newly sober Eddie Van Halen turned into a finicky creative partner. Hagar's requests to record vocals in Hawaii were nixed by the Van Halen brothers, and he found himself continually leaving his pregnant wife in Hawaii to work with the brothers at 5150 in California. "I finally ended up packing my bags and moving back to my home in San Francisco to have the baby, directly against the plans my wife and I had," he said.

With priorities scattered to the wind, Van Halen's story at this point became like the fable of the seven blind men and the elephant, where everyone saw a different, conflicting side. "Sam seemed more focused on his outside projects than he was Van Halen," Ray Danniels told *Poll-star*. "And you know what? Ed Leffler probably wouldn't have allowed that, either."

With Hagar and Eddie, the relationship had always been easy. They meshed as songwriters and bandmates. The trouble was that when things began to sour, they didn't have a vocabulary for keeping the pieces together. They could no longer look each other in the eye. The two men screaming the lyrics at each other in the "Humans Being" music video proved all too telling, as a decade of camaraderie came to a close.

Fed up with what they saw as familiar reticence by a singer whose heart was no longer in the band, Eddie finally told Hagar to be at 5150 by six o'clock to continue working on the song "Between Us Two." By this point, the process had dragged on so long that Eddie had brought in outside lyricists to work the song to his liking.

"No, I did not show up the next day at the studio like he demanded," Hagar told *Guitar World*. He was losing patience. "My wife had just gone through a difficult breach birth, and I was staying home to take care of her, period. That's the sad state of affairs my relationship with Eddie had fallen into."

The turmoil continued only briefly. After eighteen months of building hard feelings there was no avoiding the collapse. They gave up on "Between Us Two" and only finished "Humans Being" for the soundtrack. A second song, "Respect the Wind," appeared under the names of Edward and Alex Van Halen—a complete outside work with Alex on piano and his younger brother accompanying.

On Father's Day, in June 1996, hoping for help putting together a greatest hits album, Eddie called new dad Hagar for one last heart-to-heart talk. When sweet nothings came down to brass tacks, he changed his tune and accused Hagar of behaving like a solo artist, being a stubborn uncooperative partner, and always thinking of himself before the band. Eddie's wife listened at his side. "Valerie was standing next to me and counted eleven times that I said, 'Sam, all I ask is that you're a team player.'"

While Eddie came clean with his resentments, Hagar claimed that Eddie also let slip an unbelievable threat: Van Halen were already working with David Lee Roth behind Sammy's back, exploring the options in case Sam didn't shape up.

Hagar said he stood with the phone in his hand, sputtering a few incredulous sounds. He and his wife looked at each other—she went pale. Then he recalled telling Eddie, "You, behind my back, are working with Roth? You fucking piece of shit!" He elaborated in a postfight interview with *Entertainment Weekly*: "Eddie, if what you do with Roth is better than what you and I have been doing, I'll blow both of you!"

Two weeks later MTV News prematurely reported that Roth was the new singer of Van Halen. On June 26, manager Ray Danniels set the record straight: "Van Halen is in the studio working with original lead singer David Lee Roth. . . . It has also been announced that Sammy Hagar, Van Halen's vocalist since 1986, is no longer with the group. The band is currently considering a replacement."

In the opinion of Danniels, who had become Hagar's nemesis, the situation changed the day Eddie got sober. "Eddie got capable of making judgment calls that he probably let go for many, many years. The boy became a man, and he took his band back. It's as simple as that."

Sammy issued his own press release the next day announcing his departure from Van Halen over differences of creative opinion. Even though their official missive led with the Roth bombshell, the others denied that they had met with Roth except to discuss the upcoming greatest-hits record. "Sammy was telling everyone that we were talking to David Lee Roth behind his back, which we weren't," Mike said. "He started to attack the band, basically lying. He wants everybody to have sympathy for him, thinking we kicked him out, and that's not the case."

"What we thought was kind of odd was that Sammy quit and then got mad," Alex said. "I'm not a psychiatrist, but there's something wrong with that."

"They were in there with David Lee Roth, while I'm changing my new baby's diapers," Sammy vented to *Billboard.*

The band closed ranks against Sammy. Michael Anthony had grown close to Hagar during the past two tours, but throughout the split he remained loyal first to his band. In 1996, Mike didn't join Hagar in Cabo San Lucas to celebrate his birthday. "Mikey and I have always been great friends," Hagar said later. "I think the reason he didn't try to side with me during the breakup is that Ed and Al were out to crucify me, and they had gotten Mike and basically threatened him—'You side with Sam, and you're out.' So I think Mike was just smart enough to pull his head off the chopping block."

Closely tied to the drama behind Hagar's departure, Ray Danniels maintained his poor rapport with the singer. "I understand him being upset and angry," Danniels explained to *Pollstar*. "This is a guy who somehow managed to blow being a member of the biggest American rock band, period, and he's smarting. But unfortunately, he's created the situation for himself."

The problems between Sammy and the band were not high-flying tabloid fare. The partnership was dissolved over six months of squabbles about movie soundtracks, travel timetables, and whether to do a best-of collection. These were music insider problems, not something normal people could relate to. It was a strangely unfulfilling end to one of the nicest and most lucrative partnerships in rock. After all, Sammy had lasted almost as long as Roth and racked up four number 1 albums. He went out not with a bang but with a flurry of nagging details and resentments.

Van Halen's next piece of business was releasing a greatest-hits album without sounding their death knell. Sammy had shunned the idea along with Alex, saying that a greatest-hits collection was for bands whose day was done—even though he had just gone down that road himself with *Unboxed*. Fans were not thrilled about the idea, fretting that the release of a best-of would delay production of a new Van Halen album. With Hagar gone, the argument was over. Van Halen were ready to catalog their greatest hits, juicing the fans by including new music made with Roth.

By late July, Van Halen were officially recording two new songs with the original lineup. Eddie had learned of Roth's interest while playing golf with their mutual guitar tech Rudy Leiren, a valuable soft channel for communication during the lengthy cold war. Wasting no time on a respectful mourning period, and showing little interest in appeasing Sammy, Eddie brought Roth to the studio without warning—Alex and Mike were expecting Dave the helpful computer guy to drop by, not Dave Roth. Either afraid they would talk him out of it, aiming for maximum impact, or simply forgetful, Eddie got the original band back together, almost by accident.

From a slush pile of twenty unused songs, Dave chose "Me Wise Magic," scratching out producer Bruce Fairbairn's lyrics and bluntly dismissing the suggestion that Desmond Child be called to add some lines. He filled the vocal booth with potted palms to create a "Club Dave" in 5150. Eddie said that Roth humbly thanked him for digging through material to find a suitable second song, "Can't Get This Stuff No More"—the first time Roth had ever thanked him for anything.

"Me Wise Magic" was a welcome return to Roth's dark funk, though in the buildup to the chorus he shadowed Hagar by singing too high for his range. "Can't Get This Stuff" evolved from a rejected song written during the *Balance* sessions called "The Backdoor Shuffle." The song was sitting on the back burner when Roth came along and wrote new words and a vocal melody. Sammy claimed that Ray Danniels overnighted him a check for $35,000 and an apology when he cried foul, demanding credit on a song he helped write.

The typically easygoing Michael Anthony was the last member of the band to okay the reconciliation with Roth. Besides being closest to Sammy, Mike had often borne the brunt of the abuse. He hadn't spoken to Dave in eleven years. "At first I told them I didn't want to work with Dave and I wouldn't wanna tour with him," Mike told Van Halen's Dutch fan club. "Then we had a meeting with him. It's funny because he was very humble. He hasn't got a record contract. He admitted that he has made big mistakes and that he did the wrong thing. He admitted that he has a very big ego. Hopefully he's better now."

Roth took several days to nail vocals for the two new songs, and fingerprints of studio wizardry were all over the tracks. Still, the songs rekindled the spirit of '76 without abandoning the lush, flowing musicality of the later records. Eddie had installed a Fernandes Sustainer in his guitar, a special pickup to recirculate string vibrations so each note in his fast, agile noodling could hold indefinitely—or at least as long as Roth could chatter, which was pretty close to indefinitely.

MTV polled a few luminaries from the rock world, and found Billy Corgan of the Smashing Pumpkins and Kim Thayil of Soundgarden eager to see a Roth reunion. Chris Cornell of Soundgarden compared the event to Kiss touring again after fifteen years with full makeup. Even Hagar's Cabo Wabo buddy Jerry Cantrell of Alice in Chains confessed to preferring the Roth lineup.

Needless to say, the record company was pushing hard for the reunion to go further. The opportunity certainly had lucrative potential. The original lineup of Kiss had regrouped earlier in 1996 and was in the throes of a 192-date tour that would ultimately take $43.6 million at the box office, according to *Pollstar*, making them the runaway top earner of the year. The problem was that Van Halen had enough money already—they were hoping for a more powerful cocktail of money, love, creative freedom, and respect.

In early August, Van Halen still would not rule out a reunion tour, though they were proceeding with extreme caution. "After we've finished mixing these songs," said Mike, "we will be looking for a new singer." The band seemed vehement about using a brief interlude with Dave as a chance to put the eternal reunion question behind them.

Yet Sammy Hagar later said that Van Halen definitely had a European tour booked with David Lee Roth—he claimed promoters were contacting him to book his solo act in the fall of 1996, hoping to capitalize on runoff business from the monster reunion. "I might send my produce guy," Hagar told the *Los Angeles Times*. "If Roth sings one of my songs, he deserves to get a tomato thrown at him."

Nonetheless, against what all parties involved later said was their better judgment, the original Van Halen bowed to record company pressure and MTV's enticements. In a move that could only be construed by anyone watching as evidence of a reunion, David Lee Roth and Van Halen agreed to appear together onstage at the MTV Video Music Awards. A montage promo spot featuring footage of the old band and the *Welcome Back, Kotter* theme hammered home the misconception with a sledge.

As the four men walked onstage, the crowd shot out of its seats. While front-row celebrities like comedian Chris Rock applauded wildly, Roth embraced Eddie before an ecstatic audience. "This is the first time we've actually stood onstage together in over a decade," Roth needlessly reminded the crowd, ad-libbing during the tightly scripted event. Eddie yanked Roth away from the microphone after the ovation so Michael Anthony could read his lines, but the bedazzled singer danced in the background while hapless winner Beck attempted to accept the award they were supposed to present him.

The next few hours were a painful struggle between Roth's natural push for full-fledged spectacle and the band's extreme caution. Interviewed by Kurt Loder, the others squirmed uncomfortably while Roth waxed nostalgic. Roth later described the tense demeanor of the others that night as "balled up like angry pill bugs." During a press meeting, Eddie insisted almost angrily that the band was still looking for singers. Roth piped: "But they're not going to find anyone better than me!"

Playing it close to the hip, so to speak, Eddie told reporters the only thing sure was that he would undergo hip surgery in the fall. Grimacing, Roth turned on his new friend: "This night's about me, not your fucking hip!" Ed apologized, but for a moment Eddie and Mike saw Roth again as the band dictator they had hated passionately in 1984. "Yeah, you'd fucking better not!" Roth added.

"We did not tell him he was in the band—period," Eddie emphatically explained to the press.

Eddie thought he had recently bonded personally with Roth for the first time ever, but moving forward was now impossible. He thanked Van Halen tour manager Scotty Ross for preventing a fistfight. Chances of a full-fledged reunion were scratched. "You don't treat me or anybody the way Roth did," Eddie told *Guitar*. "Because you'll end up 60 fucking years old without a friend."

Roth unleashed an open letter on October 2, 1996. He claimed to be completely aware of the limitations of the reunion, that Van Halen were auditioning other singers, and that he was only back for a couple of songs. He also claimed he was against appearing together on camera for the benefit of MTV. He didn't want the public to get the wrong idea when they were only shaking their hips together this once for a "quickie."

Then he laid the blame on Eddie, crying betrayal and deception. He believed the band had secretly hired another singer as long as three months earlier and was only stringing him along for the publicity value. "I can't think of a reason Edward would lie to me about being considered for the lead singer when he had already hired someone, and then let me appear on MTV under the impression that there was great likelihood that Van Halen and I were reuniting," he wrote. "If I am guilty of anything, it's denial. I wanted to believe it just as much as anyone else."

The next day, Van Halen countered with a press missive that scoffed at Roth and promised to reveal details of their unconfirmed new singer. "We parted company with David Lee Roth 11 years ago for many reasons. In his open letter of October 2, we were reminded of some of them. For the last two weeks, we have been working with someone who we hope will be part of the future of Van Halen, although no final decision can be announced until contractual considerations have been resolved."

Without waiting for the paperwork to settle, Eddie and Alex appeared on the *Mark and Brian* morning radio show and announced that their new singer would be Gary Cherone, with more details to come. Ironically, when Cherone's old band Extreme had opened for Roth's solo band in 1991, Roth told them they were good enough to someday take the glory away from Van Halen.

That very week, Eddie, Alex, and Michael accepted awards for passing the ten-million mark in record sales with *Van Halen*. It was an occasion that Roth deserved to enjoy, except for the flare-up in renewed animosity. The remaining three members gave a thumbs-up as a plaque commemorating their rise to stardom was embedded in the sidewalk outside the Whisky a Go Go club, where they had often played for $100 a night.

Then in August 1996, Alex announced his divorce from his second wife, Kelly, after two years apart. Alex had been through the wringer before with his brief first marriage, but this time with his six-year-old son, Aric, the split was much more painful. The revelation added another problem to the pile of explanations for the general unhappiness. Complicating everything further, Van Halen's manager was now Alex's *ex*-brother-in-law.

Against all this tumult, even if the band was personally done with Roth, their record label was not. "Me Wise Magic" was released to rock radio on October 7, and its hopefulness already sounded like a regret-tinged farewell. Eddie's endless tremolo summoned images of something beautiful flying far away. Plans for a voodoo-themed concept music video were scrapped—Roth reportedly hated the idea of using actors, and he nixed a video treatment that diluted him to singing on a big screen behind the three live members of the band. It was too boxed in, seemed totally meaningless, but the band was in no shape to create a new performance video together.

The band refused to be photographed with Roth for magazine stories about the reunion. Small wonder why the initial concept of a double-disc best-of collection celebrating both singers was scrapped. Alex and Eddie now seemed embittered by frontmen as a class. "Sammy is an extremely talented guy," Alex said, "and Dave in his own way is very talented, but there's just a couple pieces missing."

"They're not from the same planet I'm from," Eddie agreed.

Dave returned to Miami and his grandmother and resumed rehearsing with the Mambo Slammers. After making so much noise in such a brief time, he remained uncharacteristically silent for the near future.

When *Van Halen* reached RIAA diamond certification in August 1996, marking over ten million copies sold, Van Halen would soon become one of five rock bands with two albums selling over ten million, joining the Beatles, Led Zeppelin, Pink Floyd, and Def Leppard. More people owned Van Halen's first album alone than lived in any of the forty least-populated U.S. states. If the album *Van Halen* were a country, it would have roughly as many citizens as Belgium, Portugal, or Greece. Overall, more Americans had paid money for all of Van Halen's albums combined than typically voted in U.S. presidential elections.

When Van Halen's *Best of Volume I* was released on schedule on October 22, 1996, the record debuted at the top of the charts—Roth's long-overdue first number 1 album. It stayed in the Top 10 for all of November, and lingered on the album charts for a year, earning double-platinum awards during 1997. The record company promoted the album with a Willy Wonka–style golden "Wolfgang" ticket packaged in one CD, granting the winner a flight to California to pick up a signed Wolfgang guitar from Eddie.

Eddie kicked more sand on Sammy Hagar's name in *Rolling Stone*, claiming he became personally embarrassed at how badly Hagar treated *Best of Volume I* producer Glen Ballard, who had just produced Alanis Morissette's phenomenally successful *Jagged Little Pill* and quit a troubled project with Aerosmith in order to work with Van Halen.

Eddie was also quick to diminish the continued importance of David Lee Roth to Van Halen. Beneath his rock titan armor, he was still bleeding from battle injuries. "No matter what we do, it will never be the same," he told *The Inside*. "You can't exhume something like that. The magic is just gone."

The world was disappointed by the false restart. Having survived the end of L.A. hair metal and the ascension of grunge and hip-hop, now it seemed Van Halen's only enemy was itself. There were cracks in the mirror, reflecting the ugly possibility that these old rockers were too bitter to reunite for the sake of love, their fans, or even money.

The Van Halen brothers let the razzing from the peanut gallery bother them like, well—milk off a duck's back. Eddie and Alex topped off the tumultuous year like strong-boned, healthy all-American boys, appearing in a "Got Milk?" ad photographed by Eddie's old friend

Annie Liebowitz. They were the first rockers to appear in a Milk Council ad, then titled "Milk: Where's Your Mustache?" Alex was pictured bare-chested and strangely drenched in bovine lactations above a caption they apparently hadn't seen beforehand: "Every time we change singers, we have an extra glass of milk. That way we're sure to get more than the recommended three glasses a day."

Still, Eddie gave guitar fans what they had wanted for years, as he stepped outside his band to cross wires with musicians whose gifts equaled his own. He assembled a band for an eight-hour benefit concert on November 17 for Jason Becker—the guitar wunderkind diagnosed with Lou Gehrig's disease one week after joining David Lee Roth's band in 1989. Dressed in black berets and wife-beater undershirts, the so-called Lou Brutus Experience included Eddie Van Halen, his close friend Steve Lukather from Toto on guitar and vocals, Roth sideman Billy Sheehan on bass, and Pat Torpey from Mr. Big on drums. They played "Wipe Out" by the Surfaris, "Little Wing" by Hendrix, "Good Times, Bad Times" by Led Zeppelin, the Beatles' "She's So Heavy," and a unique dual-guitar version of "Ain't Talkin' 'Bout Love." The ridiculous level of musical chops onstage playing three-chord rock songs was like hiring Michelin chefs to make popcorn for a slumber party.

If Eddie would continue branching out, the promise of his life beyond Van Halen could prove very exciting. "It's like when I did that City of Hope thing recently," he told *The Inside*, speaking of another impromptu gig he played in October 1996. "Depending on what tune or who you're playing with, you play differently. And it's just the interaction with the people you're with that pushes you to another level."

PART III

WHERE HAVE ALL THE GOOD TIMES GONE?

THE CHERONEAN ERA AND NEO-ROTHOZOIC AND NEO-HAGARLITHIC PERIODS 1996–2007

July 26, 1961: Gary Cherone born in Malden, Massachusetts.

1985: Cherone's band the Dream wins MTV's *Basement Tapes*.

June 8, 1990: Extreme's "More Than Words" single hits number 1.

April 20, 1992: Gary Cherone joins surviving members of Queen at the Freddie Mercury Tribute Concert in London.

October 4, 1996: Alex and Eddie announce Van Halen's new singer will be Gary Cherone.

March 17, 1998: Release of *Van Halen III*, the first VH studio album not to go platinum.

November 5, 1999: Gary Cherone leaves Van Halen.

May 2000: Texas hospital confirms Eddie in outpatient cancer prevention study.

Summer 2001: Van Halen completes at least three new songs with David Lee Roth.

January 2002: Van Halen's partnership with Warner Bros. ends after twenty-three years.

April 15, 2002: David Lee Roth and Sammy Hagar announce joint forty-date summer concert tour.

May 2002: Doctors declare Eddie Van Halen cancer-free.

July 2002: Eddie and Valerie Van Halen announce separation.

April 2004: Sammy's Cabo Wabo Cantina opens branch in basement of a Lake Tahoe casino; Cabo Wabo tequila ships over 110,000 cases for the year.

June 11, 2004: Van Halen launches reunion tour with Sammy Hagar; relations sour by the end of the summer.

November 19, 2004: Eddie smashes two Peavey Wolfgang guitars, ending his thirteen-year partnership.

December 6, 2005: Eddie and Valerie officially file for divorce.

January 2006: David Lee Roth replaces Howard Stern as morning radio DJ; lasts through April.

September 2006: Eddie Van Halen announces Van Halen will tour in 2007 with his son, Wolfgang, playing bass.

December 2006: Roth rehearses with a new all–Van Halen lineup.

March 2007: Van Halen inducted into the Rock and Roll Hall of Fame.

NO WAY OUT

During the grace period between singers, Van Halen seemed to sail right along. Eddie and Alex were nominated for a Grammy in early 1997 for Alex's piano piece on the *Twister* soundtrack. Eddie also remained central to the guitar industry, and his Peavey EVH Wolfgang won Guitar of the Year from the Guitar Dealers retail association. He increased production and added a lower-priced model for beginning players. Yet for lesser mortals the pantheon of hard rock was crumbling. *Headbangers Ball* had been dumped by MTV, the hot car on the horizon was not a Camaro but a revamped VW Bug, and guitar solos were shunned in popular music like a cause of AIDS.

Dinosaurs became extinct when their environment could no longer sustain them, allowing smaller, quicker animals to take over. Where David Lee Roth failed to send feathers flying in Vegas, in January 1997, the king of schmaltz Pat Boone laughed his way up the charts with a cover of "Panama" on the *In a Metal Mood: No More Mr. Nice Guy* album. Van Halen should have been deeply worried when a campy, ironic version of their music was considered more fun than the real thing. Young audiences in the late 1990s liked their "rock" with a wink and a nod—like nerdy Chicago indie rockers Weezer, whose "Flying W" logo was a knowing riff on Van Halen's trademark.

Piling on the chuckles, suburban pop punkers Nerf Herder released "Van Halen" in 1997, a singsong novelty hit that praised *Van Halen* and two-handed tapping, while mocking Roth's hairline and lamenting Hagar's lost cool. The Van Halen brothers, Michael Anthony, and Valerie Bertinelli granted permission for their images to be used in the video—which MTV added to regular rotation—but Nerf Herder claimed Hagar called them "faggots" and refused to sign off on the insulting tribute.

In their glory days, Van Halen had defied parody because they were more fun than the funnymen. There had always been a big fat joke hanging in songs like "Hot for Teacher," and peeling off the black fishnets to find the punch line was part of the appeal. But somewhere along the way, everyone got seriously distracted and Van Halen became an unwitting source of laughs. In Adam Sandler's 1998 retro-comedy *The Wedding Singer*, set during the 1980s, his lovable loser character warns his fiancée to stop disrespecting a Van Halen shirt for fear his favorite band will break up. Only a dope could still have faith.

Undaunted, Sammy set about showing the world how much fun he was having without Van Halen to slow him down. The Red Rocker turned a gray-sounding fifty in October 1997, ringing in the years at his Cabo Wabo club with a bongo-laden south-of-the-border retirement version of "Right Now."

Hagar's 1997 solo album *Marching to Mars* was recorded with nearly a half million dollars of his own money. He flaunted his new freedom with all-star guests like Huey Lewis, drummer Matt Sorum and Slash of Guns N' Roses, funk bass legend Bootsy Collins, and Mickey Hart of the Grateful Dead. He fell far afield from hard rock, revisiting "Amnesty Is Granted," a song he wrote and performed on a 1995 Meatloaf album.

Angry about his public bashing at the hands of Eddie Van Halen, Hagar depicted the guitarist in his "Little White Lie" video as a clueless chimp slapping a guitar. The song was about Van Halen secretly rehearsing with Roth, only to have the reunion attempt backfire. "My God, these are sick dudes, man!" he told *Rolling Stone*. "They stabbed me in the back, and now they're trying to throw dirt on me and bury me!"

After twenty years, Sammy buried the hatchet with Ronnie Montrose, inviting him to play guitar on *Marching to Mars*'s "Leaving the Warmth of the Womb." As Montrose said, "I did fire him from the Montrose band because he was on to his own thing and had many more things that he wanted to do as a band leader than he could do in our format. One of the running jokes is that it took Van Halen a lot longer than it took me to fire him!"

While Van Halen figured out what to do with Gary Cherone, just like in 1985 the band's phone rang off the hook with helpful applicants for the job of singer. One caller was Billy Squier, the radio rocker whose band Piper had been signed by A&M instead of Van Halen in 1976. The band was also strongly rumored to be courting a singer who had been moonlighing onstage in *Jesus Christ Superstar*—former Skid Row singer Sebastian Bach.

"The way I think of it, we can make any singer sound good," Michael Anthony noted. "We're going to be known as the band that can take any singer and make him famous."

As mainstream news outlets were still learning how to filter the information morass of cyberspace, a news story based on a fake Internet interview hit wire services claiming that former Whitesnake singer David Coverdale was recording with the band. Coverdale soon denied the allegations, saying he had last seen Eddie in a hotel room in 1993 where the guitarist drank a beer while Coverdale and Jimmy Page had their afternoon tea.

Also under the microscope during summer 1996 was Sass Jordan, a British singer with a music career in Canada. She lived seconds away from Eddie, and even while Sammy was in the band, Sass, Eddie, and Alex spent a lot of time together in 5150. Alex insisted he was casually interested in advancing her career, but Jordan later told Wall of Sound, "I was talking to their manager Ray Danniels and I said, 'I swear to God, I think they were thinking of having a female singer in the band.' And he said, 'Of course they were! Why the hell else do you think you were up there?'" Instead, she went on to become a judge on the north-of-the-border talent search show, *Canadian Idol*.

The editor of a music industry tip sheet issued an open letter in the summer of 1996, saying he knew firsthand that Van Halen were probably not rehearsing with Roth before Sammy left, but that they *had* hired another singer—not Cherone. In fact, according to North Dakota country rocker Mitch Malloy, he was hired as Van Halen's replacement singer in early summer 1996. He had been sleeping in Eddie's guesthouse, rehearsing with the band and recording a five-song demo including "Jump" and "Why Can't This Be Love?" On the third day, the band called him to the control room, hugged him, and congratulated him on joining Van Halen.

When the Dave reunion suddenly happened without his knowledge, Malloy claimed he wrote a letter to manager Ray Danniels backing out of the arrangement. "I thought it was a mistake and that they had just made it nearly impossible for any singer to come in and be successful cause now everyone thought Dave was back," he told MelodicRock.com. He didn't hear from the band again for several weeks.

Incredibly, Michael Anthony may have also had a hard time getting his calls returned. The band appeared not only to be playing musical singers. According to Roth, the Van Halen brothers were also practicing with new bassists at 5150 at the same time they were testing the waters with him.

Ultimately, the singer Van Halen had quickly tapped to replace Hagar was much younger howler Gary Cherone. Plucked fresh from a Boston production of *Jesus Christ Superstar* himself, Cherone had fronted Van Halen–influenced light metal band Extreme, who disbanded in 1996 after four albums. Cherone had just left Extreme to pursue his solo career, with their next album already halfwritten, shortly after guitarist Nuno Bettencourt left the group.

Like Hagar, Cherone was not discovered through an all-points fifty-state star search. Extreme also happened to be managed by Ray Danniels, who sent over Cherone's audition demo. The band was reportedly not wowed, but Eddie Van Halen felt differently about Cherone after meeting him. Cherone was a modest, unpretentious rock stylist with a decent track record and some dashing stage moves. For singer number three, Van Halen didn't want to take over the world again—they just wanted someone they could work with.

Before hiring Cherone, Van Halen put him through the ropes with a handful of songs like "Panama" and "Why Can't This Be Love?" representing the back catalogs of both other singers. Within an hour they had compiled the first song with their new lineup—"Without You," originally written to start with the line, "Hey you, wake up, get your shit together."

"There's not a hint of LSD—Lead Singer Disease," Eddie told *The Inside*. "He's a brother, a normal guy like Alex, Mike, and me."

Born north of Boston in the suburb of Malden, Massachusetts, on July 26, 1961, Cherone came into a Catholic household headed by an Army sergeant father and a gym teacher mother. He was the third of five brothers, including his fraternal twin, also a musician. In that sense, Van Halen could joke that they were keeping a spare singer on hand.

Almost fourteen years younger than Hagar, Gary grew up listening to Van Halen. As a teenager he aspired to play basketball but injured his knee and turned to music. In the late 1970s he formed a cover band called Myth with future Extreme drummer Paul Geary. Hardly surprising considering the era, they played Van Halen songs like "Ain't Talkin' 'Bout Love" and "Dance the Night Away."

After changing their name to Cherone and the Dream in 1981, the band won MTV's *Basement Tapes* in 1985, an early call-in talent search where successful regional bands battled for record contracts. Cherone learned the ropes during the 1980s, and then caught the tail end of the glam rock craze with Extreme, whose self-titled debut was released in 1989. The antithesis of airhead West Coast metal, Extreme offered deeper tunes and natural hair. The number 1 ballad "More Than

Words" from 1990's *Extreme II: Pornograffitti* CD was a career high point. Afterward, Extreme supported David Lee Roth's band on tour. Always open about their Van Halen influence, on their final tour Extreme added "Hot for Teacher" to their set list.

Though he was a much-younger suitor calling on the mother of American hard rock bands, Cherone's idols came from the same old guard that had inspired Van Halen: Freddie Mercury, Roger Daltrey, and Mick Jagger. Marking a serious notch in his belt, at the Freddie Mercury Tribute Concert in 1992, a long-haired Cherone took the helm of Queen, leading the legendary hard rock band's three surviving members in a hyperactive rendition of "Hammer to Fall." His performance endeared him to Queen fans and spoke for his potential beyond Extreme.

Oddly for a rock singer chasing their coattails, Cherone had never seen Van Halen live until joining. Describing how it felt to be chosen for the job, he joked, "It doesn't suck."

Van Halen welcomed Cherone to the family like a cute puppy who would one day be called on to pull the sled of their career. Gary took over Eddie's guesthouse, and Valerie reportedly nicknamed the new singer "Schneider," after the ever-present handyman character on *One Day at a Time*. "This is it for life," said Eddie. "He's in. If it doesn't work out for whatever reason, that would pretty much be it for Van Halen. Al and I would just move on, score movies, whatever."

Eddie delayed his much-needed hip surgery again in anticipation of a quick tour, but he ended up spending a lot of time alone in the 5150 studio. He began recording in his bathroom, writing "on the pot" where he believed God gave him frequent inspiration. His safe haven, the toilet-based studio came complete with rack effects for serious bursts of divine intervention.

The songs just kept coming from Eddie—he briefly wanted *III* to be a double album. Much of the new album featured songs passed over by Roth during sessions the previous summer, though in that time Eddie had conjured dozens more song ideas.

Out of left field, the band chose producer Mike Post, a golfing buddy of Eddie's and a five-time Grammy-winning legend in soundtrack music. Originally a musician, he played guitar on Sonny and Cher's hit "I Got You Babe" but soon became engrossed in writing emblematic cops-and-robbers music for television. His experience in rock album production began and ended with Dolly Parton's *9 to 5*.

Post penned one of the most memorable TV theme songs of all time for *The Rockford Files*, not to mention the themes for *Hill Street Blues*, *L.A. Law*, *NYPD Blue*, and *Law & Order*—basically any legendary show with a badge. He also composed for *ChiPs*, *Kojak*, and *Knight Rider*. His last brush with rock was the 1990's cult show *Cop Rock*, a Steven Bochco–produced abomination that was like *Cops* meets the "I Can't Drive 55" music video, where police officers make busts then burst into song.

Most recently Post had worked on *Lethal Weapon 4*, and the worn-out action franchise seemed like a good comparison to the blockbuster Van Halen. If the Van Halen saga had become a long-winded television series, Gary Cherone was a character brought in like Ralph Macchio in the later seasons of *Eight Is Enough*, or George Clooney at the end of *The Facts of Life*. As a late-season replacement, at least he was in good company.

Befitting its strange new cast, season *III* of Van Halen was an eclectic, sometimes incongruous collection. The album began with an instrumental prelude, "Neworld," with producer Post on piano and Eddie on acoustic guitar, hitting harmonics that led into the first single, "Without You." Eddie played the scrappy guitar lick using a quarter as a pick. He attached little pieces of Velcro to get a better grip.

"Dirty Water Dog" was an asteroid chunk that had been orbiting around Eddie for ten years, since he first performed the riff on *Saturday Night Live*. "Once" was more of a departure—white soul in the vein of eighties Wham! or Tears for Fears. It was the kind of urban lounge music Roth had been dabbling in during the nineties but couldn't cool down his personality enough to successfully master.

Cherone's gritty and emotive voice was not a radical departure from Hagar's, but he sounded more natural because he was not constantly singing at the highest limits of his range. His background in musical theater was most obvious on "From Afar," a dramatic showpiece that resembled something by Stephen Sondheim. Many songs on *III* were captured in two or three takes. The guitar solo to the Zeppelin-like "A Year to the Day" was done in one try.

Post's soundtrack experience surfaced on sound effects like the helicopters at the start of "Fire in the Hole." He let Eddie loose in his digital sample library, resulting in the timpani booms and other manipulations heard throughout the recording.

"Josephina" was completed late in the process, while an earlier song titled "That's Why I Love You" was pulled. Written quickly during a phone call, the latter song sounded too firmly planted in Van Halen's past—a dangerous place to be, Eddie felt, if the new band was ever to be accepted as legitimate.

For opposite reasons, a track called "Why? Because." featuring Wolfgang Van Halen on vocals was left off the album, judged as too "eclectic." Eddie did not want to press the patience of "all the Budweiser-drinking guys in the Midwest."

Van Halen's not-so-secret weapon Michael Anthony was mostly muzzled on *III*, as Eddie sang more backup vocals, insisting that his voice meshed better with Cherone's. In fact, "How Many Say I" showcased another side of the Eddie altogether, a pounding rumination on soured friendship that found him seated behind a piano croaking out acrid lyrics like Tom Waits in the late afternoon. Cherone stood off to the side somewhere singing softly in high-pitched harmony. The song was inspired by words Cherone wrote—lyrics Eddie praised as "not all about female body parts," unlike both Roth's and Hagar's.

Cherone was the first Van Halen singer to hand lyrics to Eddie before songwriting, instead of improvising dexterously around the guitar parts like Roth or scribbling lyrics on the hood of his Ferrari in the studio driveway like Hagar. One night while lying in bed with Valerie after putting their son to bed, Eddie read the lyrics to "How Many Say I" while his wife skimmed a script. Apologizing for interrupting their alone time, he scrambled downstairs and composed the music.

When the album was finished, Eddie spoke of finding his musical "soul mate" in Gary Cherone. "It's like he's a long-lost brother," Eddie told *The Inside*. "It's funny, when I think about it, my father was a traveling musician—so who knows?"

Though Eddie's spirits had been battered, he remained relatively sober throughout the sessions. "It's kind of hard for me to listen back to some of the old stuff," he told *The Inside*. "I was in a different place. I was in a bottle. I wasn't clear. I have a glass of wine every now and then, but I don't get fucking hammered like I used to. I don't have the reason that I used to."

"I think I caught it just in time," he continued later. "I think when you hit around 40 and you don't cut the crap, you either kick the bucket or just lose it in the turn."

Eddie began mentioning a higher power for the first time in relation to his musical gifts. "I don't mean to get deep on you, but there's some force out there, and for me to come up with the whole thing in ten minutes—it was just given to me. Anyone who thinks that they're responsible for something like that can kiss my ass. God just picked me to do this. And you try to keep your chops up so whatever he gives you, you can execute."

III had sharper teeth than much of the Hagar-era output. The band sounded more immediate than the super-size stadium rock of *Balance*. Alex's drums were tightly contained, while Eddie's guitar was pushed up front in the mix. At the same time, the record was relaxed and a little introspective—not a bombastic attempt to blow away the earlier achievements. *Van Halen III* was a stripped-down snapshot of the band in the late 1990s, with a young hopeful bravely throwing out his vocal chops.

Marking a return to rock, Eddie had grown his hair back to a respectable unruly mop of curls, and he still rapid-fired on his EVH faster than many listeners could register. As always, he seemed to be operating effortlessly in a slow-motion zone, throwing out licks and flourishes as if he had all the time in the world and everyone else was crawling along at half-speed.

The biggest complication of completing *III* was that the recordings were captured with too many microphones, which brought sonic goblins into the mixing phase. Every little tweak sent the entire mix into a tailspin, changing the relative punch of guitars, bass, drums and vocals. Then, when Van Halen proudly delivered their first new album in two years to Warner Bros.—now under new leadership—the label thanked them but said they weren't ready for it yet. Back to the drawing board went Eddie and his engineers.

Hoping for airplay on adult contemporary radio, Eddie remixed a version of "Once" with acoustic guitars, adding new vocals by Gary and female vocals by Madonna backup singer turned yoga music doyenne Donna DeLory. Eddie successfully made the track suitable for falling asleep. Despite his extra effort, the single remained unreleased—a sure sign that the record company didn't know what to do with the band as it mellowed with age. Commercial radio was certainly no longer a friend to rock music.

Alex's girlfriend, Stine Schyberg, designed the album cover, and afterward she put together the stage set and tour merchandise. For many years the band's interest in Asian wisdom began and ended with the Kama Sutra. Now, along with therapy, breathing exercises, and meditation came a dalliance with Eastern mysticism—one of Eddie's speaker cabinets had a Peavey nameplate written in Sanskrit, and Alex's bass drums read "Van Halen" in Sanskrit. By this time, Alex was a yoga-practicing vegetarian with a mystical Fu Manchu handlebar mustache. He also adopted a Zen approach to superior firepower. "We'd like it to be great the first time out," Alex stressed to *The Inside*. "This is gonna be the first time the band will be seen the way it is now. The rest is really out of our hands."

Van Halen began 1998 in freezing Sweden in the dead of January, where they filmed a video for "Without You" in a trendy ice hotel—a building made of packed snow and furnished with carved ice, a space untouched by California sunshine. Cherone had long since shorn his shaggy brown hair and was leading the band with a snappy, short hairdo, doing his part to finally update Van Halen for the 1990s.

The week before *III* hit stores, on March 12, 1998, Van Halen unveiled its new look, sound, and feel with a live radio broadcast from Billboard Live in Hollywood. Along with a few new tracks, they performed mostly Roth classics like "Unchained" and "Feel Your Love Tonight." Eddie had to relearn the gem "I'm the One" by listening to the record—the former cover guitarist covering himself. The Billboard Live club was a corporate aquamarine box on the Sunset Strip, situated by coincidence on the grounds where sleazy Gazzari's stood in the 1970s. The grittiness had been gutted, disinfected, and stuffed with padded couches. The Hollywood music scene and the Sunset Strip had grown up and gotten comfortable, and Van Halen had been a big part of that transition to legitimacy.

After introducing Cherone to fans with a simple summer tour, the band planned to return to the studio in the fall of 1998 to quickly produce a second album. The condition of Eddie's hip had improved to the point that his doctor was postponing surgery indefinitely. Alex, however, remained shackled by a neck brace, as his cervical vertebrae were inoperable. "I'm not too happy about it," he said, "but it's the price I pay for being an idiot sometimes."

Van Halen Mk. III hit the road immediately, jetting down under for the band's first ever visit to Australia and New Zealand. Debuting at venues halfway around the world gave Gary a psychological break, as the crowds were smaller and had never seen Van Halen before. Overall, he was a smart international choice, as Extreme remained very popular overseas, where his more subtle qualities connected—unlike Mr. "Voice of America" Hagar.

At the first shows, Gary seemed out of his mind, climbing fences and stalking the stage in a trim black suit and *GQ* haircut. He alarmed Hagar-era fans, who were expecting giant smiles, colorful baggy shorts, and an overflowing mop of curls. During the sampled swirling intro to "Dirty Water Dog," an Aborigine appeared with a didgeridoo to drone and gurgle along with the band.

While halfway across the world, plans to swing through Indonesia didn't come to pass. The Van Halen brothers were curious about their mother's homeland, but tracking record sales in the bootleg-ridden country proved too sketchy. They couldn't predict if they would play to thousands of people or dozens, and every day away from the States meant losing bigger opportunities.

Unlike Hagar, Cherone was game for singing old Roth-era songs like "I'm the One" and "Mean Street," as well as a few Sammy hits like "Dreams." The distinction made by outsiders between Roth and Hagar songs irritated Eddie and Alex. They reminded the public that all the songs were Van Halen material, written by the band and sung by whoever happened to be holding the microphone.

While mostly keeping barbs at bay, they liked pointing attention to Sammy's reluctance to sing old Roth-regime songs. They questioned whether Dave intimidated the Red Rocker. "Regardless of Dave's singing ability, the songs were identified with him," Mike remarked.

Even Hagar knew that his refusal to sing Roth songs had hurt him. "I didn't want to be compared to old Van Halen," Sammy admitted to *The Road*. "I did have some insecurities. I would walk out on stage every night knowing those people wanted to hear 'Jump' and 'Runnin' with the Devil.' I was a little nervous about that, but at the same time, I knew the new music we had made was powerful and strong."

Cherone brought back the Roth standards with hopes that the majority of Van Halen's fans would embrace him. Though diplomatic about not choosing a favorite forerunner, Cherone knew the Roth songs but none of the Hagar ones. "There's going to be obvious comparisons about whichever is better," he told *The Inside*. "I try not to think about it. Music's not a competition over who can sing better. It's subjective."

Crowds were delighted to hear "Mean Street," "Dance the Night Away," "Ain't Talkin' 'Bout Love," and other hallmarks of the band's formative years. During sound checks the band tested "Jamie's Cryin'" and Black Sabbath's "War Pigs." A few nuggets like the spaghetti western tribute "Hang 'Em High" remained on the shelf—it was deemed "too talky" and reliant on Roth's carnival barker repartee.

Along with the classic songs, Michael Anthony brought his long-retired Jack Daniel's bass back into active duty. Unfortunately, one set piece they cut was his bass solo, but he did step to the foreground to help sing "Somebody Get Me a Doctor." More than ever, the emphasis shifted to Eddie Van Halen's guitar playing.

For all the talk of how the band was a family, there was in fact a genuine camaraderie between the band and the staff. Tour manager Scotty Ross had been wrangling press, band, and crew on the road since 1991. Michael's bass tech Kevin Dugan, one of the creators of the Jack Daniel's bass, had been keeping his boss in picks and whiskey since the early 1980s. Beyond these familiar faces, treated as valets to the gods, were three dozen other longtime working men on the road and a handful of union guys. The only job Van Halen really had a hard time filling was lead singer.

A new and controversial conversation piece was Eddie's encore of "How Many Say I," where he wheeled out a concert piano and gargled bravely into the microphone while crowds continued roaring at typical concert levels. Philadelphia honored the band's twenty-second career performance there by declaring May 24 "Van Halen Day." All four members of the band received miniature replicas of the Liberty Bell. They also played a command performance for Donald Trump at his Trump Marina in Atlantic City in late August.

Yet the expectations should have been scaled down during the incubating period, with more small shows like at Billboard Live. For all the time spent recording during 1997, the band had spent very little time rehearsing with its new singer. Cherone inherited his rock god mantle, but he remained a prince, not a king. He looked small in comparison to his brightly colored predecessors. He remained boyish, still searching for his stage legs. He bleached his hair, but going blond would not save the day this time. "There's always a few out there with the folded arms going, 'Okay, I don't care what you do, you ain't Dave and you ain't Sammy," he told *The Inside*.

He smartly set himself apart from his peacock-plumed predecessors by dressing in subdued black suits or sweaters, dancing and shimmying in Banana Republic outfits and bare feet. But Nuno Bettencourt, who played guitar in Extreme with Cherone for twelve years, observed that Van Halen were trying to force their new singer to sound more macho. "It's like they've pushed him so hard he's not Gary anymore."

The *New York Times* called Van Halen's Madison Square Garden show "hollow, almost devoid of presence, pacing, or drama," and suggested that the newly reinvented Van Halen should have taken their no-frills show to more clubs instead of halls.

Adding to the feeling that the sky was falling, in June 1998 Alex was warming up before a show in Hamburg, Germany, when a section of plaster fell on top of him and bruised his right arm. He told Michael he felt like he'd been hit with a baseball bat. The band was removed from the stage just before another slab of ceiling dropped onto Alex's kit. His arm muscle was seriously torn by the accident, so at the eleventh hour, the remainder of Van Halen's European tour was canceled. He appeared back in the States wearing a soft cast on his arm, along with the usual neck brace and head wrap. His wounded appearance seemed to personify the damage that had been done to his band in recent years.

Van Halen III was soon widely recieved not as a rebirth but a disappointment. Peaking at number 4 in *Billboard*, it lingered briefly on the charts for three months. Stuck at gold status after August, *III* became the first Van Halen effort not to reach platinum sales. The distinction hurt—for years Van Halen had been the only act on Warner Bros. with a platinum disc for every album released. Eddie frequently protested that Van Halen weren't in it for the money, only the joy of music. But their partners at the label were definitely dollar-oriented— and it had to hurt band morale to take a step down the career ladder. It was a question of pride, if nothing else.

The specter of the 1996 debacle at the MTV Video Music Awards with Roth already hung over Cherone's every move. And as Gary acknowledged in several interviews, anything less than double platinum in Van Halen was considered a failure. Only a massive hit could have saved him, as "Why Can't This Be Love?" did for Sammy. "The album was a stiff and the tour didn't do well," Hagar remarked uncharitably during a radio interview. "That could have happened when I joined the band, fifteen years ago, but it didn't because we made a great record. And my career was in place with 'I Can't Drive 55.' It was equal to Van Halen at that time."

Hagar may have felt entitled to revise history, but increasingly it looked like Cherone would never get that far. In June 1999, he developed unusually pronounced symptoms of lead singer disease. Cherone clashed with multiplatinum alternative rock bands, though unfortunately, not on the album charts. Using his post in Van Halen as a soapbox, he wrote a public letter to Pearl Jam singer Eddie Vedder, an outspoken proponent of social causes, including abortion rights. Cherone's missive mocked the idea of a woman's right to choose as a function of whether she herself had been chosen by her parents after conception. Though his freedom to speak his beliefs could be seen as healthy, this was the first time Van Halen had been used as a mouthpiece for the Catholic Church.

The remaining songs from the 1997 sessions sat waiting to be recorded for Cherone's follow-up effort. He described one unrecorded track, "Sad Celibate," as a moody, expansive song in the vein of Led Zeppelin's *Houses of the Holy*. Alex, Eddie, and Gary all maintained that the band would return to the studio almost immediately, but their momentum was lost.

Like an underperforming CEO hired to turn around a major corporation, Cherone summarily exited Van Halen on November 5, 1999, after failing to achieve target results. "He was just the wrong choice, it's that simple," Alex said later. "No harm, no foul. I think the chemistry was just wrong."

Instead of dueling press releases, the separate statements competed to seem more heartbroken and apologetic. "Gary is a brother," said Eddie. "I had a great time singing with the band," said Gary. Neither side felt confident or warm and fuzzy about the future.

At the same time, Ray Danniels was finally fired as manager. Wrangling the sometimes competing interests of a boys' club of multimillionaires could not be an easy mission, but Danniels was unfortunately exiting with the reputation that he had misguided and misled the career of a band that sat atop the world when he inherited the reins. While Danniels, Warner Bros., and the band sorted out the resulting legal mess, Van Halen remained without management.

"I don't have any idea what the boys in the Van Halen Wacky World are going to do," David Lee Roth told KKGB radio. He sounded reinvigorated, despite his brushes with Van Halen, maintaining his fighting spirit with martial arts training and growing his shaggy bottle-blond mane back to proper rock god proportions.

"It's a bummer for Gary because it will probably ruin his whole damn career," Sammy Hagar commented to KCMQ in Missouri. "I mean, he's a decent singer, but what's he going to do now? 'Hey, he's the guy that bombed with Van Halen'? That's not a good handle to have. I kind of feel bad for him, but it's none of my business."

DEAD LEAVES AND THE
DIRTY GROUND

hen David Lee Roth finally crawled out of hiding after the ill-fated 1996 reunion attempt, he appeared before thousands of New Yorkers at the February 1997 premiere of Howard Stern's biopic *Private Parts*. Speaking the minds of a generous plurality of his fans, Stern blurted, "Van Halen is nothing without David Lee Roth. Long live David Lee Roth!"

The zealous crowd ripped into a spontaneous protest of "Eddie sucks! Eddie sucks!" which Roth downplayed. "Nah, Eddie doesn't suck—he just made a mistake."

Still unflappable, Diamond Dave seemed advancing to a new stage of public life. On his birthday in October 1997 he released *The Best of David Lee Roth*, featuring one new song, "Don't Piss Me Off." On the cover, he was pictured in his prime, tanned and golden-maned, wearing assless chaps and gazing into a makeup mirror backstage somewhere in purgatory.

The self-reflection was carrying over into another major project, a great leap from his bite-size MTV blasts. With the help of an old acquaintance from the Zero One club in the early eighties, Henry Rollins, Roth was putting together his memoirs. While still in Black Flag, Rollins had begun printing small books of poetry. By the mid-1990s, his self-run publishing imprint had released dozens of books and become the springboard for Rollins's career on the spoken-word circuit. "I helped [Dave] hook up with a few people to help him get his book going," Rollins said. "I was just kind of a catalyst, a foothold for the moment. What I've read of it is just tremendous. Dave worked very hard on it, too. The guy is a great storyteller."

The autobiography, titled *Crazy from the Heat* like his EP, hit book-stores in hardcover in October 1997. Roth had mused back in 1984 about following in the populist bootsteps of American writers Will Rogers and Mark Twain once his music career faded, and now here he was—gone literary.

Not a telling of the Van Halen story, *Crazy from the Heat* was a mental map of Roth's extended interior safari. He explained himself fully, revealing a horny romantic with few inhibitions and grand aspirations. Without naming many names or grinding unnecessary axes, he heralded the perversity of his life on the road, and gave up the goods on Van Halen without seeming too self-serving. "The emotional impact for me," he wrote of the break-up, "is once you've encountered hatred and ugliness like that, once you really become aware of just what human beings are capable of in that kind of sense, you're not so quick to rush back out onto the field with a sword in one hand and a torch in the other. I'm not so quick anymore to form a team."

Throughout the book, Roth's frequent battlefield metaphors stuck with thorns, not Velcro. He unchained his inner Jewish warrior, and compared Alex and Eddie to Hezbollah fanatics in their crusade against him. He recalled growing up around concentration camp survivors with numbers tattooed on their forearms, and admitted to delivering a downer bar mitzvah speech about how much it sucked being Jewish in WASP-land. "The best you can hope for as a Jew is to be tolerated," he wrote, adding that while leaping high off drum risers he always imagined himself landing hard on the panicked faces of his enemies.

At the same time, Sammy Hagar began his own book, tentatively titled *Red Storm Arising*, but had a falling-out with the coauthor over money. He successfully blocked the book's publication by claiming he was part owner of the interview tapes.

Like Sammy backing his own solo career, Roth paid for his 1998 album *DLR Band* himself, recording the music in three weeks. Forming his own record company, Wawazat Records, he claimed not to have a manager, agent, promoter, or publicist. "I don't have a plan for the future," he reported. "I just stand up and surf, show up every day and see what happens. Know what? Every time I've done that, and really believed in that, the greatest things have happened. Every time I've tried to grow up and act like an adult with a plan, it's blown my arm off."

Roth assembled a touring lineup of the DLR Band but scotched a self-financed tour after sales registered nothing but a blip. Even at this late stage in the game, however, he credentialed another guitar hotshot—John Lowery from Grosse Pointe, Michigan. Lowery had worked cheap for Salt-N-Pepa, k.d. lang, and former Judas Priest singer Rob Halford on the Two project. When the DLR gig stalled, he skipped off to Marilyn Manson, upgraded his name to John 5, and within five years was a bona fide guitar hero with a steady gig working for Rob Zombie.

Roth contented himself with a promotional tour, where he sold the record with a new universal angle: "You may have never bought one of my records, but you heard my voice coming out of the stereo at the local drive-in, or the beach, coming from the stereo at the lifeguard station. You heard it in the club. You heard it when you went to jail—I got you through jail. I got you through war. I've got letters from people who conceived children to my songs." Advanced egomania, possibly, but also true. "I think we're onto something that people may have already known, but may have forgotten for a while."

Pressed by a Finnish TV show about how many copies the album had sold, Roth seized the offensive with a tart one-liner. "Are you trying to hit me up for dinner? Because I'll take your whole motherfucking country out for dinner on this one." Dave could have given the TV host a break—in a country where thirty thousand CDs rates a platinum award, the actual number probably would have sounded impressive.

Billing himself as the ultimate multimedia entity in the flesh for the age of the tech boom, Roth launched an Internet television show called Dave TV—a spin-off of a concept from his "Just a Gigolo" video. The content was a flickering blitz of vintage Van Halen, live Roth, and commentary clips. Unfortunately, with broadband Internet still mostly a buzzword, the short run of five episodes hosted by Dave 2.0 dressed in futuristic cyber-outfits was largely wasted. Behind their squealing modems, only a small number of Internet users at that time were interested in guitar rock. Though money was flowing through the taps in every city in the United States, this was the age of irony—and genuine rock had just reached an absolute low point.

Even indestructible source of life "Top Jimmy" Koncek, inspiration for one of Van Halen's happiest tunes, succumbed to liver failure and died in May 2001. The loss of the signal flags up ahead called for a quick stop to check the road map. "I'm old enough to know there may not be a tomorrow," Roth said. "With my last dying breath, if you lean over to me on my deathbed, I want to be able to say I tried everything on the menu—twice."

When the Advil finally stopped working, Roth went for arthroscopy on his knee in January 2000—torn cartilage from too many hard jumps. He announced to *Rolling Stone* that he and Van Halen were attempting a trial marriage, and nothing more was said for a while. "You learn how to have fun," he said, "you learn how to be positive, you learn how to get along—then you can come to the barbecue. What I'm also going to say is don't hold your breath. These guys are unhappy. These guys are sour. They're different people now. It's not just a case of pop Diamond Dave in and all of a sudden the sun comes up."

<hr />

Edward Van Halen's only output for 1999 was a heady collaboration with Pink Floyd guitarist Roger Waters and Italian soundtrack boss Ennio Morricone on the song "Lost Boys Calling" from the film *The Leg-*

end of 1900. When in doubt, Eddie returned to the studio, adding a seventy-two-input analog mixing desk to 5150. He bought a Mellotron, a peculiar 1960s keyboard that played tape loops of flutes, choirs, and guitars like a rudimentary and spooky-sounding sampler. He also finally underwent his long-delayed hip replacement operation on November 16, 1999, receiving a titanium implant that made him partly a man of metal. His doctor told *USA Today* that the procedure had been recorded for posterity—possibly for use on a future Van Halen album. Later a mysterious source told *Blender* she'd seen Eddie's real hip on ice in a freezer.

Eddie was no longer spending much time on the Malibu coast, where he had lived two doors down from Hagar, literally looking toward the horizon over an ocean of possibility. He seemed lost up in Coldwater Canyon in the Hollywood Hills, another genius with a fortune floating in a dreamland. "I've been playing a lot of cello lately," he told *Guitar World* in 1999. He cited Chinese American cellist Yo-Yo Ma as an inspiration, and described trying to play along with his records like some pimply teen trying to learn Van Halen songs.

During 2000, Van Halen stalled for time, releasing newly remastered versions of their first six albums that fall. At the Video Music Awards in 2000, MTV lampooned the band's lack of action. The network mocked Van Halen along with MC Hammer and Vanilla Ice with a fake memorial production tribute to "artists no longer with us"— perhaps unaware that Eddie Van Halen was battling cancer.

The health problems in paradise that began with Eddie's late-eighties rehab visits blossomed during the 2000s, as years of drinking and excess came to a head in a slew of problems. After two decades, Van Halen's great legacy of sex, drugs, and rock and roll was haunting the band. Their former assets became liabilities.

In May 2000, the University of Texas M. D. Anderson Cancer Center in Houston denied that Eddie was a patient but later confirmed he was participating in an outpatient cancer prevention study. Eddie didn't further address the rumors for an entire year, until in April 2001 he came clean on his Web site, revealing he had been checked out by three cancer specialists and three neck surgeons at Cedars-Sinai in Los Angeles and was well on his way to recovery.

"Ed went through a very difficult time," Alex told the *Boston Globe*. "It was a health scare, and believe me, as his brother who didn't know if he was going to make it through the next week, it was a very strange experience."

David Lee Roth released a chipper public statement of support: "You can beat this, champ. See ya down the road." Two weeks earlier he had leaked news that he had recorded three "astonishing" new songs with the band after Gary Cherone's departure but hadn't heard from Eddie or Alex since his contract expired in July 2000. He hoped that alerting the public would juice the band into responding. All Van Halen would say in response is that they were indeed working on their next album.

As he fought his potentially lethal squamous cell carcinoma of the mouth, Eddie again began talking about God. He had been a smoker for roughly forty years, and the inevitable lightning bolt finally struck. Sammy Hagar had poked Eddie to quit, to no avail. Eddie had quit drinking occasionally but never gave up his smokes. He even smoked on the golf course. Now he went under the knife and hoped to save his life.

With surgery and treatment, about 75 percent of patients survive oral cancers. Doctors cut out roughly one-third of Eddie's tongue to eliminate the tumors. On *Live with Regis and Kelly*, Valerie Van Halen joked, "Whenever he gets smart with me, I say I'll cut more of that tongue out." Now even when sober, Eddie's speech sounded a little sloppy. "They butchered me," he later complained.

The band's latest attempt to reform with David Lee Roth began in 2000 and dragged well into 2001. They disagreed over songs that were too radio-friendly, over business details, and over one another. With Alex and Eddie running the band's business, there was no hard-nosed manager involved to make sure all the pieces fell into place. Eventually, Eddie told the *New York Post* that they finished three songs with Roth in 2001 but that they would all "probably be scrapped."

"Everything looked pretty positive about getting together, but before you know it attorneys are involved," Eddie told *Maximum Gold.* "These cats had me so beat down and confused, it made the cancer seem like a tiny zit on my ass. Everything seemed to fall apart once these guys got involved. I mean, we used to do it on a handshake. At this point, I don't have a clue what is going on."

He insisted that musically the band was still advancing, even as he supposedly underwent treatment supervised by the Mayo Clinic. "The band has always been together," he told the *Post.* "Whether we have a singer or not is a different story."

"I don't know if we had a complete album's worth of stuff, but we were pretty damn close," Michael Anthony told a Japanese magazine. "For the most part it was actually pretty good. I don't think Ed would ever let it out, though. I've got some demo stuff at home, they didn't even really want me to take any stuff home, but I ended up with some stuff, anyway."

WEA International, the megacorporate cousin of Warner Bros., tested the waters by releasing two Van Halen box sets in Japan—one box containing the first six albums from 1978 to 1984 with a metal VH key ring, the second offering four Sammy albums from 1986 to 1993 including the live album and two bonus tracks. Though WEA also had rights to put a Van Halen box out in the United States, it respected the band's wishes and waited for the time being, hoping to preserve its good relationship with a rock and roll mega-entity.

Meanwhile, Sammy told the *Philadelphia Inquirer* that a Las Vegas businessman had offered him, Van Halen, and David Lee Roth $50 million to play two pay-per-view concerts in Sin City. He claimed everyone but Roth shot down the offer immediately. It was hard to tell whether Van Halen were beginning to cash in their chips—or whether their chips would soon be cashed in for them.

After twenty years, a good-size general audience still wanted to hear Eddie's guitar playing and Roth's attitude, preferably in combination. But in the past five years, the public had heard enough Van Halen drama—it was time for new music or nothing.

On the bright blue morning of September 11, 2001, religious fanatics commandeered four commercial airliners and flew two of them into the symbolic heart of America's financial empire, the World Trade Center in New York City. The director of Van Halen's celebrated "Right Now" music video, Carolyn Mayer Beug, died aboard American Flight 11 when it collided with the North Tower, 1 World Trade Center.

The next month, while the country still remained in chaos, Valerie Bertinelli and Eddie Van Halen were amicably separated. "This is something Valerie tried very hard not to have happen," her mother told *People*, "but it finally came to a breaking point. I believe it will result in a divorce. I think Valerie is going on with her life."

They had seemed the perfect couple for twenty years and six months, since Valerie was a tender twenty-one years old. During that time she had played virtually every kind of suffering female role imaginable. Eventually, her marriage to a perfectionist alcoholic guitar god became too close to a sad made-for-TV melodrama. She and Eddie began living apart during the summer of 2001, when she moved to Salt Lake City for a role alongside Della Reese on *Touched by an Angel*. She lasted the remaining fifty-nine episodes until the show was canceled in 2003. The marriage did not.

David Lee Roth and the tabloids had claimed that Valerie left Eddie previously in 1992, but nine more years together quieted that gossip. Now there was no denying the marriage was done. Eddie paid Valerie a settlement in one lump payment, and he was a single man for the first time since he was twenty-six. The parents shared joint custody of ten-year-old Wolfgang, though he lived with his mom throughout the separation.

"I can't say that we're really great friends," Valerie had told an interviewer during a rocky period in 1990. "We don't have a hell of a lot in common, but we'll always be connected like brother and sister."

At least Eddie soon had his health. After doctors declared him cancer-free in May 2002, Eddie relayed the news via the band's Web site. "I'm sorry for the delay but I wanted to let you all know that I've just gotten a 100 percent clean bill of health—from head to toe."

The hardships brought lifelong musical partners Alex and Eddie closer together. The cool, contained older brother stepped out of the shadows. "Eddie always knew he would get better. I didn't," Alex told the Dutch publication *Telegraaf*. "All we had in those difficult times was our music. It was therapy. We played for months and months working on new songs."

Eddie also reached out to Alex, who had protected him since they were fresh off the boat from Holland. "There is a huge misconception about this band and that is without my brother, Alex Van Halen, who is the key, the band would not be. He is and has been there for me since before I was born," he told *Guitar World*. Eddie promised to get back to making music quickly, but though he and Alex played frequently, Eddie still seemed hampered by his old brainwashing voiced after 1984—that the public might not accept music from him outside certain defined lines.

During this time, Eddie did talk with Indiana country rocker John Mellencamp about an acoustic tour, a quiet change of direction. He also quietly continued to work against cancer. On *The Howard Stern Show* in 2006, Eddie offered a series of bizarre revelations. He proclaimed himself totally cancer-free, not simply in remission, then denied that thirty years of chain-smoking had brought on the disease. "I live in an electromagnetic field about fourteen to eighteen hours a day in my recording studio with a metal pick in my mouth. It's basically like playing golf in a lightning storm."

Eddie also claimed to be funding McClain Labs, a pathology lab with twenty-nine employees in Smithtown, New York. As loony as his explanation of how he beat cancer sounded, the technique he described was in fact at the cutting edge of oncology. The experimental lab cut a tiny healthy piece of his tongue, then grew the cells and conducted all the tests outside of Eddie's body before administering treatment. "I didn't have to drink the Drano," he said.

He acknowledged mysteriously on *The Howard Stern Show* that the technique was not yet legal in the United States, and suggested that the billion-dollar pharmaceutical industry was more interested in selling people chemo drugs and radiation therapy. "Cancer is a multidimensional disease," he explained. "It's spiritual, it's how you think, and it's emotional." For someone best known for playing guitar really fast, Eddie sounded a lot like a would-be prophet.

⟫⟫⟫⟩⟩⟩

In January 2002, Van Halen drifted further off course, splitting with Warner Bros. after more than twenty-three years in business together. Their contract wasn't up, according to *Billboard*, and the label described the break as simply a business decision, "not a function of where the band is at musically." It was the culmination of a clean sweep that began in 2000, when most of the band's long-term employees were shown the door. Along with the label, Van Halen also replaced the lawyer who had been with them practically since Sammy joined. For the first time in nearly twenty-five years, Van Halen was an unsigned band—and they would remain untethered, floating loose for years.

Warner Bros. still possessed the master tapes to most of the early albums and more or less had legal rights to release outtakes and compilations. The original tapes to later albums, beginning with *1984*, mostly still resided at Eddie Van Halen's house—the label had never thought during the band's fiscal heyday to send over a courier in a silver limo to demand the originals back. Warner representatives began compiling a box set including rarities, demo tapes, and alternate takes, but when they contacted acting manager Alex Van Halen, they were initially told to forget the idea.

Even the most dedicated fans began to fade during this period. After six years, Van Halen's fan quarterly, *The Inside*, ceased publication. The glossy magazine had begun in 1995 and for a while became the semiofficial mouthpiece of the band, offering editors tours of 5150 and access to tour rehearsals. The last two Van Halen studio albums published the magazine's address. But now publisher Jeff Hausman stopped the presses, citing "a big lack of news." For all his trouble, David Lee Roth sued Hausman afterward over licensing issues but dropped the claim in May 2002 after agreeing *The Inside* had done nothing illegal.

It took him a while, but Roth eventually accepted that reunion negotiations had collapsed, and his three or four new songs with Van Halen had no future. Afterward, he was brutal—yet behind his well-crafted words was genuine sorrow. "I'm about right here, right now. What the Van Halens are about is wasted time. If you think one second isn't valuable, then ask the little girl who just missed getting a gold medal at the Olympics by one second. If you think one month is not valuable to somebody, then ask the lady who just had a premature kid how valuable that month is. Eddie Van Halen and his sister have wasted years."

GET THE PARTY STARTED

Meanwhile, Sammy Hagar ventured forth successfully as a solo artist reborn, often with Michael Anthony in tow. With his new wife, Kari, and a growing young family started during his last months with Van Halen, Hagar was buoyant. After turning fifty, he had become an all-around lifestyle impresario on the back of his music and the Cabo Wabo Cantina. "It's almost like Cabo Wabo in some ways broke the band up the first time," Sammy told KSHE. The band had bailed on the club after discovering a whopping bill for back taxes. "Van Halen didn't want to do it, and they were part of it, and they wanted to give it to the government. I said no way, you're not gonna take my place from me, that's crazy. So I bought them out. And ever since then, they hated it, because it's been successful."

Twenty years after he began drinking at age thirty, Sammy the son of a terminal alcoholic had become a tequila magnate and self-promotion machine. The success of Cabo Wabo Cantina made it possible in 1996 for Sammy to partner with the small Miravalle tequila factory from Jalisco, Mexico, supplier of his house tequila. Rebranded as Cabo Wabo after a successful trial run in Hawaii, the elixir made its way to upscale liquor stores nationally with the help of distributor Wilson Daniels. In 2000 and 2001, all three varieties of Cabo Wabo tequila won Taste Award Gold Medals and Best of Show medals from the American Tasting Institute, a trade group of thirty thousand restaurant workers.

Fortune profiled Sammy in 2000 and estimated Cabo Wabo's catch that year at $19 million. Hagar figured that he made more money from tequila than record sales but claimed his partner Shep Gordon was the bean counter. As far as the public was concerned, Hagar's role was fun-loving tequila promoter and taster-in-chief supervising the product down to its hand-blown glass packaging. "When a fan of mine pays this much for a bottle of tequila, and he probably doesn't even like tequila, I want him at least to have a nice vase to put on the table."

The brilliance of Hagar's burgeoning empire was how the music sold the tequila and vice versa. His friendly, outgoing personality already endeared him to casino and club owners. Now bars that stocked his booze promoted his music around the year—while, in turn, gigs once or twice yearly in casinos in Atlantic City or Foxwoods in Connecticut jacked up awareness of Cabo Wabo. "The way I live my life is the Cabo Wabo lifestyle," he told *Tequila Aficionado*. "Everything I do, it promotes itself because I don't have to go out and say I am selling this, I am Mr. Cabo Wabo! Between the club, my stage show, which is built around the Cabo Wabo, and the tequila—it's like a snow ball thing, it all promotes itself."

The annual Branded Entertainment Summit conference was impressed enough to invite Sammy to host a luncheon at the Beverly Hills Hilton. "While known for his rock n' roll exploits," the press release read, "Sammy is also an extremely successful entrepreneur and someone who naturally recognizes the value in a brand."

Sammy seemed to be beachcombing for the blown-out flip-flops of Jimmy Buffett, the musical entrepreneur whose midlife-crisis anthems spawned a multimillion-dollar empire of T-shirts, paperbacks, clothing, and music celebrating the vacation mind-set of Key West, Florida. As Buffett's fans called themselves Parrotheads, the Red Rocker's followers became Redheads and put on red afro wigs. When a branch of the

Cabo Wabo Cantina opened in the basement of Harvey's Casino in Lake Tahoe, California, in 2004, Jimmy Buffett cover bands became a staple, alongside looping videos of Sammy Hagar with Van Halen.

Sammy had figured out how to sell not just music, but a part-time party lifestyle to middle-aged businessmen who looked at him and saw one of their own. With his sunburned nose, beachcomber shades, and shorts, he looked more like a tourist who had recently lost his inhibitions than the spry rocker of the early 1980s. "I don't like hats, I don't like socks, I don't even like shoes," he said. "I don't even like clothes period but you know you gotta wear a T-shirt and some shorts."

Rock fans of a more selective morality began calling him "$pammy" Hagar. The potshots came all too easily, but the very nature of his goofy enthusiasm deflected criticism. For one thing, Hagar was still genuinely enthusiastic about playing music.

While Eddie made infrequent appearances at celebrity golf tournaments, Hagar continued to record and perform, pausing only for a guest appearance as a bartender on a 1998 episode of *Nash Bridges*. After leaving Van Halen in 1996, Sammy formed the Waboritas with boyhood pal and drummer David Lauser, who introduced bassist Mona Gnader. The band's hotshot guitarist, Vic Johnson, came from the Busboys, a versatile eighties crossover act that had been featured alongside Eddie Murphy and Nick Nolte in *48 Hours*. Waboritas keyboardist Jesse Harms was another old friend, a producer of solo Hagar prior to Van Halen, as well as albums for REO Speedwagon and Eddie Money.

At first the band were weekend warriors, but 1999's *Red Voodoo* album rose to number 22 on the *Billboard* album chart. Returning to the fresh-faced hard rock of his pre–Van Halen solo albums, Hagar showed that he had emerged from years of sensitive balladry and electro-pop unscathed. A reworking of Gary Glitter's stadium singalong "Rock 'n Roll Part 2," Sammy's "Mas Tequila" served as both a commercial for his drink empire and a slap in the ruddy faces of old bandmates who couldn't hold their liquor.

As he thrived in his new life, his appearance completely changed. Wine and pasta added some pounds to his midsection. He went under the shears in November 1999 on *The Tonight Show*, cropping his trademark curls for the benefit of Locks of Love, a nonprofit organization producing human hair wigs for children with long-term medical hair loss. Afterward, with giant red shorts and shades, he looked like a mascot for a minor-league baseball team, or the footloose descendent of Cyndi Lauper's former manager, Captain Lou Albano.

By 2002, the Waboritas were upbeat purveyors of party rock par excellence, rampaging through two-hour sets with Hagar solo hits, Wabos originals, and Hagar-era Van Halen songs like "When It's Love" and "Finish What Ya Started." He still stayed away from Roth-era songs, claiming he didn't know the words. As Sammy rifled his Rolodex, his band welcomed guests ranging from Ted Nugent to Metallica, who joined him onstage for renditions of old Montrose songs and hard rock standards, such as a crowd-pleasing Led Zeppelin medley of his own design called "Whole Lotta Zep."

Sammy Hagar and the Waboritas's 2002 album *Not 4 Sale* kicked off with "Stand Up," which he'd written for the fictional heavy metal band Steel Dragon in *Rock Star*. Though the movie story was based on Judas Priest, who had replaced their singer with someone from a Priest cover band, the comparison was funny—the movie told the story of a replacement singer going through the ropes with a brand-name hard rock band.

Sammy claimed Van Halen's inactivity was not his fault. "I think if they could do anything right now they would have done it," he said in early 2002, after they had ignored calls to join him or Dave for any kind of Van Halen tour. "No one has heard anything, they don't have a record deal. They've just fallen completely apart. I think it's the worst thing that could have ever happened to one of the greatest rock bands in the world."

〜〜〜〜〜

Heralding a strange new century, in 2002 the former Van Halen singers Sammy Hagar and David Lee Roth teamed for a rivalry-packed summer tour dubbed "Song for Song: The Undisputed Heavyweight Champs of Rock and Roll." The Sam & Dave package was announced on April 15, the dreaded deadline for income taxes. When the pair finally met for the first time, they seemed to regard each other with the affection usually reserved for IRS agents.

In the years since he commanded center stage, Roth's quirky personality had accelerated to the hilt. Flaunting his bare chest and wearing low-cut flare pants as he approached fifty, he immediately jump-kicked into grizzled warrior mode, reportedly dismissing Hagar as "a mediocre talent." He had begun 2002 on the wrong end of a lawsuit from a booking agent who accused him of nonpayment of tens of thousands of dollars in fees.

"I never knew Dave," Hagar said. "I suspected from what everyone's always told me that he's not an easy guy to get along with. He's like an egomaniac—in a positive sense, that he really, really thinks he's the greatest thing that ever walked the planet."

As details of the forty-plus concert dates solidified, the appeal of seeing two eras of Van Halen merge onstage became clear—the pair possibly trading verses of "Jump," or the off-the-wall possibility that Roth might take a stab at a latter-day hit like "Runaround." Sammy held even higher hopes—to reconcile with the Van Halen brothers after seven years and possibly instigate a full-fledged Van Halen tour. "My idea was that that maybe this Sam and Dave tour would motivate a Van Halen reunion," he said, "which would still be one of the greatest things ever for the fans."

With the two foils alternating headlining slots in each city, the bout was Diamond Dave, with highly processed and aged blond mane, dressed in blue-sequined suits, against the Red Rocker, who dressed like a beach bum or a hockey fan, draped in Mardi Gras beads and fronting an energetic band that included an ex-machinist girl bass player and a black shredder guitarist. In his corner, Roth had plucked guitarist Brian Young from Atomic Punks, a Van Halen tribute act that was doing very well at giving the public the classic Van Halen it wanted.

The two came out from their corners fighting. "Sammy Hagar is upset with me because he knows I'm better than he is," Roth told a TV interviewer.

Tempers flared backstage at the Universal Amphitheatre in Los Angeles, where Hagar and his band were relegated to a small backstage dressing room while Roth scored a sumptuous receiving area with colorful furniture and wardrobe. Roth delayed his arrival until Hagar was nearly ready to perform, then attempted to steal the show with an entourage of a half dozen security guards and a trio of masked blonde Playboy models wearing silver bodysuits and cat ears. "This is the parade down Main Street—this is P. T. Barnum," Roth told VH1 while Hagar simmered.

Crowds appeared at the "sans Halen" shows waving anti-Eddie signs and mutilated cardboard Eddie cutouts. The spats in the audience were minimal—fans from the Roth and Hagar camps tolerated each other like teenagers told to share a backyard party with younger siblings. Hagar and Roth split a basic crew, though they hired separate sound and lighting specialists to hedge against sabotage. Beneath the enmity, the two did seem to share a psychic survivors' bond—it just happened to be a very bad one, joined in a very harmonious understanding about not liking each other.

In Detroit, Kid Rock tried to broker an onstage collaboration between the pair, which Hagar had wanted since before the tour began. Though Roth agreed, the powwow never materialized. Kid Rock learned it was easier to marry bombshell Pamela Anderson and lure her to Michigan than to unify the oppositely charged particles of David Lee Roth and Sammy Hagar. Hagar put on a futile show of banging on Roth's backstage door every night, making a game of his rejected overtures. Roth stopped answering the door.

Hagar couldn't resist getting in his digs in the press, laced with lots of jokes about Roth's hair. "Dave comes out with all his glitter and glamour, and we come out with the real deal—it all just folds together into one great rock show."

Michael Anthony joined Sammy and the Waboritas onstage as a guest for many dates, his first appearances onstage in over three years. He reported that back at home the Van Halen brothers did not have a problem with him joining the tour—at least not with Hagar, though anger at Roth was still a definite possibility. He also let slip that he hadn't spoken to Eddie or Alex since February.

On August 1, before the tour rolled into the Big Apple, the *New York Post* broke a sensational headline: VAN HALEN'S GETTING VICIOUS. Given a platform to vent his frustration with Dave, Sammy delighted in comparing Roth to Liberace, criticizing his hair and calling him an "asshole." Roth retorted two weeks later in a Nashville interview, joking about Sammy's increasingly portly physique. "I think I saved Sam from having to do celebrity boxing for a living."

The karate black belt Roth and the ex-boxer Hagar mostly exchanged verbal blows from a distance, but they did appear onstage together once during the tour at Radio City Music Hall in New York City. They traded scripted banter as they presented an MTV Video Music Award to Linkin Park. "Relax, Dave, all these people aren't here to see you," Hagar read from the prompter. "It's really good to see you after fifty-five shows—where have you been all summer?"

"I've been on the Celebrity Deathmatch tour," Roth said, laughing.

While in New York, Hagar arranged a free show at Irving Plaza, giving out five hundred tickets over the radio, and reserving another five hundred for uniformed police and firefighters. One year after the September 11 attacks, Sammy's gesture was appreciated. A grateful official representative presented Hagar with a 9/11 memorial plaque. A cop in the audience went further and gave Sammy the uniform off his back. As Sam puffed a joint and slapped hands with the crowd, it was hard to tell who needed to blow off steam more: the shell-shocked first responders of the World Trade Center disaster, or the working-class singer who had been forced to battle all summer with sharp-tongued David Lee Roth.

Also at the Irving Plaza show, two former Van Halen frontmen sang together on the same stage for the first time—Sammy Hagar and Gary Cherone. Though Cherone had toured with David Lee Roth while still in Extreme, he had never met Hagar before joining Van Halen. With Michael Anthony pumping away on bass, Hagar and Cherone clasped one another and banged out Led Zeppelin's "Rock and Roll."

Three years onward, Cherone was starring in a community musical theater production of *The Wall*, and preparing to release the first record by his new band, Tribe of Judah. He showed no signs of bitterness toward Van Halen. "I guess due to some personal, frustrating moments on my part, it just seemed the time and place to move on," he said. "All I can say is that those guys were absolutely great to me."

After the show, Hagar beamed to Mike. "It's the same shit as the old days—only on some other level." He still wanted to compete with young rock bands, and he still had things left to prove. Ultimately he had to be satisfied climbing back onto the Cabo Wabo jet as an older man, still sweating, still reigning over a joyous room, whether the press or the music insiders understood his success or not.

Business-wise, the tour succeeded beyond expectations. Apparently fans felt two ex-singers doing Van Halen songs was better than no Van Halen at all. The Sammy Hagar and David Lee Roth summer dates did $9.6 million worth of business, selling over three hundred thousand tickets. On a personal level, Sammy got to know David Lee Roth. "There's just so much about Dave I don't like," he admitted.

Maybe surprising themselves, most audiences gave the decision to Sammy's show over Dave's. Still, Sammy wondered whether it was worth it. "I spent five years of my life with the Waboritas, building my audience, trying to shed myself of Van Halen," he told *Guitar World*. "Once I got involved with Dave, I realized that I was thrown right back into the Van Halen arena and all I was was an ex–Van Halen singer."

Whether the tour would rouse Eddie and Alex from their slumber remained to be seen. Hagar still kept a house down the road from Eddie's vacant Malibu digs. "If Eddie calls me, I'm going to be suspicious and have my restrictions," Sammy said. "But if we just ran into each other, it could either be a fistfight, or it could be good vibes."

The faithful neutral party Michael Anthony also mused publicly about Van Halen teaming again with Dave, Sammy, or both, if only for the sake of putting a lid on the past. "Roth would kind of pull his hat down and just walk by me," Mike told *Burrn!* "One of the first shows that I did with those guys I had a few drinks and I went into Dave's dressing room after the show and I just unloaded on him, on what was his problem that we could not make this reunion work."

Soon, however, Michael was again fending off rumors that he had been kicked out of the band, forcing a public statement in November 2002. "I haven't met with any lawyers, and I haven't quit Van Halen. I'm still the bass player for the baddest rock 'n' roll band on the planet and always have been!"

〰〰〰

After the summer sunshine, the days seemed darker for David Lee Roth. His demeanor had changed—he now seemed frustrated by the role of sex god. He routinely vented some fucked-up male sexuality, inviting pretty soccer moms in the front row for a drink from his trademark Jack Daniel's bottle, and then shaking the stage prop at groin level while ejaculating about a quart of whiskey on the heads of his bewildered conquests. Who knows how many times he had enacted the same scene backstage with willing participants during his halcyon days, but now his soaking of his loyal admirers revealed the impotent anger of an aging Adonis.

As the holiday season commenced in 2002, Roth filed suit against Van Halen and their record label for unpaid royalties. According to *Billboard*, Roth still received a 25 percent share for his records as per the contract he signed when he left the band. Now he claimed that Eddie, Alex, and Michael had renegotiated their album royalties with Warner Bros. in 1996, and that he was due $200,000 extra for album sales through the end of 2001. He was still being paid according to the skimpy deal they had struck back in 1976. "When you buy *Van Halen I* now, if I make 10 cents the bass player makes 30 cents," Roth argued. "I've always maintained that I should make 25 percent." Lawyers filed dozens of motions and complaints as the suit propelled through September 2003, when all parties involved reached a settlement and Roth dismissed the lawsuit "without prejudice."

Released in April 2003, Roth's next album, *Diamond Dave*, was mostly covers of Jimi Hendrix, the Steve Miller Band, Savoy Brown, and the Beatles. The young production team was wet behind the ears, but the methods were vintage and the musicians mostly recorded live. Roth called the album "post-modern," though the concept was much less complicated. "Classic rock in the USA is a fixed playlist, they set them in stone maybe seven years ago," he told *Classic Rock*. "So I consciously did an album that was classic, otherwise how would I get airplay?"

While swinging with old chestnuts, Roth also reprised "Ice Cream Man" yet again, this time with Edgar Winter on sax and Nile Rodgers on guitar. That and the easy-listening "Bad Habits" were the highlights of a mostly routine-sounding album. Like *DLR Band*, this was an album named after himself—but more than ever the muscle needed to come before the marketing if he wanted to jump-start his career. Roth's ego needed huge ambition to be justified, but *Diamond Dave* fizzled out after selling fewer than thirty thousand copies.

The signature line in "Just a Gigolo," when Roth wondered if life would go on without him, was starting to chime louder. At the House of Blues in Myrtle Beach, South Carolina, his equilibrium was rattled by a spinning mic stand during his encore, "Jump," which gashed open his forehead and required twenty-one stitches. He finished the show but canceled a slew of upcoming tour dates while he recovered at one of his tricoastal crash pads in California, New York City, and Miami.

Roth could still kick some kind of ass, however, as a Pasadena neighbor of his soon learned. The man tried crossing Roth's property in the middle of the night to break into his own house. Neighbors called the police when they heard breaking glass. The cops arrived to find Roth pointing at a man lying facedown in the grass, a knife lying a few feet away. They arrested the intruder for methamphetamine possession, and Roth issued a press release stating he had used a twenty-gauge shotgun to detain a knife-wielding intruder. "What are you doing in my backyard at 3:15 in the morning without a backstage pass?" Roth challenged. "Anyone found bearing arms here at night will be found here in the morning."

Meanwhile, the hermitlike guitar god Eddie Van Halen made his annual appearance before mere mortals at the 2003 NAMM convention. Time had ravaged him. While a throng of hundreds waited, he sat in a private section wearing a floppy brown hat, conducting business and chatting with his peers. Much later than planned, he sat down to show off some new guitar work. He promised new music and new gear from Peavey in the following year, and then security dispersed the waiting crowd. The reaction to Eddie's appearance and behavior was an unusual mix of pity and anger.

Goldmine reported ex-manager Ray Danniels saying that Eddie's problem was that he'd been a rock star all his life, and had lost touch with reality. "That's an understatement!" Danniels emphasized.

Sammy Hagar agreed there was a problem. "Otherwise he'd be playing music, and the guy hasn't played music for I don't know how long," he told MelodicRock.com. "Yes, I'm really down on Eddie for wasting his life."

In 2003, Van Halen became eligible for the Rock and Roll Hall of Fame, raising hopes that they would be inducted—an excellent inducement to leave the house and play. "It's very rare that you run into a McCartney-Lennon or a Jagger-Richards kind of thing," Roth told Howard Stern. "That's a luck scenario that you should happen to geographically collide with somebody with the same inspiration and enthusiasm. And I treasure it and salute it whenever I hear it on the radio. Makes me drive a little bit faster."

Van Halen made the first cut of thirty potential candidates, yet the band seemed to be a can of worms the Cleveland rock boosters didn't want to touch. The museum put Mike's original Jack Daniel's bass on display and left the rest to conjecture. "I don't know how Sammy would react, and it really doesn't matter at this point," Alex once mused to *The Inside*. "If anyone would feel awkward playing together, it would be Roth."

Asked about reuniting for the Hall of Fame by the *Oregonian*, Roth described the scene in his head. "I'm going to look at Mike Anthony and say, 'It was a great time, and you were there.' I will look at the drummer and say, 'We were creative and fearless, and you were there.' I will look at Eddie and say, 'Hey man, we made a contribution, and you were there.' I will look at Sammy and say, 'You weren't there!'

"There will have to be an intervention with Eddie before we even start talking again about going out on tour or making an album," he continued. "I don't want to get everybody worked up again with all of the millions of dollars of expectations. On the positive side, I think 'hope springs eternal' is an axiom to live by."

A GRAND DON'T COME
FOR FREE

Six years after Van Halen last toured supporting *III*, Sammy Hagar passed through California for a family wedding. While in the area, he phoned Alex Van Halen, and the two estranged friends spent a day together testing the water, fishing for whatever might be left of their chemistry. While Sammy had at least been on the road playing Van Halen songs with Michael Anthony and the Waboritas, Alex had only infrequently been able to rouse his main collaborator, Eddie, for an occasional jam session. After spending dinner talking about brighter times, Alex was ready to consider playing with Sammy again—if Eddie felt the same.

Eddie had not exactly deluged the world with soundtrack music or solo records in the four years since Van Halen had virtually shut down. He claimed to have countless hours of songs ready for release, material he described as "a fat fucking cabernet." Vowing to "serve no riff before its time," he was very aware that the world was still waiting for his next notes, and insisted he was being productive. "If I dropped dead right now, there'd be music for at least twenty to thirty CDs," he said. Caught at home early one morning by Iowa radio hosts Dwyer and Michaels, he played and sang them a song he was working on: "Death by Hollywood, a little too fabulous for his own good."

According to MTV, Eddie's guitar had come out of the case in early 2003 during a bizarre audition for Limp Bizkit, who were then conducting a national public search for a guitarist. When Eddie jammed with the band, they reined in their typical down-tuned rap metal and played sharp hard rock in the vein of classic Van Halen. Not exactly a pipeline to the future of rock music, the real-life mash-up was a crazy tear in the fabric of the rock universe. The story grew strange, however, when Eddie allegedly returned to the rehearsal area twenty minutes after leaving, agitated and looking for his guitar. They insisted he had taken it with him, but he persisted in grilling them suspiciously.

Shortly after his reconciliation with Alex in early 2004, Sammy took a deep breath and called Eddie. "It's like old times as friends, but nothing more than that," Hagar said afterward. "It's great to have open communications with some old friends again, much better than being in a maze."

Before long, temptation called the Hagar era of Van Halen back into active duty. No apologies were offered, but the band could communicate enough to work together. "Some people have different memories of what happened," Hagar said. "We decided to leave it at that. We started out like it never happened."

Now that he and Sammy were back on the same team, Alex offered CNN his opinion on the 2002 Sam & Dave tour: "I felt bad for Sam, I'll tell you the truth!"

In March, Van Halen hired a booking agent at the William Morris Agency. The band also signed with a manager, Irving Azoff, after nearly five years adrift. Longtime minder of Journey and more recently Christina Aguilera, Azoff had also looked after Sammy Hagar's business for several years. The allegiances of managers with potential conflicts of interest had caused problems in Van Halen before, but at this stage the band desperately needed a cohesive business strategy.

Hagar put the Waboritas on temporary hold while Van Halen booked a massive summer reunion tour. Offers reportedly materialized from Kiss, Aerosmith, and Bon Jovi to assemble a package, but Azoff proceeded with caution. Calling the process "admittedly dysfunctional," he kept press interviews to a minimum and distributed only one new photo of the band. Bringing Van Halen back to life was a delicate operation—for example, most of the band's crew now worked for Hagar and were reticent to return to Van Halen after being unceremoniously dumped during the late 1990s.

"I'll speak for myself," Alex told *USA Today* about how things went down in 1996. "We made a mistake. The whole thing unraveled. We were buddies for 11 years, and all of a sudden it stopped. We'll take full responsibility for what happened, but there were outside forces that tried to drive wedges between people, and you don't always get the full picture. Before you know it, decisions are being made for you."

After Sammy and the Van Halen brothers were on board, Eddie astonishingly didn't want Michael Anthony involved in the tour. The two men had not spoken to each other in two years, and Mike claimed he was forced to take a pay cut in order to participate, that basically he and Sammy were contract employees. "I don't know how he was going to call it a reunion," Anthony told *Burrn!* "but I basically had to work out a deal with Irving Azoff's management company in order to be part of this thing."

Said Mike, "I had to sign off on any kind of rights I had as far as the name or the logo or anything I do with the band. That was something that Eddie was controlling."

The brothers had been subtly knocking the bassist for years, often telling interviewers they didn't bother putting bass in their stage monitors. Outside the band, few knew how tenuous his position had become. "I've always felt sorry for Mike," Sammy Hagar later commented to *The Road*. "I was the only guy who stood up for him. He's in trouble now, because he's got no one to stick up for him. I fought for Mike all the time. The brothers just got him by the balls."

With their house coming in order, the refreshed Van Halen signed a one-record deal with Warner Strategic Marketing for another greatest hits compilation. The double-disc *Best of Both Worlds* was released on July 20, 2004, and went platinum in six weeks—reassuring everyone that the commercially flatlined *III* was just an aberration that could be blamed on pushing the record-buying public one singer too far.

Suffering from oddball sequencing, *The Best of Both Worlds* opened with "Eruption" and more or less zigzagged between Roth and Hagar songs, an agonizing dilemma for loyalists from both camps who dreaded sitting through "Dreams" to hear "Hot for Teacher," or vice versa. Curiously, not a single picture of Roth appeared in the package except on two postage-stamp-size album covers, and he was only mentioned twice in the liner notes. Worse yet for Gary Cherone, none of his songs even made the cut.

Like *Best of Volume I*'s new tracks with Roth in 1996, *The Best of Both Worlds* featured three new Sammy cuts: "It's About Time" was a caustic staccato nod to nineties headbangers like Pantera. "Up for Breakfast" was a raunchy dirt-road rocker with sexual metaphors by Sammy based around breakfast food. The third new song, "Learning to See," was a soul-searching bag of countrified sap out of Bon Jovi's hymnal, recorded using a waterlogged guitar that Eddie clamped onto barstools and played horizontally like a jerry-rigged lap steel.

After returning to Eddie's creative incubator, Hagar vouched for the library of unreleased songs scattered around 5150. "There is enough music for one hundred years in that studio laying on the floor," he remarked. Yet for the first time in Van Halen's history, these new compositions were not credited to the entire group. Michael Anthony was excluded. In fact, Eddie played bass on the three new songs, strengthening suspicions he had recorded bass on other tracks throughout the years—a practice Roth claimed began as early as *Fair Warning*. By the time Mike was asked back, all that was left for him to do was add backing vocals to the essentially finished tracks.

The collection made it pretty clear which world the band thought was best—besides beginning with three new Hagar songs, the double-disc set ended with three live Hagar versions of "Jump," "Panama," and "Ain't Talkin' 'Bout Love." While punishing Roth for being a pain in the ass during negotiations, the whole package served as tour promotion: a reminder to Van Halen fans to put the kids to bed and sneak out for a pricey night on the town with Van Halen.

Van Halen's 2004 tour began on June 11 in Greensboro, North Carolina, their first show since 1998. The stage was a giant VH circle logo, with the band running around the rings or confined to the triangular center, while a chosen group of fans watched from within the stage in the vein of Metallica's famous Snakepit design from the early nineties. Unknown bands like Silvertide, Shinedown, Laidlaw, and Rose Hill Drive were chosen to open various shows—mainly to make sure the equipment was working while the crowd arrived and found their seats. Guitarist Nick Perri from Silvertide said admiringly that Eddie still disappeared into a backstage "closet"—now a large dressing room—to warm up for hours before a gig.

Compared to the jolly tranquility of the Van Hagar era, this meeting of Van Halen and Sammy Hagar rocked way harder. The band teased its way through the night, tossing off familiar riffs then jumping into different songs. The show began with a bang, as Sammy shouted, "Hello, baby," signaling the start of "Good Enough," only to rip into "Jump." In fact, Sammy performed plenty of songs he had shied away from during his ten years in Van Halen, even the notoriously Roth-stamped "Unchained." Standing right in the eye of the storm, the band also played "Humans Being," the song from *Twister* that had contributed so much to their breakup, while giant video screens ran clips of tornado footage.

Dressed in red stage clothes with a "Red Rocker" inlay fretboard on his guitar, there was no masking of Sammy's solo artist identity this time. After marinating in the Waboritas for five years, his voice was loose and raspy, and he was wisely willing to howl in a lower range. For some reason, the hard rock heartthrob Sammy Hagar I had immediately become the soft rock siren Sammy Hagar II when he joined Van Halen in 1985. The recent years as a solo artist saw the rougher edges flourish again—this thick, squat Sammy Hager III finally had the balls to own the microphone and sing for Van Halen.

Unfortunately, when Sammy cleared the stage for solo showpieces like "Eagles Fly," the sappy "Learning to See," or Bob Dylan's dopey "Rainy Day Women #12 & 35"—better known as the "Everybody Must Get Stoned" song—the Sammy Hagar II of headset microphones hijacked the night. During the unlikely segment that resembled a Bryan Adams concert more than a Van Halen reunion, Sammy played guitar solos while the rest of the band sought refuge behind the amps.

As could be expected given his lowered status, Michael Anthony's bass solo was painfully short, but with his Jack Daniel's bass recalled to duty he remained the raging bull of the evening, squalling into his wall of amplifiers and bounding over the stage. Trading off for the short solo, he sang most of the lead vocals to long-lost classic "Somebody Get Me a Doctor." Sammy pitched in, but Mike's impossibly high backing harmonies still rang clear.

Alex seemed to be bashing for his life. Far from out of practice, time away from the band seemed to have honed his chops. He had only begun practicing classic drum rudiments in the early 1990s, with eight Van Halen albums already under his headband—a career point where most drummers slack off considerably. Though he continually came across as aloof and detached after shows, his lack of interaction was just advancing with his hearing loss—his long-suffering ears were now ringing down to the brain stem.

Back from the edge after beating cancer, Eddie was screaming to be useful—a lit-up hellion, not the smiling waif of past tours. He indulged in onstage jamming when the mood struck. His lengthy solo tied "Eruption" with "Cathedral" through a flurry of connected riffs. He used his whammy bar like a clarinet player would use breath control, swooping notes upward then downward with extra momentum. Though no longer an enfant terrible, he looked as fit as Bruce Lee and couldn't stop the high jumps and knee slides he had been doing since Van Halen started playing stages big enough to fly across.

When at his blazing best onstage, Eddie proved to still be the original high-speed shredder, in total command of the guitar. Some nights, he seemed to be off his bearings, as in Chicago, where he petered out and excused himself to the fans, saying "I done run out of gas!" He insisted he was following through on his newfound freedom. "This was the first time ever that I wasn't nervous when I got onstage," he told radio hosts Dwyer and Michaels. "I was actually writing onstage, coming up with stuff while I was playing."

The years were flying fast. Hagar was now fifty-six, and Eddie forty-nine. Since they last played together, MTV's *Headbangers Ball* had been canceled, forgotten, and resurrected. Van Halen returned in a whole new era. Like Rip Van Winkle, they had awakened to a torrent of new realities. Life was no longer as easy as walking out onstage and blazing through "Eruption"—although audiences were paying upward of $100 each for tickets hoping Van Halen could prove that it could be.

Reviewers came away with mixed reports, often from the same show. The band sounded rough and raw—they opened the gates to classic Van Halen spontaneity—not the tightly calibrated war machine that made them great, but actual chaos, which was almost as good. They had never really rocked with Hagar before, and the pop audience weaned on "Right Now" sometimes interpreted raucousness as sloppiness. For one thing, this was the Sammy trained on seventies rock and now shaking coconut trees every night in clubs, not the highly processed poofster of the 1980s. Meanwhile, a whole new generation of fans who know Van Halen only through Internet downloads of their glory days were shocked that the brightly lit boys of 1978 were now old grizzled men.

The fans in 2004 were themselves a far cry from the hearty Pasadena teenagers who had overturned police cars while fighting for their right to party. The typical ticket buyer in 2004 had been a horny undergrad in 1992, and had gotten laid at a dorm room kegger with the help of "Right Now." Now their kids were entering junior high school, standing right next to them, seeing their first rock concert. The only backyard parties these folks were hosting were suburban barbecues, careful not to piss off the homeowners' association with loud music.

Playing to upward of forty thousand faces some nights, the tour was a financial success—yet it was a creative wash, and an interpersonal flop. "We had a few bumps because old things came back up again from time to time on the road between Sammy and Eddie so it was a little bit shaky," Mike told *Burrn!* Bad blood between Sammy and Eddie put the kibosh on early plans to extend the reunion to Europe, Asia, and South America, scratching the chance to return to the Van Halen family homeland, Holland.

Following in his pal Hagar's footsteps, Anthony was delving into foodstuffs with a boutique hot sauce launched in 2004. Like Hagar, he won peer approval—two awards from *Chile Pepper* magazine. Yet he claimed that Van Halen lawyers called every radio station in the United States in advance of their interviews to warn against promoting Cabo Wabo tequila or Mad Anthony hot sauce. A St. Louis radio DJ was asked to change his Cabo Wabo shirt before the before the band arrived for the sake of keeping the peace. "Isn't that one of the benefits you're supposed to reap from all these years of success?" Anthony complained.

The edges were not as sharp, but the band impacted with blunt force. In South Dakota, an overexcited thirty-year-old fell fifteen feet from the balcony and injured his head and shoulders. The Winnipeg show marked the end of an era, as the city-owned Winnipeg Arena was shuttered after forty-nine years as soon as Van Halen left the stage.

In Boston that June, Eddie showed off his talents and his demons. He commandeered the grand piano in the Ritz-Carlton hotel lounge, but rather than hammer away like a rock idiot, he dazzled guests with exquisite jazz standards. He also allegedly wandered into a small restaurant wielding a bottle of wine, stuck his fingers in the water glasses of a young couple, and flicked water on them to give his blessing. But if Eddie was behaving erratically, the public was forgiving. "When you're Eddie Van Halen and you've weathered a hip replacement, overcome tongue cancer, and watched your marriage dissolve after 20 years, you deserve the ovation," wrote Melissa Ruggieri of the *Richmond Times-Dispatch.*

Eddie missed his former partner in crime by a few days—on

Independence Day 2004, David Lee Roth performed "California Girls" and "Jump" during a nationally televised appearance with the Boston Pops. Dressing his age in an open-necked linen shirt and vest, he could still summon a couple of high kicks and 360-degree twirls for the all-American congregation of flag-waving picnickers.

At Van Halen's Meadowlands appearance outside New York City, Eddie played a blazing solo, then appeared to start to cry. He sat down to play "316"—the song named after his son's birthday—and was immediately joined onstage by thirteen-year-old Wolfgang, ready to perform the song as a duet.

An exceptionally proud dad, Eddie gushed about Wolfie at every opportunity. Speaking openly about his emotions as a father, he echoed Jan Van Halen when he proclaimed he knew no better feeling than having his son follow in his footsteps. Eddie also touted the boy's talents as a guitarist, bassist, and drummer in superlative terms. "When his balls drop, he's my new lead singer," he had joked in late 2003.

For Christmas in 2003, Eddie gave Wolfie one of his three original Frankenstrats, last used on the *1984* tour. The guitar had been in its case for nearly twenty years. Eddie installed one of his patented D-Tuna mechanisms, but didn't even change the funky old strings. "It's fun showing people I can play guitar," Wolfgang told *Rolling Stone*, "even though I'm better on drums. I'm gonna keep practicing. Someone's got to carry on the family name."

"It's a bummer that my dad never got to see him," Eddie later told *Guitar World*, speaking of his son, "but for all I know he may be my dad."

During the 2004 tour, Van Halen played for as many as twelve thousand people per night in Los Angeles, Chicago, and New York City—the Mandalay Bay Center in Las Vegas sold out in half an hour. Yet some dates in the Dakotas and Kentucky were more like four thousand, and not even half full. Overall in 2004 Van Halen sold 716,650 tickets, according to *Pollstar*, grossing $54.3 million. They reported merchandise revenue at ten dollars per person. On the backs of over half a million CDs sold in 2004, the band went over the margin and added six additional multiplatinum awards to their walls. Still, the bar had been set very high, with guarantees as high as $1 million at some shows. *Rolling Stone* thought the band had missed its mark, and would have to "settle for less" with its next tour. Then again, the magazine had ranked Eddie the number 70 greatest guitarist of all time in August 2003, only two spots above Joni Mitchell—their metrics were hardly more than idle chatter.

The 2004 tour operated on thin high-stakes margins, however, and one cancellation led to a $2 million lawsuit. In April, the Baltimore Orioles offered the band a cool $1 million to play at their outdoor Camden Yards baseball field, which Van Halen rejected. The proposed date was too difficult to route into the existing schedule, plus Van Halen's show was geared toward indoor arena venues. The Orioles countered in June with a generous $1.5 million plus 80 percent of merchandise sales, which the band accepted. A few weeks later, however, the Orioles organization cooled on the deal, and in late July reneged on the offer. Incensed, Van Halen pursued the lawsuit, asking for damages to the tune of $2 million. They were no longer in the position to be building relationships—they were collecting on their prestige and legend and did not like being jerked around.

≈≈≈≈≋≋≈≈≈≈

Eddie's slurring during some interviews could be written off after his tongue operation, but it was apparent that a lot of nights he was plainly drunk onstage. "I hate to talk smack about anyone in the band or whatever," Michael Anthony said reluctantly during a radio interview, "but Eddie's still doing a bit of drinking and everything. There were nights where it was kind of like a roller coaster, up or down. I would have liked to see him totally clean up if we were going to take this further, because gosh, we could have gone all around the world with it."

"He was pretty out of it the whole tour," Sammy Hagar told Melodic Rock.com. "There were nights when I didn't even know what song he was playing. Nobody else did either. We just stayed on the same song while he stumbled around the neck of the guitar. I think Eddie is as innovative as Jimi or anyone else. Together we wrote some of the greatest songs in rock history. With Dave they wrote some of the greatest songs in rock history. I would sooner leave it alone and say let this thing go down as one of the greatest things. I don't want to keep going out there and butchering it."

Separate dressing rooms and limos soon became separate jets. Mike Anthony bemoaned the lack of camaraderie. By the end of the tour, Sammy was no longer appearing for soundchecks. One of the few bands bigger than Van Halen, their former opening act Metallica, released a soul-searching documentary during the 2004 tour. Titled *Some Kind of Monster*, the all-access film covered the painful spats, alcoholism, and opulent waste that brought a six-year delay between studio albums and nearly broke up the band. Sammy Hagar didn't think that confessional approach would work for Van Halen. "We already went through the misery once," he told *USA Today*. "Why relive a horrible experience?"

Hagar had learned lots of new tricks since his tenure in Van Halen, and his approach to fan interaction rankled others in the band. Wielding a microphone in one hand and a pen in the other, he signed all the shirts and posters thrown onstage—a crowd-pleasing turn that distracted the others. The clashes ultimately became evident offstage. Hagar appeared on KSHE in St. Louis with seventeen shows left. "I like my band better, I'm sorry," he said. "I think the Van Halen thing is great, it was really my idea. I made the initial call, and I'm glad I did. It could have been better than it was. I think it was past its trip—it should have happened a few years ago. God help us if we waited any longer!"

Before 4,300 fans in Tucson, Arizona, on November 19, the final show of the tour, Eddie smashed two Peavey Wolfgang guitars and so ended his thirteen-year affiliation with the manufacturer. During the past decade, the Peavey 5150 amps had become extremely popular with heavier forms of music, used by grungesters Alice in Chains, Swedish death metal band Arch Enemy, and Ozzfest mascara metalcore lads

Atreyu. Eddie himself had been given over two hundred EVH Wolfgang guitars. Speculation at the Peavey shop centered on whether Eddie was miffed at sharing their attention with guitar guru Joe Satriani, who had joined forces with them for an amplifier.

After the breakup, Eddie kept the rights to his Wolfgang guitar, while Peavey restyled the 5150 amplifier as the Peavey 6505, retaining the same electronics and design. Interestingly to guitarists, one EVH Wolfgang collector went public with photos and descriptions of two versions of an EVH Wolfgang hollow-body prototype made by Peavey during the 1990s. He claimed the instruments had never been shown to Eddie, for fear the increasingly temperamental guitarist would fly off the hook at the sight of a mellow version of his trademark riffing monster.

The same night that he smashed his guitars, Eddie almost belted Sammy. "We almost got into it after the last show," Hagar told *Billboard*. "They just pulled him one way, and me the other. We didn't even say goodbye to each other. It was a horrible way to end the whole thing."

While the media questioned Eddie's stability, actual working musicians put a lot of amplifier royalties into his pocket for his contributions to the Peavey 5150 amp. Young guitarists didn't buy the equipment simply for Eddie's name, either—bands like In Flames were buying 5150s for their juicy distortion and multiple gain stages, not just because the guy smiling in the "Right Now" video designed them.

Not leapfrogging to a new guitar endorsement just yet, Eddie tapped the nostalgia market with a pricey EVH Art Series reproduction series from one of his original suppliers, Charvel. Three varieties of striped guitars aping Eddie's glorified Frankenstrats were available for a few thousand dollars apiece, summoning the sound and feel of a San Dimas 1975 guitar if not the do-it-yourself attitude.

Chasing the momentum of the 2004 tour, as late as October Alex was still saying that Van Halen planned to record a new album with Hagar.

By the end of the year, however, feelings had soured. Sammy claimed that Eddie was working too slowly, unable to finish his solos. "I don't get along with Eddie anymore, and that's all there is to it," he said. "I don't know what his problem is, but he's miserable and he likes to make everyone around him miserable."

Disappointed, Hagar moved his family to Cabo San Lucas, put his daughters in school, and spent time cooking, gardening, and managing his Cabo Wabo Cantina, tequila empire, and solo career. Whatever battering Hagar took, like his boxer father he did not allow himself to be knocked down. He was well practiced at making contentedness look convincing. "Whatever makes you happy," Hagar advised, "you need to get more of that in your life"—and none of those things had the last name Van Halen.

Whatever momentum Van Halen summoned was sapped—which was sad for many reasons, not least because when Eddie's energy was bottled up in this band, he could be explosive. Left free to wander, he hadn't revealed as much music to the public in years. Privately, he wasn't doing so well. He had long ago given up tall cans of Schlitz Malt Liquor for a full-bodied syrupy red wine called Smoking Loon, a far more potent and absorbing vice.

He was reportedly redesigning the Wolfgang guitar and his signature amps for the following year's NAMM show. "Very few people keep up with my ass," he told Iowa radio station KCQQ during a 4 A.M. interview. "I'm always doing something. People think I take on too much, but no I don't. But when someone tells me they can do something, I expect them to pull through sometimes. I am probably the simplest guy you'll ever meet."

The next Saturday night, December 8, 2004—the anniversary of John Lennon's killing—heavy metal guitarist "Dimebag" Darrell Abbott was shot dead onstage in Ohio by a deranged ex-marine. It was a horrible moment for anyone attached to the electric guitar in any capacity. Dimebag had been a member of Pantera for over twenty years with his brother Vinnie Paul, and had racked up an impressive portfolio of gold and platinum albums while continually speaking his adulation of Eddie

Van Halen. During the lean era of the 1990s, Pantera kept stadiums filled with faithful hard rock fans eager for guitar solos.

In their post-Pantera thrash band Damageplan, Dimebag and Vinnie Paul had lobbied hard for a support slot on Van Halen's 2004 reunion tour, stating they had already toured with reunited Judas Priest, Kiss, and Black Sabbath lineups—Van Halen would complete their four main heavy metal childhood heroes. The Abbott brothers had just visited backstage with Van Halen in Wichita, Kansas, on November 6.

Eddie appeared at Dimebag's memorial service. He held his cell phone to the mic and played a voice mail Dimebag had left him days earlier. "Thank you so much, man for the most awesome, uplifting, euphoric, spiritual rock and roll extravaganza ever," Dimebag had said.

Then came an awkward several minutes when a drunk Eddie repeatedly interrupted the farewell from Zakk Wylde, guitarist in Ozzy Osbourne's band and one of Dimebag's closest friends. "I don't know what the hell happened to Ed," Wylde told *Revolver*. "He hasn't just gone off the deep end, he's living in Atlantis! It was like he thought the whole thing was about him." But in a lasting sign of deep respect, Eddie buried the black-and-yellow tape-striped guitar pictured on the back cover of *Van Halen II* with the slain guitarist.

Hopefully Eddie's desire to play guitar wasn't also buried. During 2005, he seemed to slip deeper into a funk. At least at his son's junior high graduation in June 2005, he played a song with Wolfgang's band Die Sheise—German for "the Shit." "I've recorded so many songs with Wolfgang already," Eddie said. "I've got hundreds of songs I haven't released. I'm playing with Wolfgang every day."

Then, after having beaten back his own disease a few years earlier, Eddie suffered the loss of his mother, Eugenia Van Halen, at age ninety in the summer of 2005. He was reaching an all-time low. In another sad chapter to the golden boy's downfall, Valerie officially filed for divorce on Tuesday, December 6, 2005, citing irreconcilable differences.

While Sammy still occasionally spoke with the Van Halen brothers, Michael Anthony had not heard from them since the 2004 tour ended. "Mike's a buddy," said Alex. "He's typical suburbia. He's a very easygoing guy who's got lots of friends from many walks of life. He's got a lot of heart and is a stocky little guy." But apparently Eddie did not share his brother's enthusiasm.

One of Eddie's closest friends since 1980 was Steve Lukather, a versatile session player with over five hundred albums to his credit ranging from Alice Cooper to Aretha Franklin. Lukather played bass and rhythm guitar on Michael Jackson's "Beat It," and more recently sang recorded background vocals on *F.U.C.K.*, *Balance*, and the new songs on *The Best of Both Worlds*. "He is fine," Lukather said about Eddie. "He went through a really rough spot. Let's face it—it is tough on a cat. There is still a lot of good music left in Ed. You just have to let him go through what he is going through. He is just a fucking man who is trying to raise his son and get his health and his mind right. Give the guy a fucking break."

ALL THE RIGHT REASONS

When the going got tough, the tough got weird. In June 2005, Paul Anka recorded a version of "Jump" with an eighteen-piece orchestra that accomplished what Roth had been trying to nail for years. With veteran lounge-lizard swagger, Anka confidently strolled down Roth's velvet carpet, reclaiming the terrain with booming drums, piercing horn stabs, bubbly piano, and vocal ad-libs before the solo break. Anka sounded like Big Daddy come down from entertainment heaven to tell Roth to "roll with the punches." Around the same time, a novelty band called Lounge Against the Machine took a decent swipe at "Hot for Teacher."

Following an aborted attempt to develop a new adult-oriented show in Las Vegas, Roth unexpectedly resurfaced far from the velvet curtains. With little fanfare, he had become a fifty-year-old emergency medical technician, and in late 2004 started riding ambulances in poor neighborhoods in New York City. He went on over two hundred calls just to be certified as a paramedic so he could volunteer one weekend a month. "I was working in neighborhoods that were almost exclusively black and Spanish-speaking," he told the *Los Angeles*

Times. "Only about twice out of 200 clients was I recognized. I was working in Brooklyn, down in Coney Island. . . . I've been in more project apartments than Jay-Z and Diddy combined."

When the EMT card was in his pocket, he went to Fort Sam Houston in Texas for training at the site where U.S. Army medics are schooled. Roth certainly wasn't performing public service for the money—proceeds every time "Jump" was played in some sports arena kept his yacht washed and waxed. Diamond Dave was saving lives and pursuing the family business, following his father and two uncles the doctors, and his grandfather the surgeon—a line of work almost as prone to God complex as rock star.

After high school, Roth had worked as a hospital night orderly for two years, prepping and cleaning up after surgeries. "I was with the guy before they put him to sleep," he told *Rolling Stone* in 1985, "and the last one he saw before he went out, and some of them never woke up again. It had a very striking effect on me. It's very difficult to disassociate yourself from it once you've left. So I'm not as affected by pain and death and misery as I was before I worked there."

Less altruistically, Roth was simultaneously threatening to revive his movie-star dreams on the basis of a slew of VH1 commentator appearances that rekindled his love of being on camera. He also played himself as a poker-playing acquaintance of the Jersey mafia in a 2004 episode of *The Sopranos*. Riffing on accountants and income tax, he delivered his line deadpan: "I used to be able to write off condoms."

Then at the beginning of 2006, David Lee Roth showed up large on billboards and the sides of public buses across New York City. Filling the silence left by the departure to satellite radio of his longtime friend Howard Stern, he began a rollicking experiment in morning talk radio that listeners found either refreshingly urbane and unpredictable or just plain annoying. Stern had already predicted the hiring back in July 2005, hoaxing his listeners for the first hour of his show with an arrogant Roth imitator who bebopped and shoobedooed over Van Halen loops.

Once installed for real, Roth seemed truly appreciative of his new platform. His main experience focusing his boundless energy and free-

flowing patter behind the mic was the short-lived Internet radio experiment five years earlier RothRadio.com. His new show seemed to have
no producers, as it booked very few guests and left the singer to extem-
poraneously improvise for hours each morning.

While lashing out against the insular culture of "celebutards," he
welcomed Latin listeners and soldiers tuning in via Internet, rocking the
limits of both his format and his New York–based market. Though his
loosely organized rants seemed ill-suited for high-powered morning
drive-time radio, a more nuanced and interesting view of the world's
most eligible and aging himbo emerged. He lectured audiences on the
concept of *balance*, how he would alternate orgiastic backstage excesses
with humility exercises like scrubbing a motel room clean with a tooth-
brush. He promoted deep album tracks by long-lost funk-rock bands
like Mother's Finest, and his love of his own life showed.

His envy appeared, though, whenever he talked about modern rock.
He tore apart popular bands like Green Day and Linkin Park, bashing
their safe choices and lack of sophistication. Of course, he couldn't help
banging the pulpit on the subject of Van Halen. Roth had been ridiculed
into silence during the 1990s, but now he could monopolize the conversation. When the radio show was inevitably canceled on April 21,
2006, he came out smiling. "At the end of the day, I sing for my dinner, and I kept my day job," he told Fox News.

After a silent period of a few weeks, Roth's mouth was back on the
job. Capitalizing on the profile boost of four months of mostly negative
press about his radio show, he immediately booked a summer tour,
appeared on *Strummin' with the Devil*, an album of Van Halen songs
performed by a fast-picking bluegrass band, and sashayed into the
talk-show circuit to parade his happy trails.

Playing with a country band, Roth found his Indiana roots and his
relevance to the new conservative, rule-bound America. He swore by his
cornfield beginnings as fiercely as he had once played his connection to
footloose Uncle Manny and bohemian New York. He appeared onstage
in a white fedora and a striped stock trader's shirt, still kicking over his
head in time to "Hot for Teacher." The attention-stealing, egomaniac

frontman was carrying on with the show long after the spotlight banged off—just another human lump with an oversized need to be loved.

The crowd still shouted for Van Halen. Shouted, shouted, shouted. Of course, the question hovered—whether Roth would rejoin his first love. "Paging Eddie Van Winkle," he quipped on Fox News. "I think he's the only one resistant now. I think it's inevitable. That material is as familiar as 'My Country' Tis of Thee.' How hard is it to sing 'Dance the Night Away'? To avert that would be a sin."

—————

Even if they were fighting on different fronts, David Lee Roth and Sammy Hagar had both survived the Van Halen wars. Sammy and the Waboritas were going strong into 2005, playing long nightly sets to crowds of thousands. Hagar's straightforward act had expanded into a farcical reenactment of spring break in Cancun, complete with sandpit volleyball, bikini-clad waitresses dispensing tequila and temporary tattoos, and a donkey wearing a sombrero. Meanwhile, the Cabo Wabo brand remained literally center stage, painted on a giant hanging backdrop—and permanently tattooed on Sammy's left bicep.

"Hagar's success isn't because he's a great singer, a great guitarist, or a great songwriter," said David Lauser, a friend of Sammy's since high school. "He's in touch with his heart, and people will pick up on that. I guess that's what makes you a great artist."

Advertising Age reported that Cabo Wabo was on track to ship over 110,000 cases in 2004, putting the super-premium tequila well behind Patrón but still in the top five high-end brands. Perhaps anticipating the future of the concert business, Sammy announced he was making enough money from tequila sales and merchandise that he hoped to be able to tour for free. "It's a year or two early from being able to do it for free, assuming the company keeps growing the way it is," he said.

When he appeared on Craig Ferguson's late-night talk show just days after Roth, he fidgeted through questions about Van Halen, pretending to walk off the set after being asked about another reunion. "I would love to if everything could be cool," Sammy told Ferguson, "but it just ain't happening anymore. It's like a marriage that's gone bad. I'm not going to go back and date my ex-girlfriend." Badgered by Ferguson about whether Eddie might be crazy, Hagar reluctantly said, "Listen, I'm crazy, too, but I'm user-friendly."

Since early 2002, Sammy and Michael Anthony had been working on a semi-supergroup called Planet US, writing music Hagar described as a blend of Led Zeppelin and Tool. Joining half of Van Halen would be Journey guitarist Neal Schon and Journey drummer Deen Castronovo. Former Guns N' Roses guitarist Slash initially agreed to play with the group but never made a rehearsal.

Van Halen's 2004 tour had scotched the Planet US project, but Sammy and Mike still wanted to get a band going. They retooled their party band Los Tres Gusanos to include not just Waboritas drummer David Lauser but also Waboritas guitarist Vic Johnson. Billed as the Other Half, the quartet played an hour of Van Halen songs and resurrected Mike's epic bass solo. "Van Halen is us four with the brothers," Mike said, "but if nothing's happening with the band, the fans want to hear it, and we want to go out and play it. I'm not going to sit around and do nothing."

Angry that the pair would dare play without him, Eddie Van Halen offhandedly but cruelly slammed the Other Half on *The Howard Stern Show*. "They're both a little chubby, I think they're both a little wider than they are tall. They're out there selling hot sauce and tequila, playing all my music. That don't bother me, just makes them a cover band."

Surprisingly, Eddie appeared on Howard Stern's show in 2006 to say he was "open to anything," including touring with "Diamond" David Lee Roth—though he rapped him as "Cubic Zirconium." Eddie called Roth a loose cannon, but said he could deal with loose cannons—and went on to act like one himself, insulting the hell out of Michael Anthony and Sammy Hagar, calling the former "Sauce Sobolewski" and the latter a "little red worm."

Eddie claimed to be pissed off at Mike's forays outside Van Halen, playing bass with Hagar and with Ohio guitar ace Neil Zaza. In any case, like Jan Van Halen gigging with his high school sons, Eddie turned to a sideman he could trust implicitly and biologically. "I'm pretty much open to anything, but what's going to happen is there's a new Van Halen member involved, and that's my son," Eddie said. "My son is in, and 'Sauce' Sobolewski can do whatever the hell he wants. The name Van Halen is going to go on way after I'm gone, because this kid is just a natural."

In June 2006, Sammy projected that Eddie would need "an overhaul" before a Van Halen regrouping of any kind was possible. Although something of a gourmand, he also told a reporter he ate in greasy-spoon diners that didn't demand that he change his clothes.

"If I was ever a genius at anything," he told the *San Francisco Chronicle*, "I found everything I like to do and where I want to live and I rolled it all together. I got a business. I can play music at my business. I love tequila and that whole lifestyle, the Mexican food. I've got a Mexican restaurant. I have the tequila that goes with it. I have the whole lifestyle rolled into one."

After sponsoring a successful booze cruise to Mexico for his diehard admirers, Hagar was last spotted signing bottles of Cabo Wabo at a Costco—happy as he could be, a true human phenomenon. His gusto was rewarded in June 2007, when Italian liquor titan Campari paid $80 million for an 80 percent stake in the Cabo Wabo Tequila company.

At the end of 2005, Alex Van Halen and his third wife, Stine, were named Neighborhood Emergency Assistance Team members in their community of Hidden Hills, California, and awarded backpacks and hardhats to use in case of earthquakes or other emergencies. The way things were going with Van Halen, they might need to duck and cover sooner than they thought.

Speculation about Van Halen's plans spiked in 2005 with word the band would be seeking a new lead singer on the CBS reality show *Rock Star*. INXS had successfully humiliated themselves during the show's first season, and now rumors that Van Halen was next in line surfaced from MTV.com and America Online. Van Halen's publicist didn't help matters with the statement, "I'm not denying it. I'm not going to answer any questions about it." On his radio show, Roth claimed he had been handed an open-call audition sheet from producers. After six months in the news, a "vehement denial" from the band and CBS put the rumors to rest.

Eddie Van Halen's presence was needed, but when he appeared the reaction was not entirely a good one. His weary appearance at Elton John's March 2006 Oscar party underscored the urgency. Drained by divorce, surgeries, and drink, thirty years of eternal eruption had left Eddie a worn, gray-haired fifty-year-old man. Once the envy of millions, he looked like the walking wounded. Heartless Internet wags dubbed him "Smeagol Van Halen," an unflattering comparison to Gollum from *Lord of the Rings*. Even in his Dutch hometown of Nijmegen, Eddie only placed seventeenth in a newspaper popularity contest ranking the "Greatest Nijmegeners." You couldn't help but hope that all he needed was a return to the precious power of Van Halen.

The Van Halen brothers kept a jealous eye on all their exes, especially Roth. Weeks after his cornpone bluegrass outing, Eddie and Alex ambled out of the garage to the Home Depot Center in Carson, California, where they joined country star and frequent Hagar sidekick Kenny Chesney in loose renditions of "Jump" and "You Really Got Me." Mechanical hip be damned, Eddie ran through his old gymnast routines like a wounded bird testing its wings and flying once again.

Before long, a few of his much-touted 5150 projects finally saw the light of day. He released music videos for two new songs, "Rise" and "Catherine," written for Goth-porn movies by director Michael Ninn. Embracing the sex movies, Eddie invested money into their production and allowed scenes and a couple of music videos to be filmed at his home. In the fall of 2006 he hosted a launch party for the flicks at his house, now a bachelor pad, playing a slew of early Van Halen songs on a backyard stage.

The "Catherine" video, directed by Michael Ninn, was an expression of aimless sadness, capturing Eddie alone in 5150 in the darkness, cigarettes in his headstock, shirtless and sweating heavily while he cried out a sustained guitar solo over piano, strings, and drums. Cut-in shots showed him playing the other instruments as well. At the close of the song, he threw down his guitar on the hardwood floor and gulped from a bottle of red wine. The poignant isolation of the three-minute film seemed the clearest picture of what Eddie had been doing since 1999.

He was rootlessly looking for an outlet but was fenced in by unrealistic expectations that ruled his actions. The optimistic story that began on a boat from Holland had all but turned into *Citizen Kane*, with Eddie losing his mind like Orson Welles at his Xanadu estate. Instead of a glass snow globe labeled Rosebud, Eddie dropped his red guitar, and his malfunctioning path was just as enigmatic as Charles Foster Kane's in the movie. He had turned a few guilders and a piano into limitless riches and adulation, and had built his American dream house at 5150, yet King Edward had become a prisoner in his castle—a cautionary tale instead of a shining inspiration.

VAN HALEN IV

Pressing Van Halen back into service at this dark hour, the Rock and Roll Hall of Fame came calling a few days before Halloween 2006, nominating the band along with eight other acts for the following year's five available slots. If nothing else, winning the vote would jolt the flatlining band into appearing publicly.

Suddenly, in November 2006, Van Halen's apparent new spokeswoman—a porn publicist who had become Eddie's girlfriend—announced that Van Halen were rehearsing for a summer 2007 tour. Speculation ran rampant about who would sing, alongside surprise over confirmation that Michael Anthony had been canned and replaced with fifteen-year-old Wolfgang Van Halen.

At first, the old dance partners Eddie and Roth moved awkwardly. "I'm telling Dave, 'Get your ass up here and sing, bitch! Come on!'" Eddie told *Guitar World*. "The ball is in Dave's court."

Roth let the rumors simmer. He continued to serve his fellow man as a paramedic, riding an ambulance on New Year's Eve 2006 instead of hosting a TV party as he would have done twenty years ago.

He compared the Van Halen soap opera to a NASCAR race that spectators watch just to see the crashes. Sammy Hagar was less circumspect. "Dave and Ed working together? I don't see it in a million years," he told the *Cleveland Plain-Dealer*.

In fact, Roth had rehearsed with Eddie, Wolfgang, and Uncle Al during December. Wolfgang had apparently been the unifying force, directing his older bandmates with cues from a Van Halen–loaded iPod. "The chemistry is combustible," Roth told *Rolling Stone*. "There's an explosive sound there that . . . unless you were there, which most folks weren't, then you may have forgotten."

The road to hitting the highway in a tour bus was still bumpy. Regardless of the latest reconciliation with the considerably wiser Roth, Eddie let it be known that he would not let the band's former dictator push him around. "We're not holding out for anyone, and we're not demanding anyone," he told *Rolling Stone*. "We're not putting our eggs in any one basket. There's not just one person on this planet that can sing."

The Rock and Roll Hall of Fame pressed a decision, however, as Van Halen were chosen for honors in 2007 along with R.E.M., Patti Smith, the Ronettes, and Grandmaster Flash and the Furious Five. From their separate outposts, the band members past and present issued low-key statements of acceptance. "That music is a part of American culture," Roth commented, "beyond just a stack of tunes."

The Hall of Fame simplified matters somewhat by leaving Gary Cherone off the invite. "Nothing against Gary, but I would've voted against getting him in," Hagar told MTV.com. "He was really just a moment in Van Halen. There was questions about me getting in, because I've only been in the band 21 years!"

Ever gracious, Cherone congratulated the five inductees on the honor, downplaying his exclusion gracefully. "To answer the few fans who are wondering whether I should or shouldn't be included—while, yes, I was a small part of their history, I was certainly not a part of their legend, and that is what we, the fans, are celebrating."

For the first time in years, Van Halen seemed to be getting something done. At the January 2007 NAMM convention, Eddie announced a milestone partnership between his own EVH guitars and industry granddaddy Fender, commencing with a top-line run of three hundred precise replicas of his red-and-white-striped Frankenstrat. Obsessively crafted by builder Chip Ellis, complete with cigarette burns, bicycle reflectors, and nonfunctioning front pick-up, the copy of the axe that Eddie built for under $300 in 1976 was priced in 2007 at upward of $25,000. Announcing the partnership and praising the replica guitar as fooling even himself, Eddie seemed distracted and awkward before the adoring crowd. He plugged in and proved he could still play guitar if it ever again became necessary.

As rumors reached a shrill pitch, on February 2, Van Halen "officially" announced a summer tour—only to run adrift two weeks later. Despite a breaking announcement on Billboard.com, a reunion newsflash on the Drudge Report, and a "99% likely" forecast by the *Las Vegas Review-Journal*, the latest Roth adventure was soon postponed. An unnamed executive from concert promoter Live Nation told the *Los Angeles Times* that Van Halen's 2007 tour had "shut down."

"We have fragile politics in Van Halen," Roth said almost sadly. "Please accept that as a partial answer."

All eyes turned to the Rock and Roll Hall of Fame induction ceremony, just a few weeks away at the Waldorf-Astoria Hotel in New York City. If the reunion/renewal lineup of Van Halen with Wolfgang and Roth were in any shape to perform, they would surely unveil themselves that night.

The question hung heavy: What form of Van Halen would appear at the ceremony? Though a great opportunity, the event was fraught with hazards. Roth shunned Sammy's overtures toward singing a duet at the event, explaining that the two men played entirely different kinds of music. Meanwhile, the Van Halens reserved a table at the event, though manager Irving Azoff told Sammy they were not planning to attend. "We're not gonna know until that day arrives," Alex cryptically told *Rolling Stone*.

Eddie didn't sound very certain. "Alex and I have been doing this for so long that there aren't very many things that we haven't won," he added. "I remember the last award I accepted from Bill Maher, when he was doing *Politically Incorrect* [in 1996]. They wanted me to get up and make a speech, so I said 'Thank you.' But I told everyone from then on to wait until I'm eighty—stick everything in a box, and send it to me then."

Then four days before the Rock and Roll Hall of Fame was due to induct him, Eddie's ceaselessly upbeat assessment of the band's health was countered with a sobering admission of his ongoing alcohol addiction. Instead of touring or accepting any awards, he would be returning to rehab, possibly as a precondition of doing any business with mega-promoter Live Nation. "Some of the issues surrounding the 2007 Van Halen tour are within my ability to change and some are not. As far as my rehab is concerned, it is within my ability to change and change for the better. I want you to know that is exactly what I'm doing," Eddie wrote in a public letter.

Alex announced that he would not be attending the ceremony without Eddie, leaving the interesting entourage of David Lee Roth, Sammy Hagar, and deposed bassist Michael Anthony to accept the honor. Roth had repeatedly requested to perform at the induction ceremony, with or without the Van Halens. Though the organizers were set on having Velvet Revolver play Van Halen songs, they offered Roth the chance to sing "You Really Got Me." He insisted on an original Van Halen song, not the Kinks cover. Velvet Revolver, however, backed away from learning "Jump."

His conditions rebuffed, on the Friday before the ceremony Roth decided not to attend. "I don't make speeches for a living," Roth told the *Los Angeles Times*, "I sing for my supper." In its attempts to please the Van Halen brothers, both singers, and now Velvet Revolver, somehow the Hall of Fame had dishonored an honoree.

A weekend was a long time in Van Halen's lives, however. Nobody was sure what would happen at the Waldorf-Astoria ceremony come Monday, March 12. What soon transpired was every Van Halen fan's worst fear—the validation became a debacle that bordered on tragic.

First, Velvet Revolver—a celebrity rock project consisting of former

Stone Temple Pilots singer Scott Weiland fronting the remnants of Guns N' Roses—read a perfunctory statement listing a few career highlights, nothing surprising or exciting. The band's botched performance of "Ain't Talkin' 'Bout Love" proved they were probably the only hard rockers of their age to have never covered the song. The supposed balance—a version of Hagar-era "Runaround"—was much worse, a lackluster abomination consisting of Slash and company repeating a riff while Weiland yelled "round and round" over and over. At least one member of the black-tie audience noticed, objecting loudly as they cleared the stage: "That wasn't Van Halen!"

Cheered by their families, Sammy and Mike graciously thanked Dave and wished the Van Halen brothers the best. Sammy specifically thanked the Hall of Fame for including him. Mike recognized Gary Cherone for his contributions. Then they joined Paul Schaeffer and the house band for a squeaky, off-version of "Why Can't This Be Love?" that wasn't even saved by the horn section.

The entire event made Van Halen seem like a slipshod, overpartied footnote on rock history. It was inconceivable that Dave didn't suddenly appear with an acoustic guitar to sing "Ice Cream Man," or pop up with inductees Grandmaster Flash and the Furious Five for an impromptu mash-up of "Runnin' with the Devil." As Michael Anthony told the press afterward, "I was waiting for Roth to come busting through at some point during the speech." So were we all.

<hr>

In the end, everyone in Van Halen has taken a turn as villain. All the band members have bent the truth for convenience and used the media to stall the fans, mask their true intentions, forward their own plans, and polish one side of a controversy. The truth is more muddled by emotion, personal politics, and the haze of altered states than anyone can admit without upsetting whatever tender relationships remain, if any. The only shining side of the coin is that all the players involved have a decent track record for coming clean after enough time passes.

Thirty-five years after the Trojan Rubber Company rocked its first high school gym, the simple fact remains—Van Halen ain't over until David Lee Roth sings. His return to Van Halen remains a great unanswered question of rock music. Since stepping down from morning radio, he has remained in the public eye, a constant reminder that one of the great love stories of the hard rock era awaits its proper conclusion.

Roth never enjoyed a proper number 1 album with Van Halen, but the sales speak for themselves—twice the millions of albums were sold in the United States with him than with Hagar—though time and upgrades to CD from vinyl and cassette allow Roth a head start. An entire generation born after 1985 is already past the legal drinking age. Though they were not alive when Roth led the band, they still buy the music and the $100 vintage T-shirts on eBay. The legacy of vintage Van Halen survives on grainy Internet videos.

As much as his old bandmates resent his ballhog antics, they need to put the pieces together and reconnect the electricity before it's too late. A hundred million Van Halen fans still want to live happily ever after. As Roth already stressed when he made his early-nineties push for a reunion, "I want some fireworks! I want some color! There might be some conflict, but maybe that's what made great music."

The failure of the 1996 reunion has dissipated. In 1996, Van Halen were deluded. Now they have a chance to redeem their chips for real. They could take inspiration from Gary Cherone's midyear 2006 work with Extreme after ten years—start small, rehearse plenty, and play like you want to be remembered.

A brilliant diamond fell from Roth's mouth during a 1991 interview: "With Van Halen, you got all five sides of the coin, whereas most musicians intentionally flatten it into a one-dimensional image: easily palatable, instantly digested. We never did that in Van Halen. You would have elements of brooding and great celebration, often in the context of the same song, so that you could reinterpret infinitely what you were hearing."

Tired and twisted though Van Halen might be, nobody wants to see the band fail. The hope for a reunion is that after all these years, it is possible to go back to a happy summer day in 1977, 1982, or 1984, one of those nights when the perfect swagger came along as if by accident. Sammy Hagar couldn't come between a love this strong—as he well admits. This is Richard Burton and Elizabeth Taylor love, Luke and Laura love, Tommy Lee and Pam Anderson love, meant to attract and repel again and again.

Most frustrating of all, almost everyone involved is currently performing classic Van Halen material. Roth's recent tours have provided almost exclusively Van Halen-centric playlists, and he has strained his voice mightily to deliver his point. He tells long, sappy stories about how the songs were written. He flubs the words. But for a reunion, he can inject whatever steroids into his neck that Tour de France cyclists allegedly use to scale the highest mountains. He *must*.

At exactly the same time, Michael Anthony has toured extensively with Sammy as the Other Half, playing Van Halen songs plus his incomparable extended bass solo. Even Eddie conceded to the demand for Van Halen, when he hosted a late September 2006 bash at his house and got onstage with ex–Mötley Crüe singer John Corabi to play classic Van Halen hits like "Panama" and "Ain't Talkin' 'Bout Love."

Now that the seal has been cracked on the possibility of a new tour with Roth, the ouster of Michael Anthony remains toubling, especially for his replacement, Wolfgang Van Halen. The enormous pressure on Wolfgang if that comes to pass should probably prompt a child services investigation—how can a teenager be expected to patch up the damage done by decades of lawyers, lead singer disease, and unlawful behavior? Yes, there's a certain amount of logic to Eddie's declaration. Jan van Halen left Holland and sacrificed to found a musical dynasty. If Eddie never makes another record—and he already hasn't in ten years— then he passes his son the torch. But doing this now, he's throwing his only son down an aching chasm. Interviewed by *People* magazine, Wolfgang has already expressed his doubts.

First things first—this concept of a Van Halen dynasty lasting centuries can only be built on a refreshed memory of what made the band great in the first place. Sure, all this talk of a reunion is unfair—like asking any forty-something to run a basketball play like he did in high school, clear every board of Pac-Man on one quarter, or jump a BMX bike over the canyon on a plywood ramp. But Van Halen doesn't need to point the way back to what they were as much as point the way forward.

The fact is, Van Halen have never suffered irreparable tragedy like so many of their peers. No death in the band like the Rolling Stones, the Who, Metallica, Nirvana, or Ozzy Osbourne. No murdered members like the Beatles or Pantera. So many supporting characters in the Van Halen saga have already passed away—like George Harrison, who jammed with Eddie in the early 1990s, Top Jimmy of the Rhythm Pigs, and manager Ed Leffler. The Beatles reunion never happened, and now it never will. Van Halen should. "We are in this for life—if I hit eighty, I'll still be making music, blazing on," Eddie promised after Roth first left the band.

At the end of the day—a time that is fast approaching, like it or not—the question never goes away, because in the minds of many, the original members of Van Halen are still together. The louder Eddie or Alex protests, the more the fans nod knowingly, insisting that they still love Roth. The first love is always the strongest. The tragedy of Van Halen will be if they wither away without a good-bye kiss—and it's a slow-burning tragedy already building over the last decade.

"What we sell is that we make all the guys feel young and invincible, and all the girls feel young and desirable," Roth recently reminded the *Los Angeles Times*.

Maybe the future of our civilization doesn't depend on Van Halen reuniting—maybe it does—but "Happy Trails" doesn't sound right unless David Lee Roth, Eddie Van Halen, Michael Anthony, and Alex Van Halen sing it together. There's still a lot of Van Halen left in the rest of us, and we need Van Halen to come along with the spark of life and bring it out. At the end of the story, everybody still wants some more.

BONUS TRACK A

EDDIE VAN HALEN
EXTENDED DISCOGRAPHY

Nicolette Larson, *Nicolette* (Warner Bros., 1978): guitar solo on "Can't Get Away from You"

Dweezil Zappa, "My Mother Is a Space Cadet"/"Crunchy Water": 12-inch single (Barking Pumpkin, 1982): co-producer with Donn Landee, guitar intro

Michael Jackson, *Thriller* (Epic, 1982): guitar solo on "Beat It"

Brian May & Friends, *Starfleet Project* (EMI, 1983): guitar

Tim Bogert, *Master's Brew* (Accord, 1983): guitar, as "A. Havlenen"

Original soundtrack (OST), *The Wild Life* (MCA, 1984): composer, music on "Donut City"

Sammy Hagar, *I Never Said Goodbye* (Geffen, 1987): bass, vocals, co-producer

OST, *Over the Top* (CBS, 1987): guitar, bass, producer on "Winner Takes It All"

Private Life, *Shadows* (Warner Bros., 1988): co-producer

Private Life, *Private Life* (Warner Bros., 1990): co-producer

Thomas Dolby, *Astronauts & Heretics* (Giant, 1992): guitar

Sammy Hagar, *Unboxed* (Geffen, 1994): producer on "High Hopes" and "Buying My Way into Heaven"

Black Sabbath, *Cross Purposes* (IRS, 1994): uncredited coauthor of "Evil Eye"

Rich Wyman, *Fatherless Child* (Apricot, 1996): co-producer, guitar and bass on four songs

OST, *Twister* (Warner Sunset, 1996): guitar on "Respect the Wind."

Various, *Tribute to Jeff: David Garfield and Friends Play Tribute to Jeff Porcaro* (Zebra Records, 1997): guitar, vocals

Steve Lukather, *Lukather* (Sony International, 1998): songwriter, bass on "Twist the Knife"

OST, *The Legend of 1900* (Sony Classical, 1999): guitar on "Lost Boys Calling"

Steve Lukather & Friends, *Santamental* (2002): guitar on "Joy to the World," "Greensleeves," and "Carol of the Bells"

Sacred Sin DVD (NinnWorx, 2006): videos for Eddie's solo songs, "Rise" and "Catherine"

BONUS TRACK B

HOLY GRAILS: UNRELEASED VAN HALEN RARITIES

Alex Van Halen told Australia's *Undercover News* in 2004 that Van Halen has virtually no finished unreleased material. "There may be two or three songs that were partially completed, but if those songs were really worthwhile we would have released them back when they were written."

For that to be true, you have to take "finished" to mean packaged with artwork and UPC code, practically sitting on store shelves. Van Halen has always been prolific, and they are sitting on a mother lode of unreleased recordings that would put Tupac Shakur to shame. Forget about *Best of Michael Anthony's Bass Solos, Vol. I*—here's a small selection of the bounty that will keep rock archivists busy for the next hundred years:

Live tapes and rehearsals by the "Covers Band from Pasadena," 1974–1976 Plenty of soundboard and audience recordings remain—why should bootleggers have all the fun? We've all heard Van Halen play the Kinks, now let's have their versions of Black Sabbath, Led Zeppelin, and KC & the Sunshine Band.

The Gene Simmons demos, 1976 Not the first Van Halen tape, this ten-song demo presents the first professional picture of "Woman in Love," "Fools," and "Runnin' with the Devil." This ten-song demo features early versions of "Runnin' with the Devil" and "House of Pain," not to mention some unreleased live standards like "Woman in Love" and "Big Trouble."

The Ted Templeman demos, 1977   When the band first met its long-term producer Ted Templeman, he immediately snared two dozen or more well-honed songs from Van Halen's live set. Most of the tracks surfaced on *Van Halen*, *II*, and *Women and Children First*, but "We Die Bold" and "Young and Wild" are time capsules from the Sunset Strip days.

Oakland, California, June 1981   The three Oakland shows on the *Fair Warning* tour were supposedly filmed by Warner Bros. Only a couple songs have ever surfaced, notably the "Unchained" live video.

US Festival '83, May 29, 1983   Van Halen were paid $1.5 million not just to play the US Fest but also to mix and edit a radio broadcast and TV special.

Castle Donington, August 1984   A full hour of fine-tuned Van Halen captured before a frantic British crowd just days before Roth's final performance.

The original "1984"   The intro to *1984* was cut from thirty minutes of synthesizer swishing sounds concocted by Eddie at his brand-new studio, 5150. This is probably just a fraction of what Eddie recorded while Moog-merized in his studio exploring the possibilities of electronic music.

Singer tests   Eddie likes to use tape, so it's a fair bet that the record button was pressed when Van Halen tried out singers like Sass Jordan and Mitch Malloy—especially since they've said so.

Dallas, Dececember 4, 1991   Probably the grittiest Sammy-era show ever recorded, this makeup date performed at midday on the streets of Dallas by a grungy, stubble-faced band was filmed.

Eddie's jam tapes   Sammy mentions hundreds of cassettes kicking around 5150, ranging from bare electric guitar to full songs recorded with Alex and Eddie.

Molson Ampitheatre, Toronto, August 1995   The band went to pains to record this stop on the *Balance* tour, but months later Sammy was out of the band.

Australia, April 1998   Likewise, this document of Gary Cherone's brief tenure was filmed for a pay-per-view concert and shelved.

DLR Revisited, 2002   While the fans clamored for a reunion, the band has been sitting on three or four unreleased new tracks recorded with David Lee Roth in 2002.

Van Halen IV, 2006   Eddie, Uncle Alex, and Wolfgang Van Halen have been jamming at 5150 for years. Let's hear this dangerous new band.

BONUS TRACK C

PICTURES ON THE SILVER SCREEN: VAN HALEN IN THE MOVIES

Tim Robbins learns to dance in space in *Mission to Mars* to "Dance the Night Away," David Arquette screams out "Runnin' with the Devil" with a van full of nuns in *Ready to Rumble*, and Van Halen's music plays during the party scenes of too many movies to name. Here are a few must-see moments of VH-TV:

***Back to the Future*, 1985**   Michael J. Fox puts a tape labeled "Van Halen" in his Walkman to scare Crispin Glover with futuristic interplanetary guitar sounds.

***Better Off Dead*, 1985**   Overimaginative fry cook John Cusack brings raw hamburger meat to life, creating a giant Claymation figure of cheeseburger that plays a red-and-white-striped guitar and entertains a grease pool of female fries while "Everybody Wants Some" blasts.

***Weird Science*, 1985**   Roth's "Just a Gigolo" video is prominently featured.

***Saturday Night Live*, 1987**   A skit called "Dinner with the Van Halens" lampoons life with Eddie and Valerie, as a quiet dinner with friends at home is ruined by the constant interference of overzealous roadies Kevin Nealon and Dana Carvey—who inexplicably speaks in a British accent.

***Café Americain*, 1993**   Eddie Van Halen appears as a street musician in the "Home Alone" episode of this short-lived TV show costarring his wife, Valerie.

***Frasier,* 1993**   For the episode "Call Me Irresponsible," Eddie lends his voice as a radio caller named "Hank."

***Airheads,* 1994**   Honorable mention for hinging the plot around Van Halen. When record company weasel Harold Ramis comes to sign Brendan Fraser's band, the suspicious Fraser asks which side Ramis took in the David Lee Roth/Van Halen split. Ramis says, "Van Halen," and the door slams shut in his face. "It's strictly a judgment call," he sputters in protest. "They sold a lot of records after Dave left the group!"

BONUS TRACK D

THE MENU:
THE COVERS BAND FROM PASADENA

Sometimes they faked it, sometimes they nailed it. . . . Before the well-known Kinks, Martha and the Vandellas, and Linda Ronstadt covers, here are a few of the hundreds of songs Van Halen kept on hand to play while cutting their teeth as a cover band.

- Aerosmith, "Sweet Emotion," "Walk This Way," "Last Child"
- Bad Company, "Can't Get Enough," "Live for the Music," "Rock Steady"
- Beatles, "Drive My Car"
- Black Sabbath, "War Pigs" (Eddie on vocals)
- Tommy Bolin, "The Grind"
- David Bowie, "Jean Genie"
- Budgie, "In for the Kill," "Living on Your Own"
- Captain Beyond, "Bright Blue Tango"
- Eddie Cochran, "Summertime Blues"
- Cream, all of it
- Deep Purple, "Might Just Take Your Life," "Hallelujah," "Maybe I'm a Leo," "Woman from Tokyo"
- Rick Derringer, "Rock and Roll Hoochie Koo," "Still Alive and Well"
- Foghat, "Slow Ride"
- Grand Funk Railroad, "Some Kind of Wonderful"
- Humble Pie, "30 Days in the Hole"

- Isley Brothers, "Twist and Shout," "It's Your Thing"
- James Gang, "Funk #49," "Walk Away"
- KC & the Sunshine Band, "Get Down Tonight"
- Kiss, "Rock and Roll All Night," "Firehouse"
- Led Zeppelin, "Nobody's Fault but Mine," "Houses of the Holy" "Trampled Under Foot," "The Rover," "Hots On for Nowhere"
- Montrose, "Make It Last," "Rock Candy"
- Mountain, "Mississippi Queen"
- Elvis Presley, "Heartbreak Hotel"
- Queen, "Now I'm Here"
- Rainbow, "Man on a Silver Mountain"
- Paul Revere and the Raiders, "Kicks"
- Rolling Stones, "If You Can't Rock Me," "It's Only Rock and Roll"
- Rod Stewart, "Stone Cold Sober"
- Scorpions, "Catch Your Train," "Speedy's Coming"
- Slade, "Goodbye to Jane"
- Spooky Tooth, "Wildfire"
- Sugarloaf, "Don't Call Us, We'll Call You"
- Ten Years After, "Goin' Home"
- Thin Lizzy, "Jailbreak"
- The Troggs, "Wild Thing"
- Robin Trower, "The Fool and Me"
- Edgar Winter, "We All Had a Real Good Time," "Keep Playing That Rock and Roll"
- Johnny Winter, "Still Alive & Well"
- Stevie Wonder, "Superstition"
- ZZ Top—"Beer Drinkers & Hell Raisers," "La Grange," "Waiting for the Bus," "Brown Sugar," "Chevrolet," "Tush," "Francine"

BONUS TRACK E

UNCOVERED:
VAN HALEN TRIBUTE BANDS

Van Halen's light schedule in recent years has encouraged the rise of a cottage industry of scores of tribute bands based all over the globe. It's fitting that Pasadena's greatest cover band should find itself copied into infinity. Not surprisingly, the population skews heavily toward Roth-era acts, mostly dolled up in scarves and stripes. A notable exception is the Other Half, the highly qualified party band featuring Sammy Hagar and Michael Anthony, and described by Hagar as "the ultimate Van Halen tribute band."

"I think it's great," Alex Van Halen said approvingly of tribute act Atomic Punks. "Music is an art form, and as long as you're doing something that you get a kick out of and other people get a kick out of, and if you don't have any expectations of going multinational, but you're doing it to have a good time, why not?"

Atomic Punks (Los Angeles) Billed as the number one early Van Halen tribute act (get in line). Michael Anthony played with them in 1998 and 2003, plus two guitarists have gone on to work for the real Roth.

Diver Down (Plymouth, MA) Active since 1983, they play the entire six Roth albums, *plus* the two 1996 Roth comeback songs, *plus* "Yankee Rose" for good measure. Feature an ex-Extreme drummer, and Gary Cherone has joined them onstage.

Eat 'Em and Smile (New York, NY) All Roth, all the time.

Eruption (Vancouver, Canada) Billed as the "most accurate Van Halen tribute band in Canada."

Eruption (Los Angeles)   Very convincing early Van Halen copyists, even with a blond Michael Anthony. Their Roth once made a surprise appearance singing "Runnin' with the Devil" with Sammy and Mike.

Eruption (Hampton, VA)   Not only does their bassist like to drink whiskey, he also whomps a Jack Daniel's bass.

Fair Warning (Chicago)   Formed back in 1987, their Roth-alike plays the part to the hilt, complete with bone necklaces and aerial splits.

Fair Warning (Northern California)   Props include leather chaps and a homemade striped EVH Peavey guitar.

Fan Halen (Holland)   Not only can their singer do aerial splits, but these guys are Dutch—tough to fake.

5150 (Australia)   Playing *Diver Down* down under.

5150 (United Kingdom)   Cover the Roth and Hagar eras.

Hans Valen (Australia)   Share their name with a Canadian house painter named Mr. Hans Valen, lucky guy.

Hot for Teacher (San Francisco)   They designed tricky flying HFT wings in the style of the classic VH logo, and just like Van Halen in the early days they've opened for Y&T.

Hot for Teacher (Concepción, Chile)   Hot Chile? Very funny!

Mighty VH (New York)   This Dave-era band blew away Manhattan at "Mockfest" in 2004 with Ozzy Osbourne, AC/DC, and Iron Maiden cover bands.

Ice Cream Men (Italy)   I wish they only played the pre-rock covers like "Ice Cream Man," "Big Bad Bill," and "Happy Trails."

1984 (Ontario, Canada)   Honest Roth-era interpreters who admit, "We sure don't look like Van Halen."

Mammoth (Long Island, NY)   After all, when Van Halen were called Mammoth they were a cover band, too.

Mean Street (Pittsburgh) (New York) (Maryland)   Seems like every town has a Main Street, too.

Panama (Orange County, CA)   Except for the keyboard player, the historical reenactments of *Van Halen* portraits are spot-on.

Rattle Rattle (Italy)   Maybe inspired by the baby on the *1984* cover?

Romeo Delight (Austin, TX)   Atomic Punks invaded their turf.

Romeo Delight (Northern New Jersey)   Also a great name for a pizza joint.

Romeo Delight (Italy)   They hail from the birthplace of the real Romeo.

Spanish Fly (Argentina)   Not such an obscure song in South America.

Unchained (Morristown, NJ)   The closest the world will ever come to seeing David Lee Roth sing "5150."

Unchained UK (United Kingdom)   They can't drive 88 kilometers per hour.

Valerie's Revenge (Cleveland, OH)   Now known as Virtual Halen.

Van Hagar (Sydney, Australia)   Somehow this band has gotten away with using this name for almost ten years, though it's kind of an insult.

Van Heaven (North Carolina)   Shooting for the "#1 *touring* Van Halen cover band" title.

Van Hielan (Glasgow, Scotland)   Hide your sheep, lads!

Van Wailen (Toronto)   The drummer and guitarist also had a tribute band called the Stone Temple Co-Pilots.

VH—The Van Halen Tribute Band (unknown):   VH? These Roth-heavy tributeers skirt the lines between homage and identity theft.

WDFA—short for "We Don't Fuck Around" (Northern California)   Van Halen's unofficial motto and the first runner-up title for this book. Their drummer played with bassist Cliff Burton in his pre-Metallica band Trauma.

Xhalen (Australia)   "Australia's only tribute to the mighty Van Halen," at least until they see this list.

BONUS TRACK F

VAN HAGAR FOR DUMMIES

In the spirit of world peace, here are seven quick steps for stubborn David Lee Roth loyalists to get a handle on the ten years Sammy Hagar spent in Van Halen, seven songs from five albums, totaling thirty-seven minutes—longer than almost all the band's studio albums. Season them with the instrumentals of your choice. Though it is doubtful that anyone will convert to the dark side after downloading these, Hagar foes may shake their heads a little less vigorously in opposition. Now, here they are, the least worst songs of Van Hagar:

1. **"5150" from *5150*** This is definitely not the first song here to convert any nonbelievers, but a very good version popped up on the Internet recently, supposedly by Axl Rose and Guns N' Roses. That tribute never happened, but the obscure cover band behind the grittier version definitely nailed the pathos of this track. Eddie's arpeggios land on the guitar neck like thick Texas rain on the roof of a tin shed. Though Sammy sounds syrupy, he's believable—plus the thumping electronic drum rolls are a hoot!

2. **"Mine All Mine" from *OU812*** More cheesy synths and fake-sounding drums here, and Hagar's emoting can be pretty hard to take—but the driving pace pushes the urgency. If not a great song, it's a perfect picture of where the band's head was at the time, making this the one track from *OU812* that classic Van Halen fans can stomach without retching.

3. **"Runaround" from *For Unlawful Carnal Knowledge*** Five years into his tenure, Hagar finally finds his feet, loosening his collar to sing in a lower voice. This is just another rave-up on an album full of bawdy rockers, but "Runaround" builds around choruses

and hooks that would have done any of his early-eighties solo albums proud. He even tries a sultry spoken voice in the middle section without aping Roth. Eddie's playing is subdued, focusing on rhythm like on some of Van Halen's earliest songs.

4. **"Pleasure Dome" from *For Unlawful Carnal Knowledge*** Surprisingly summoning a semi-science-fiction landscape for this galloping epic, Sammy narrates the lonely tale of a lost desert wanderer. Why the band waited so long to live its boyhood comic-book fantasies is a mystery—and the image of Sammy Hagar in any kind of "Pleasure Dome" is best left alone.

5. **"The Seventh Seal" from *Balance*** Another majestic Zeppelinesque stormer from late-era Van Hagar, this cataclysmic album opener is classic heavy metal in the vein of Iron Maiden and Judas Priest, filtered through the washy stadium rock of U2. If Hagar wanted to leave the band at this point, the brothers were making him work hard for his supper, as he screams his way across a constantly changing landscape of pulsing bass, intricate drums, and multilayered guitars.

6. **"Aftershock" from *Balance*** Funny that throughout his time with Van Halen, whenever Hagar really throws down he sounds like Tina Turner. On his way out the door, he dishes some hard howls about his recent divorce wounds—which just as easily apply to his impending exit from the band. Unlike so many of his commercially potent songs, this one is not background music—saddling up next to greatness, "Aftershock" demands your full attention.

7. **"It's About Time" from *The Best of Both Worlds*** Shameless nineties guitar riffing aside, Hagar jumps right back into the fold for this quick rekindling of the Van Hagar chemistry. Thirty years after the birth of Van Halen, Eddie still comes up with some guitar parts that warrant "how did he do that?"

LOOK AT ALL THE PEOPLE HERE TONIGHT!

Backstage All-access: My partner in all things, Dianna Dilworth, my esteemed editor, Stephen S. Power and his crotchless leather pants ("chaps," he claims), and one-man rhythm section and negotiator-in-chief, Peter McGuigan.

VIP Area: Kimberly Monroe-Hill, Hannah Gordon, Steven Tackeff, Jason Perlman, Trey Azagthoth, Brian Kehew, Jose Mangin, Alex Porro, Greg Steele, Tom Wilkinson, Jess Besack, Jeff Stone, James Lo, Matt Sweeney, Omid Yamini, Rob Dyrenforth, Portia Jane Cook, Tim Donovan, Steve Loschi, Todd Sentz, Doug Messenger, Jeff Kitts, Christoffer Jonsson, Patrick Delaney, Millicent Souris, Austin Hill, Denise Korycki, Greg Fiering, Adrienne Bradley, Bret Witter, Albert Mudrian, Martin Popoff, Dennis Sobolewski, Ben Daughtry, Monte Conner, Richard Kreis, Johnny Kreis, Sjors Soulburn, Metal Opie, Kris Durso, Mike Nicoletti, Eric O'Brien, Steve O'Malley, Traci Terrill, Rob Grobengeiser, Nigel Cox-Hagan, Jeff Hausman, Vinny Cecolini, Liz Ciavarella, Derek Yip, Rob Womack, Scott Rosenfeld, Vinnie Paul, Rob Halford, David Rensin, Neil Zlozower, Gibbs Chapman, Adam Chapman, and Andy "Right Now" Ryan.

To everyone who couldn't pick up the phone—I hope you're feeling better.

EVERYBODY WANTS SOME ONLINE
www.soundsofthebeast.com

Photographer's Note: As a sixth grader, Kevin Estrada was suspended for squirting a VH logo on the school walls with mustard packets. When he was twelve, he shot the photos of Van Halen's 1978 tour that appear in this book. Raised in Arcadia, California, Estrada grew up in Van Halen country, and he was constantly bumping into his favorite band, getting them to autograph a bag of chips or an ever-present Van Halen album. A family dinner at the local Mexican restaurant Peppers led to a chance encounter with Michael Anthony's birthday party—and Estrada's dad mistaking David Lee Roth for Peter Frampton. While filming the "Panama" video, Roth nearly drove over Estrada and his friends in his red lowrider.

In high school, Estrada took guitar lessons at Dr. Music, Eddie Van Halen's favorite gear shop. Eddie gave him a guitar pick one day, but Estrada had other ideas. "All my friends wanted to be Eddie Van Halen, but I wanted to be the guy down there shooting Van Halen."

He began sneaking his camera into concerts, duct-taping it to the back of his neck. When he was fifteen, a bouncer caught him and sent him flying across the room with a punch to the head. Incredibly, he took most of the photos for this book from the crowd. He could only afford one roll of film the final time he shot classic Van Halen, on the *1984* tour. "I had to be very careful that night," he says.

Estrada now lives in Burbank, California, with his wife and two daughters. He has photographed acts including Nirvana, the Cure, and Slayer, and his work also appears in *Johnny Cash: From the Editors of Rolling Stone* and *The Heroin Diaries* by Nikki Sixx.

INDEX

Twenty-finger Guitar Hero: Eddie Van Halen erupts in 1979
Kevin Estrada

Taking flight in 1979
Kevin Estrada

Gigging the German Phoenix Club: (left to right): Jan Van Halen (saxophone), Alex Van Halen (drums), Ria van den Berg (accordion), and Theo Kreis (bass)
Courtesy of Johnny Kreis

The Van Halen
brothers at Texxas
Jam I—Dallas,
1978
Kevin Estrada

• Tortomasi–Haley Productions •
PRESENT ANOTHER
LIVE DANCE CONCERT
$100,000   8000 WATT SOUND SYSTEM •

VAN HALEN
SMILE
INTRODUCING
SMOKE HOUSE

FRIDAY, FEBRUARY 18th   8pm until 1am

ALL ADMISSIONS
AT THE DOOR
$3.25
2.75 WITH FLYER

«»
REFRESHMENTS

PRESENT THIS
ADVERTISEMENT
FOR YOUR
50¢
DISCOUNT

PASADENA CIVIC   300 E. GREEN STREET

Air Van Halen
Kevin Estrada

David Lee Roth, 1979
Kevin Estrada

"Jump"-start: Roth in
ecstasy and Eddie
Van Halen midflight
Kevin Estrada

Alex Van Halen
Kevin Estrada

Michael Anthony,
1980
Kevin Estrada

Mike and Dave on fire
Kevin Estrada

Black leather Eddie
Kevin Estrada

Barbarians at
the gate, 1981
Kevin Estrada

"Ice Cream
Man," 1979
Kevin Estrada

Shag-head Ed, 1980
Kevin Estrada

Million-dollar smiles: Valerie and Eddie with Apple
Computer cofounder Steve Wozniak, US Festival '83
Dan Sokol

Facing page:
"Look at all the
people here
tonight!"
DLR, Fair
Warning era
Kevin Estrada

Popping the whiskey bottle bass and tapping the Frankenstrat in 1984
Kevin Estrada

Sammy Hagar; the Red Rocker in black—*Balance* tour, 1995
Kevin Estrada

Shorn: Eddie sheds
and shreds in 1995
Kevin Estrada

VH3: Gary
Cherone points
forward in 1998
Steven Tackeff/
Tightedit.com

The aging Adonis: "Diamond" David Lee Roth in 2002
Kevin Estrada

Older, Budweiser—Sam and Ed in 2004
Jason Perlman/Musicohio.com

Van Hagar on the 2004 reunion tour
Jason Perlman/Musicohio.com

The countdown to another break-up begins
Jason Perlman/Musicohio.com

Happy trails—or everybody wants some more?
Kevin Estrada